GHOST
TOWNS

and other
quirky places in
the New Jersey
pine Barrens

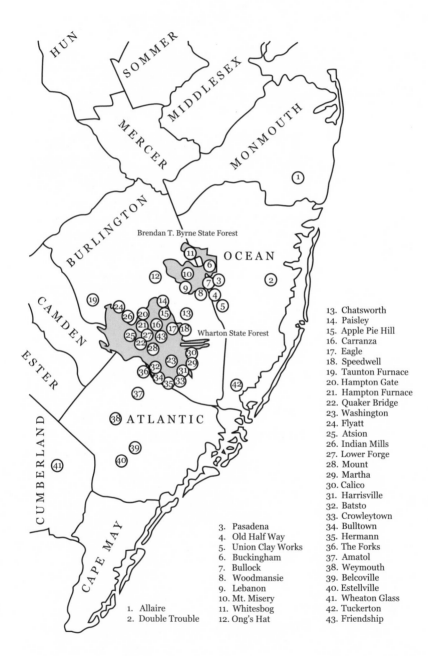

HUN

SOMMER

MIDDLESEX

MERCER

MONMOUTH

BURLINGTON

Brendan T. Byrne State Forest

OCEAN

CAMDEN

⑪
⑫ ⑩ ⑥
⑨ ⑦③
⑧④
⑤
②

ESTER

⑲
⑭
㉔ ⑬
㉖ ⑳ ⑮
㉕㉗⑯⑰⑱   Wharton State Forest
㉒㊸
㉘
㉓㉚
㊱㉜ ㉙
㉞ ㉛
㉟㉝
㊲

CUMBERLAND

ATLANTIC
㊳

㊴
㊵

㊶

㊷

CAPE MAY

1. Allaire
2. Double Trouble

3. Pasadena
4. Old Half Way
5. Union Clay Works
6. Buckingham
7. Bullock
8. Woodmansie
9. Lebanon
10. Mt. Misery
11. Whitesbog
12. Ong's Hat

13. Chatsworth
14. Paisley
15. Apple Pie Hill
16. Carranza
17. Eagle
18. Speedwell
19. Taunton Furnace
20. Hampton Gate
21. Hampton Furnace
22. Quaker Bridge
23. Washington
24. Flyatt
25. Atsion
26. Indian Mills
27. Lower Forge
28. Mount
29. Martha
30. Calico
31. Harrisville
32. Batsto
33. Crowleytown
34. Bulltown
35. Hermann
36. The Forks
37. Amatol
38. Weymouth
39. Belcoville
40. Estellville
41. Wheaton Glass
42. Tuckerton
43. Friendship

GHOST TOWNS

and other quirky places in the New Jersey pine Barrens

Barbara Solem-Stull

Plexus Publishing, Inc.
Medford, New Jersey

Second Printing, December 2005

Ghost Towns and Other Quirky Places in the New Jersey Pine Barrens

Copyright © 2005 by Barbara Solem-Stull

Published by: Plexus Publishing, Inc.
                 143 Old Marlton Pike
                 Medford, NJ 08055

Publisher's Note: The author and publisher have taken care in preparation of this book but make no expressed or implied warranty of any kind and assume no responsibility for errors or omissions. No liability is assumed for incidental or consequential damages in connection with or arising out of the use of the information contained herein.

Library of Congress Cataloging-in-Publication Data

Solem-Stull, Barbara, 1947–
   Ghost towns and other quirky places in the New Jersey Pine Barrens / Barbara Solem-Stull. -- 1st ed.
      p. cm.
   Includes bibliographical references and index.
      ISBN 0-937548-60-X (alk. paper)
   1. Pine Barrens (N.J.)--History, Local. 2. Cities and towns--New Jersey--Pine Barrens. 3. Automobile travel--New Jersey--Pine Barrens--Guidebooks. 4. Walking--New Jersey--Pine Barrens. 5. Bicycle touring--New Jersey--Pine Barrens. 6. Canoes and canoeing--New Jersey--Pine Barrens--Guidebooks. 7. Pine Barrens (N.J.)--Tours. I. Title.
   F142.P5S64 2005
      917.49'610444—dc22

                                                              2005020580

Printed and bound in the United States of America.

President and CEO: Thomas H. Hogan, Sr.
Editor-in-Chief and Publisher: John B. Bryans
Managing Editor: Amy M. Reeve
VP Graphics and Production: M. Heide Dengler
Book Designer: Kara Jalkowski
Cover Designer: Michele Quinn
Sales Manager: Pat Palatucci
Copyeditor: Dorothy Pike
Proofreader: Bonnie T. Freeman
Indexer: Sharon Hughes

Cover photo of Main Street, Harrisville courtesy of the Howard Feyl Collection.

Contents

Chapter 1 - Before You Go

Chapter 2 - Atsion and Hampton: Where Iron, Cotton, and Cranberries Ruled

Chapter 3 - Old Tuckerton Stage Road

Chapter 4 - Harrisville and Martha: Industry Deep in the Pines

Chapter 5 - The Chatsworth to Carranza Loop

Chapter 6 - The Forks to Hermann

Chapter 7 - Brendan T. Byrne State Forest and Vicinity

Chapter 8 - Whitesbog Village and Double Trouble: On the Cranberry Trail

Chapter 9 - Weymouth, Belcoville, and Amatol: Of Iron, Paper, and Munitions

Chapter 10 - Batsto, Allaire, and Wheaton Villages: Living History in the Pines

Acknowledgments

One of the highlights in researching *Ghost Towns and Other Quirky Places in the New Jersey Pine Barrens* has been the interesting and wonderfully generous people I have had the pleasure of meeting along the way. Foremost, I am deeply indebted to Budd Wilson, noted archaeologist and Pine Barrens historian, who spent countless hours traveling with me to many of the sites mentioned in this book. Budd has also read and commented on the entire manuscript, offering valuable suggestions at every stage of the writing process. Budd's knowledge of the New Jersey Pine Barrens is extensive, and it has been my great pleasure to spend time with and learn from him. Budd generously provided me with many of the old photographs that appear in this book.

Through Budd I met Steve Eichinger of Wading River, a man with vast knowledge of the Tuckerton Stage Road. Steve, who has researched and charted much of the Old Tuckerton Stage Road, spent a day with me traveling its path and sharing its history. I am very appreciative of the time he was willing to spend with me as well as for the information he so generously shared.

Also through Budd Wilson, I was fortunate to become acquainted with Scott Wieczorek, a young archaeologist who had just completed research and an excavation of the mysterious Pasadena Terra Cotta Company site. Scott didn't just share his research but also provided me with a personal tour of what we now know is the Brooksbrae Brick Company site. Scott's work has been a great help, and I am grateful to him.

I think highly of Richard Regensburg's work on the "first people" of the Pines and appreciate his willingness to answer all my questions, no matter how inane. Through Richard I met Joan Berkey, a historian from Atlantic County who most generously shared her recent work on Weymouth and Belcoville. Joan also took the time to read and comment on what I had written about these two old towns. I am most appreciative of Joan's kindness and expertise.

Joan introduced me to George Flicker, park superintendent of the Atlantic County Park at Estell Manor. George generously spent time with me to share his knowledge of Belcoville as well as to provide information about the other treasures located in the Estell Manor Park. He shared important documents, showed me where the most interesting ruins were located, and provided access to some wonderful old photos of Belcoville.

Thanks to Maria Peters of the P.I.N.E.S. program for sharing information about Buckingham, a ghost town I had never heard of. A special thanks to Chris Bethman, superintendent of Brendan T. Byrne State Forest, for his willingness to share his personal research into the forest he supervises.

I would also like to thank Tom Darlington, nephew of Elizabeth White and grandson of J. J. White. Tom graciously spent an afternoon sharing the history of Whitesbog Village, interwoven with delightful family stories. Thanks, too, to Janet Robbins, tireless Whitesbog volunteer, for her very informative tour of the historic village.

A very special thank you to Lois Morris, who spent a day with me in the Pines, taking me to the Crossley Preserve and to "Sacrificial Bog" at Webbs Mill. Lois has a vast knowledge of the Pine Barrens and a wonderful way of sharing what she knows. Through Lois I met George Burke, a park ranger at Double Trouble and, most interestingly, someone who had actually grown up in the village before it became a state park. George's father was a foreman at the Double Trouble Cranberry Packing and Sorting House, and as a young man George also worked in the cranberry bogs. I was most fortunate to have the opportunity to tour the old packing house with George as my personal guide.

I am particularly indebted to the good folks at the Main Branch of the Burlington County Library for their willingness to lend me many of the wonderful old photographs that appear in this book. I also appreciate the extensive collection of Pine Barrens books and materials available at the New Jersey Room and the assistance provided by Paula Lynch Manzella, reference librarian, in locating information.

Ghost Towns and Other Quirky Places in the New Jersey Pine Barrens would be incomplete if not for the very special contribution of Berminna Solem, talented artist, dear friend, and (lucky for me) loving relative. Facing all kinds of weather and, at times, treacherous road conditions, Berminna accompanied me deep into the woods as we sought out the old places. Her descriptive site maps will surely help readers locate all that remains in each of the old towns while also giving them a glimpse of how these places may have appeared long ago. Her beautiful illustrations help to bring the story alive by providing realistic renditions of old structures and scenes.

I particularly want to thank my sweet husband, Gordon Stull, for all his assistance in the completion of this manuscript. Gordon has accompanied me on many trips into the Pine Barrens searching for the old towns and places. On more than one occasion he has dug us out of a frozen-over mud hole, saving us a costly tow charge as well as a long walk back to civilization. He has traveled with me time and time again over the same old dirt roads so I could accurately record routes and locations. He has provided a range of technological assistance. He has read the entire text and provided valuable editorial feedback. He has encouraged me when I was feeling frustrated and unsure of my ability to complete the task I had taken on. And last, but certainly not least, he has taken most of the wonderful photographs that appear in this book.

I also want to thank John Bryans, my editor at Plexus Publishing, for his belief in me and in the Ghost Towns project. His support, encouragement, and friendship are much appreciated. Many other talented people at Plexus contributed to the book in important ways, notably Amy Reeve, Kara Jalkowski, Michele Quinn, Heide Dengler, and Pat Palatucci.

Finally I want to acknowledge all of the talented authors who have so skillfully recorded the rich history of the New Jersey Pine Barrens. Much of the information that appears in this manuscript has been in print before in one form or another, and without the fine work of these authors, this book would not have been possible.

Foreword

The Pine Barrens are extensive—a million acres in the middle of a megalopolis. Their natural importance has drawn international attention. To most the Pine Barrens are a wonderful pristine place, a rich ecological treasure that has escaped major environmental problems. The fact is the Pine Barrens supported an 18th- and 19th-century industrial area that laid waste the environment. It has taken 140 years to heal the effects of that destruction.

The region was inhabited for more than 4,000 years before Henry Hudson saw it burning in the predawn hours of September 2, 1609. The region, first referred to as the Pine Barrens in 1675, has always been prone to fire, both natural and intentional.

First came the woodchoppers, then the sawyers, and then the colliers. The colliers supplied the charcoal for the blast furnaces and for four kinds of forges. There were 17 iron furnaces, and each furnace needed 1,000 acres of pine annually to stay in operation. The pine was made into charcoal. The charcoal pits were covered with floats that were comprised of turf from the forest floor. There were thousands of charcoal pits.

The blast furnace and forges needed ore such as that found along the edges of Pine Barrens streams. The digging of this ore destroyed the original configuration of the waterways. A large furnace could produce 750 tons of iron a year with a volume of ore five to 10 times the volume of the iron it produced. Consequently, the bog areas of the Pine Barrens were strip-mined for the ore.

The iron furnace plantations, although large, were only part of the industrial base of the Pine Barrens. There were sawmills, gristmills, cotton mills, fulling (woolen) mills, paper mills, glass houses, turpentine stills, tar kilns, shipyards, and landings.

There were agricultural towns built around cranberries and blueberries. There were towns located along railroads that cut through the pines. For every town that blossomed during the railroad period, there were 20 real estate ventures that died. There were towns that were built and died within two years. There were famous people who lived here and visited here. There were people who later became famous, and there was a group of people who became infamous but who never actually existed.

All of the early industrial towns had adjacent farmland. The larger acreage on these farms was in pasture and grain fields. The smaller acreage was for orchards and gardens.

The Pine Barrens was a busy place where people traveled on roads and rivers that still exist, where raw materials were made into products for a new nation. It was a time when smoke from charcoal meant production, not pollution, and where the noise of the blast furnace meant men had jobs. It was a time when taverns, not television, were a citizen's source for the news of the day.

The book you now hold is Barbara Solem-Stull's second. While her first publication, *The Forks: A Brief History of the Area,* centered around one historic place on the Mullica River, this one is broader, telling the story of many of the industrial towns that were scattered throughout the Pine Barrens during the 18th, 19th, and early 20th centuries. Barbara and her husband, Gordon, live in the Pine Barrens and have walked or kayaked all the places mentioned in the book. Her passion for the topic is evident in these pages.

Ghost Towns and Other Quirky Places in the New Jersey Pine Barrens has been written to whet your appetite for adventure. If your first venture is tomorrow, the trips could take a lifetime. I hope you may enjoy them as I have. This book is a good place to start.

Budd Wilson
March 25, 2004

Introduction

The New Jersey Pine Barrens—in spite of its inhospitable reputation—has sustained humans for over 10,000 years. In the late 17th century, the European settlers named this place the "barrens," but somehow those who settled here found a way to harness the resources of the area and to carve out a life for themselves and their families. This book tells the story of these hardy settlers and of the industries and towns they built. The stories of the people and old towns of the Pines are filled with ambition, promise, success, and failure. It is a history that is an important part of early America, but it is a past whose remains are quickly disappearing because of two irrepressible forces—looting by vandals and the overgrowth of the forest.

Ghost Towns and Other Quirky Places in the New Jersey Pine Barrens focuses on the core of the Pines and tells the stories of the old towns and places in Burlington, Atlantic, and Ocean counties. It is primarily a field guide designed to take the reader to the sites of the forgotten Pine Barren towns and settlements of the 18th, 19th, and early 20th centuries. In some places the ruins give the reader a clear view of how the town or settlement may have appeared during its heyday. In other places the only remains are sandstone cellar holes and a few crumbling building foundations. But there is a story in each of these places that tells of the towns and the people and the industries they created.

Chapter 1, "Before You Go," includes safety tips on traveling in the woods, as well as information on the history of the region. The rest of the chapters in the book focus on specific towns or groups of towns and places. These chapters are organized as suggested day trip itineraries but also include side trips as an option for an extended outing. Day trips may be combined, abbreviated, or extended as time permits. The amount of time needed for each trip will depend on how thoroughly the visitor intends to explore each site or location.

The author has found that in some cases multiple trips to a site are needed in order to locate everything of interest.

Driving directions are provided to guide the reader to the old towns or settlements featured in each chapter. Site maps are included, showing the location of any remaining ruins within the towns. Each chapter begins with an overview that is designed to briefly orient the reader to the site. The overview highlights information about walking, driving, kayaking, or biking routes, as well as alternate ways to reach or explore a location. Each overview is followed by "A Deeper Look," which provides in-depth historical background on the site. Although it is not necessary to read the in-depth section prior to exploring a site, it is recommended, as being knowledgeable about a location will enhance the explorer's experience.

Relatively little remains of the old, forgotten towns of the Pines. In some cases all that are left are a few bits of slag from an iron furnace, a depression in the ground where a dwelling once stood, or a crumbling old dam downstream from an open meadow. Often just locating these old towns and places is a daunting task, but my hope is that *Ghost Towns and Other Quirky Places in the New Jersey Pine Barrens* will help you do just that, as well as inspire you to learn more about each location. There is so much to know, and after all, the real adventure will begin once you start to unravel the mysteries of the past firsthand.

before you go

Before You Go

AVOIDING MISHAPS IN THE BACKWOODS

Whenever one ventures into the woods, leaving civilization behind, there is potential for encountering difficulties. With a few simple precautions, most problems can be easily avoided. Following are a number of commonsense suggestions born of many years of experience in exploring the New Jersey Pine Barrens. Although many of the day trips outlined in the book will not take you deep into the forest, when you do travel to backwoods areas, you'll want to be sure to take all appropriate precautions.

GETTING STUCK

The sugar-sand dirt roads of the Pinelands are usually hard packed and easy to travel. In some places, however, the dirt roads are soft and deep, creating difficult driving conditions even for four-wheel-drive vehicles. A more common problem encountered by the backwoods driver, especially after heavy precipitation, is getting stuck in one of the many deep potholes found along the old dirt roads of the Pines. When you come to a flooded area in the road, it is important to check the depth of the water as it may be deeper than it appears. When potholes are covered by ice and snow, the situation is particularly treacherous, and great care should be taken before driving through them. Getting a tow truck to pull a vehicle out of a backwoods pothole is difficult and time-consuming, not to mention costly, so I recommend you carry self-rescue equipment when going into deeply forested areas. Having been stuck on many occasions myself, I now travel with a winch for pulling my car out of a ditch, a shovel, and a tow-chain.

3

Author's husband checking out water-filled potholes
on back road to Apple Pie Hill.
(*Photo by Barbara Solem-Stull*)

GETTING LOST

Although each excursion covered here is accompanied by a map
and driving directions, it's not hard to get lost in the back roads and
trails of the Pine Barrens. When traveling in the woods, it is wise to
bring along U.S. Geological Survey Maps (USGS quads) of the area.
USGS quads of the Pine Barrens can be purchased at the Visitors
Centers within the Wharton and Brendan T. Byrne (Lebanon) State
Forests or at local map stores. Taking along a compass and a Global
Positioning System (GPS) is also a good idea. It is certainly useful to
bring a cell phone, but be prepared for poor or nonexistent reception
when deep in the woods.

Whenever traveling into the backwoods, it is important to let
someone know about your intended route and destination. Always
take an ample supply of water and be sure to have a full gas tank
when driving into the heart of the Pines as gas stations are few and
far between.

GETTING BIT

Ticks are the most common problem encountered by those spending time in the woods. Deer ticks, often no larger than the head of a pin, can carry Lyme disease. Other larger ticks can also carry dangerous diseases, such as Rocky Mountain spotted fever. The best way to protect oneself from ticks is to wear long-sleeved shirts and long pants with socks pulled over the pant legs. Spraying clothing with a permethrin-based insect repellant is also recommended. Check yourself carefully, from head to toe, after a deep woods excursion.

Chiggers, which are tiny mite-like arthropods, are another potential risk for those spending time in the woods. Chiggers are most numerous in the summer and generally live in low, damp areas where vegetation is heaviest, but they are also found in drier low places such as lawns and parks. Although it is commonly believed that chiggers burrow under the skin, in actuality they insert their mouthparts into a skin pore or hair follicle. Their bites produce small reddish welts on the skin, accompanied by intense itching. The best way to avoid chiggers is to stay on cleared trails and roadways (especially in later summer, when chiggers are at their most plentiful) and to wear long-sleeved shirts and long pants with socks pulled over the pant legs. Permethrin-based insect repellents are also very effective against chiggers.

Other species of insects, including mosquitoes and flies, may be present in the Pines in warmer months. Insect repellents sprayed on the clothes and skin are effective at keeping these critters at bay.

Although it is always exciting to come in contact with wild animals when venturing into the woods, they should never be disturbed or harassed. Harassment includes throwing stones, chasing, or invading an animal's habitat. Typically, wild animals are fearful of people and unless ill or injured will shy away from humans. It is important to be respectful of the flora and fauna of the woodlands and never to remove anything, including wildflowers, turtles, and snakes, from their natural habitats.

GETTING HURT

In many of the old ruins of the Pines there are crumbling walls and foundations of dwellings. These ruins should not be climbed upon because they are fragile and may easily collapse. For personal safety and to protect what remains of the ruins, it is important to avoid leaning against or climbing on remaining structures. Cellar holes also abound in the old towns, so keep on the lookout for these, especially if you are accompanied by small children.

In some areas the state or county has posted and fenced off especially fragile ruins. Be aware that trespassers who ignore these posted areas and fencing may pay a stiff fine if caught by state rangers. Taking items from the sites is strictly forbidden, even items that may seem insignificant, such as old bricks or stones from the foundations. These should never be removed, as they are an important piece of the original historic site.

Traveling in the New Jersey Pine Barrens is generally a low risk, safe experience. By following a few simple guidelines, you can avoid most potential mishaps and ensure a pleasant and stress-free experience.

HISTORICAL BACKGROUND

The Pine Barrens of New Jersey, which encompass 1.4 million acres extending approximately 90 miles north to south and 40 miles east to west, lies within a geologic area known as the Atlantic Coastal Plain. One-hundred million years ago this area was covered by oceans that were alternately rising and receding. Approximately five million years ago the seas retreated from the Atlantic Coastal Plain for the last time, leaving the porous and nutrient-leached silica sands and the deeper water-saturated sands that are part of the current environment. During the last Ice Age, which began about one million years ago and ended approximately 12,000 years ago, ice deposits created subarctic conditions in the areas of southern New Jersey. With the retreat of the last glaciers, the tundra environment disappeared, and the many plant and animal species that inhabit the area today emerged.

Today throughout these heavily forested Pine Barrens stand the rapidly deteriorating remains of once flourishing industries and the communities they supported. In this dense wilderness with its miles of sandy roads, silent woodlands, and tannin-stained rivers, important industries such as iron mining, lumbering, and glassmaking once thrived. The Pine Barrens of New Jersey, now a place preserved for its beauty and unique ecology, was once the site of many prosperous settlements that held great promise for future development. It is a place where fortunes were made and lost; where people toiled, lived, and died; and where generations of families found a way through hard work and ingenuity to survive lean times. These tranquil forests, scattered with sandstone cellar holes, have a story to tell, a story about resourceful men and women who found a way to carve out a living for themselves in a strange and harsh land while making important contributions to a young country.

When the European settlers arrived in the area in the late 17th century, they referred to the region of the New Jersey Pine Barrens as the "barrens" because they could not cultivate their crops in the sandy acid soils of the area. Soon, however, they found the "barrens" offered much that could sustain them, as it had the indigenous people before them.

THE HUNTER-GATHERERS

Modern archeological research suggests that there was more prehistoric use of the Pine Barrens than once thought. Although Paleo-Indian (10,000–8000 B.C.) sites in the area are scarce, it is believed that small wandering groups probably used the Pine Barrens for hunting, fishing, and collecting food while they camped beside its streams and vernal ponds. The animals during this time of subarctic conditions were browsers and nut eaters and included mastodon, moose, elk, caribou, and reindeer. Cold-water fish and mollusks lived in the rivers and estuaries. Aquatic birds were various and abundant. It is likely that the Paleo-Indians stalked and killed both the large mammals and the smaller game that inhabited the tundralike environment.

Archaic Indians followed the Paleo-Indians and were in the region from 9,000 to 3,000 years ago. This group established small, semipermanent base camps with temporary locations. Archaic Indians, like the Paleo-Indians, were hunter-gatherers. With the retreat of the glaciers and the arrival of the warmer climate, the wildlife and plant food hunted and gathered by the Archaic Indians were altogether different. Now there was an abundance of nut trees and an increase in mast-eating animals such as deer, moose, elk, bear, woodland bison, and turkey. The gathered edible food, which probably made up two-thirds to three-quarters of the Archaic Indians' diet, included nuts, berries, leafy plants, roots, tubers, eggs, and shellfish.

Archeological excavations done at Batsto in the 1960s indicate that this site was a temporary though repeatedly visited site during both Archaic and Woodland periods. In 1978, a major Pinelands Prehistory Survey conducted by Rutgers University and Monmouth College assessed over 1,000 prehistoric archeological sites in the Pine Barrens, demonstrating human habitation as early as 10,000 B.C. Since the 1978 study, archeological research has continued, and hundreds of additional sites have been located and recorded.

The Woodland Period (1000 B.C. to 1600 A.D.) brought pottery making to the Native American tribes, who continued the hunting-gathering way of life. Plant cultivation was introduced around 700 A.D., as was the use of the bow and arrow.

THE LENAPE

During the last phase of the Woodland Period, Native Americans called the Lenape, or "First People," settled in the area. When the first Europeans came to the region about 1600–1700 A.D., the Lenape were found to be occupying traditional settlements along riverbanks and inner coastal plains. The Lenape, who were hunters and gatherers, were also known to have cultivated a number of wild plants, including corn, kidney and lima beans, squash, pumpkins, and tobacco. The wild foods they gathered in the Pine Barrens included crabapples, cranberries, strawberries, and huckleberries. The game they sought included mountain lion, bear, rabbit, turkey, beaver, and deer. They used the meat of an animal for food and its fur for their clothing. The Lenape, as part of their hunting routine, had a common practice of burning the forest to drive game as well as to encourage new plant growth for themselves and the wildlife they hunted.

Across the Pine Barrens, the Lenape created networking trails that were used for hunting expeditions, traveling to different settlement sites, and conducting trade. Although it is generally believed that tribes would migrate to the seashore only during the summer months to feast on shellfish, it is now known that permanent Native American settlements did exist there. Studies of the shells found at the Tuckerton Shell Mound indicate that shellfish were harvested throughout the year, not just in the summer months.

Many of the trails of the Lenape later became the stage roads of the colonists and the roadways of today. One famous path, the Manahawkin Trail, started in Camden; ran through Marlton, Medford, Shamong, Washington, and Bass River; and finally ended in Tuckerton. Portions of this trail later became known as the Tuckerton Stage Road, sections of which are still in use today.

The Lenape, who were living in semipermanent settlements by this point, stayed in areas only as long as the game they hunted and the food they gathered were plentiful. When the soil on which they grew their crops gave out and the game became scarce, they settled in a new location, thereby giving the depleted wildlife and the land resources time to replenish.

When the European settlers came to the region, the Lenape were friendly and welcoming. They shared information about where to find the wild foods that grew in the forests and how to locate the most favorable hunting grounds. They showed the Europeans how to cultivate corn and tobacco and took them to the areas where the shellfish were plentiful. In exchange, the Europeans sold them liquor that their bodies could not easily metabolize, cheated them in land deals, and gave them diseases against which they had no immunity.

The Quakers of Burlington County, who saw early the adverse effect liquor was having on the Lenape, called a conference with them in 1678 to consider the problem. Chief Ockanickon, who attended this meeting, was quite possibly the orator of the following eloquent speech:

> Strong liquor was first sold to us by the Dutch and they were blind, they had no eyes, they did not see that it was for our hurt. The next people who came among us were

the Swedes, who continued the sale of strong liquor to us; and they also were blind, they had no eyes, they did not see it to be hurtful to us to drink it although we know it to be hurtful to us; but if people will sell it to us we are so in love with it we cannot forbear it. When we drink it makes us mad, we do not know what we do; we then abuse one another, we throw each other in the fire. Seven score of our people have been killed by reason of drinking since the first time it was first sold to us.

The introduction of contagious diseases, such as small pox, was even more deadly to the Lenape, spreading from one village to another, leaving a long list of dead in its wake. By the middle of the 18th century, with most of their land gone, the Lenape still remaining in the area were so reduced in number and living in such poor conditions that they petitioned the New Jersey legislature to provide them a tract of land for their exclusive use. The New Jersey legislature, receiving pressure from influential Quakers and Presbyterians, agreed to this request. In return, the Lenape forfeited title to all land in the Providence of New Jersey still in their possession. On August 29, 1758, 3,044 acres were purchased for their use at a place called Edgepillock, near the present village of Indian Mills in Shamong Township. All Delaware (Lenape) Indians south of the Raritan River were encouraged to move to what would become known as the Brotherton Reservation, the first and only Indian reservation in New Jersey.

During their tenure of the land, the Lenape used the natural environment to satisfy only their most basic personal needs for food and clothing. The Europeans, on the other hand, saw the abundant forests and wildlife of the region as ripe for exploitation. Their impact was huge. Unlike the Lenape, the Europeans did not live lightly on the land.

THE WOODCUTTERS

When the European settlers first came to the Pine Barrens in the early 1700s, they saw abundant forests with rivers that offered great waterpower. These combined resources made it the perfect place for the lumbering industry, and soon many sawmills set up business in the Pines. The Pine Barrens had vast stands of oak, pine, and white cedar needed for fuel and the construction of homes and ships. Oaks were particularly sought after for use in shipbuilding, as was pinewood, which was often used for spars and mast stock. Cedar was much prized for roof shingles and clapboards in house construction as it was resistant to the elements. Eventually pinewood was used in the making of charcoal, which fueled the many furnaces and forges that dotted the early landscape of the Pine Barrens.

The woodcutters came in large numbers and quickly created such devastation in the forests that concern was raised over the swift and immense loss of woodland. Even in those times, when little attention was paid to conservation, people like Ben Franklin spoke out urging sustainable forestry practices.

BOG IRON

Soon after the woodcutters came, bog ore was discovered in the streambeds of the many Pine Barren rivers and bogs. Bog ore, which is a naturally occurring and renewable resource, is formed when the iron-rich soils of the Pine Barrens are carried into the streams and bogs by continually flowing springs. By complex processes, the water-soluble ferrous iron salts become oxidized either by exposure to air or by being acted on by certain bacteria. The resulting iron oxide is deposited along the banks and bottoms of streams and in bogs where, mixed with mud, it accumulates and becomes bog ore. Although bog ore is a renewable resource, it takes considerably longer than 20 years, as previously thought, to regenerate.

As early as 1765, Charles Read purchased land in what is now known as Medford, Medford Lakes, Batsto, and Atsion for the purpose of erecting a chain of iron furnaces and forges. The remote Pine Barrens was chosen as a location for these ironworks not just for its abundance of bog ore but also for its immense forests and great waterpower—both of which were needed to run the furnaces and forges. The waterpower was made by damming streams to create ponds. The fuel for the furnaces came from small pine trees that were made into charcoal by colliers. A thousand acres of pine were needed to keep one furnace fired for the 10 months or so it was in blast each year. Flux was also needed to run the furnaces, and this was supplied by the nearby seashore in the form of oyster and clam shells.

When the furnaces were "put into blast" after the ponds thawed in the spring, workers labored seven days a week in 12-hour shifts. The furnace ran 24 hours a day until the ponds froze again in late December or January, when the water wheel could no longer power the bellows.

The iron furnace resembled a flat-topped pyramid and stood approximately 25 feet high on a 20-foot-square base. It was generally built from Jersey Sandstone, although bricks were sometimes used.

Traditionally, in order to make one ton of iron, two and a half tons of bog ore and 180 bushels of charcoal were required. All ingredients, in specially measured amounts, were taken to the top of the furnace and dumped by layers into its stack. Workers below used water-powered bellows to keep the furnace fire going. As the process proceeded, molten iron would settle in the crucible, and the slag would float to the top. Molten iron was then released through the bottom tap hole and guided into a series of trenches called "pigs" (because it was said they resembled a mother pig suckling her young) or ladled into molds for cast products. The pig iron was sent to forges for further processing into wrought iron products.

In its heyday, the iron industry in the Pine Barrens numbered 17 furnaces and at least as many forges. It was the Barrens' most important industry, lasting until the middle of the 19th century. The decline of the bog iron industry in New Jersey began around 1820, when the natural stores of bog iron were almost depleted. Many furnace owners were forced to import bog iron from locations as far away as New York and Delaware. The final blow to the Pine Barrens iron industry came when richer ore and a more efficient fuel, in the form of coal, were discovered in Pennsylvania.

CHARCOAL

Charcoal provided the fuel that ran the forges and furnaces. Charcoal was made in pits that resembled an upside-down bowl covered with turf. To build a charcoal pit, an eight- or nine-foot pole was set vertically in the ground. Eight to 10 cords of pinewood were stacked closely around the pole and then covered with turf and sand. A hole was left open at the top to allow smoke and gas to escape. A collier would light the pit by dropping burning kindling into the apex. The wood would then smolder in a slow, controlled burn. To assure that the wood burned at just the right speed and temperature, the collier lived near the charcoal pit in a small open hut to keep close watch on the process. When the fire burned out (in about a week)on the collier would wait several days for it to cool down before he raked out the finished charcoal. Even after the collapse of the iron industry, charcoal continued as a Pine Barren industry for several more decades and lasted into the 20th century in a few locations.

During the Revolutionary War, many of the iron furnaces and forges of the Pine Barrens made munitions and other wartime products for the Continental Army. Batsto was considered so pivotal in this process that in 1778 the British sent a fleet of ships to destroy the ironworks and the nearby army storehouses at The Forks. The British never reached Batsto or The Forks, however, as they turned back at Chestnut Neck after learning of an impending attack by the Continental forces. General Washington, aware of the planned attack by the British, had sent a legion of men led by Count Pulaski to fend off the assault, allowing Batsto to continue its munitions production.

COMPANY TOWNS AND TAVERNS

During the iron era, company towns grew up around the furnaces and forges. These towns typically contained workers' homes, a gristmill, a sawmill, a blacksmith, a company store, and often a school and a church. With all the buildings in the town belonging to the owner of the company, it often resembled a feudal village. The owners often paid the workers in company script that could be used only at the company store to buy all of their household supplies. The workers, often in debt to the company store long before payday arrived, found themselves continually indebted and dependent on the company. Company towns also grew up around the glass houses, paper mills, and cranberry farms of the 19th and early 20th centuries. During World War I, company towns were built around munitions plants and depots.

Taverns, though not housed in the company towns, were usually built close by and became an important part of the life of the inhabitants of these villages. This was the place to come to hear all the news of the outside world and to discuss what was going on with your neighbors. During the Revolutionary War and the War of 1812, army recruiters came to the taverns to enlist men. During the war years, taverns became the meeting places for local militias to train troops. The local tavern often served as post office for the local community and in some cases as a tax collection center. Weddings and other special events such as court hearings were also held here. The taverns were important not only to local residents but to those traveling by horse and stage. Most often built on stagecoach roads, taverns (sometimes referred to as "jug taverns") became the place where weary travelers could stop for a meal or just to fill up their jugs with beverages to be consumed on their journeys. Most taverns also provided overnight lodgings for those on longer journeys. When railroads replaced the stagecoach as the preferred mode of travel, most of the taverns on the old stage roads shut down.

GLASS

Glassmaking became the next important industry of the Pine Barrens. Beginning in 1837 and running through 1869, five factories were built in Washington Township within a five-mile radius. Hermann, the largest of these factories, was built between 1872 and 1873 and lasted less than one year. The nearby Bulltown and Crowleytown operations lasted a little over a decade. Batsto, with its bog iron business about to collapse, opened a glass factory in its village in 1846. The Green Bank glass factory was built in 1837 and was in operation for 21 years. The glass products made at these five facilities included window glass, bottles and jars, and specialty glass items such as Christmas ornaments and buttons. Crowleytown is reputed to have been the place where the first Mason jar was manufactured.

The Pine Barrens glass houses used the natural resources of the area in their production of glass. Silica (basically sand) is the main ingredient in glass and is found in abundance throughout the Pines. Lime (seashells) could also be found nearby; therefore only soda ash needed to be imported.

Glassmaking involved the heating of the silica, soda, and lime. These ingredients formed the "batch," which was heated for five or six hours in calcining ovens to rid it of moisture and organic matter. After the batch cooled, it was sifted and put into specially constructed pots to be melted into molten glass. Once this occurred, the process was turned over to the master blowers, who, working with long, hollow, iron pipes, would gather a gob of molten glass (metal) on one end of the blowpipe. In the production of window glass, the blower would inflate the ball of molten glass by continually blowing and swinging the pipe while he stood over a swing pit. He would continue this until the molten glass ball lengthened into a large cylinder. The cylinder was taken to a flattening oven and opened into large sheets. After cooling, the sheets were taken to the cutting room, where they were cut into individual window lights.

Other glass products, such as bottles, were not free blown but were blown into the desired shape within a mold. To make a bottle, molten glass large enough to form an elongated ball would be gathered around the blowpipe. This gob of molten glass would then be placed into an open mold. After the mold was closed, the blower would blow the molten glass into the desired shape.

The heyday of the glass industry in the Barrens was between 1830 and 1890. Many factors contributed to the decline of the Pine Barrens glass industry, including the long distance from developing railroads and a growing lack of fuel. The most important reason for the decline was that the local iron-rich sand did not produce a clear glass. The glass produced from the Pine Barrens sand was of a light blue or green coloring, which, although distinctive, was not preferred by the end of the 19th century.

PAPER

Paper mills were another important industry in the Pines during the 19th century. In 1835 William McCarty, a Philadelphia merchant and bookseller, opened a paper mill at what would become known as McCartyville and later as Harrisville. The plant operated successfully for a number of years and closed in 1896 while under ownership of the Harris family.

At the time of the opening of McCarty's plant, there were 29 other paper mills operating in the state. Prior to the mechanization of papermaking, paper had been made by hand from linen and cotton. McCarty had discovered a formula for papermaking that used salt hay, which could be found in abundance in nearby marsh areas. Other ingredients in McCarty's papermaking process included old ropes, rags, paper scraps, and bagging material.

With the emergence of papermaking as a successful Barrens industry, other paper mills opened at Pleasant Mills (previously a cotton mill) in 1861 and at Weymouth (previously an ironworks) in 1866. Both paper mills operated successfully for a number of years.

In 1861 the Raritan and Delaware Bay Railroad built a line through the Pine Barrens and opened a station 11 miles to the north of Harrisville. Although the paper mill used this station to ship its products, its distance from the town, which was reached by mule teams, created a difficulty that later contributed to the collapse of the company. Prior to the installation of the rail lines, a proposal had been floated that would have brought the railroad directly through the town of Harrisville. This direct connection to the New York and Philadelphia markets, had it occurred, would have surely improved the ability of the Harrisville plant to do business and may have temporarily prevented the company's demise.

Where the railroads did or did not go made all the difference for the towns of the Pines. As late as 1897, the Tuckerton Railroad was proposing a rail line that would run from Hammonton to Tuckerton with stops at Pleasant Mills, Batsto, Herman City, Green Bank, Harrisville, and Bass River. Had the railroads come, these towns might have reached an industrial prominence unimaginable today as you view the sleepy little villages they have become.

COTTON, CLAY, AND REAL ESTATE

The cotton milling and clay mining industries of the Pine Barrens were short-lived and established in only a few locations. In 1821 a cotton mill named Pleasant Mills of Sweetwater was established near Batsto, but after operating at a profit for 27 years, it was eventually converted to a paper mill. The cotton mill at Atsion, although originally built as a paper mill in 1852, was in its heyday a successful operation employing upwards of 170 people, turning out 500 pounds of cotton yarn weekly. But the mill was only intermittently successful and finally closed its doors in 1882.

The clay industry in the Pine Barrens enjoyed success during the brief period from the late 1850s until the turn of the century. Several companies operating in Ocean County made pottery, bricks, stoneware, and drainpipes from clay mined in the area.

Throughout the 1800s, realty development was also a business that thrived in the Pines. Thousands of acres of land were bought and sold, offering prospective buyers good homesites and investment properties. Some communities, such as Egg Harbor City and Hammonton, succeeded. Most of these real estate promotions failed, however, after too few sales forced companies to abandon plans of developing huge tracts of heavily forested land. As a result of these failures, many deeds were not recorded, and in some cases the same land was resold to unsuspecting new owners. According to John McPhee in *The Pine Barrens*, more than a million people bought or otherwise acquired lots in the Pine Barrens on which no houses were ever built. At places like Apple Pie Hill, Fruitland (Atsion), Paisley, and Pasadena, land developers subdivided large tracts of land (mostly on paper) and advertised the sale of these lots to prospective buyers in faraway cities like New York and Philadelphia. Some subdivisions were cleared, but rarely was even one house built. Eventually the abandoned properties became overgrown with vegetation, leaving behind many acres of ground with murky land titles.

AGRICULTURE

Two of the important industries of the Pine Barrens that continue to this day are the cultivation and harvesting of blueberries and cranberries. The cranberry industry in New Jersey, nearly all of which is now confined to the Pine Barrens, makes New Jersey the third-largest cranberry-producing state in the country, behind Massachusetts and Wisconsin. New Jersey is the second-largest blueberry producing state after Michigan.

The cranberry is a native North American plant that grows wild in low fields, meadows, and bogs and along streams. Native Americans used the cranberry as food and for medicinal purposes. Gathered for food by the early European settlers, it was eventually cultivated in Massachusetts around 1820 and in New Jersey sometime between 1825 and 1840.

Cranberries are now grown in man-made bogs. The bogs are drained in spring after the last frost to ready the ground for an early bloom in June. In September and throughout October, the bogs are flooded for the wet-harvesting process that was started in New Jersey in the 1960s. Before the advent of wet harvesting, cranberries were picked by hand, and after 1925 they were picked using large wooden cranberry scoops. When the bogs are flooded in the wet-harvest method, the buoyant ripe cranberries lift off the bed of the bog and float toward the top. Workers then move around the flooded bogs with "beaters," mechanical cranberry machines designed to free the berries from their vines. The cranberries, freed from their vines, are guided onto loading conveyors. After the harvest, the water in the bogs is drained until the first freeze, when the bogs are again flooded to protect the plants from disease and frost.

Wild blueberries were also an important food for Native Americans and early European settlers. In 1910, Elizabeth White began work with Dr. Fredrick Coville in an attempt to cultivate the first blueberry. White—the daughter of Joseph (J. J.) White, who was the owner of Whitesbog, a cranberry farm near Browns Mills—and Colville became the first persons to successfully cultivate the blueberry in 1916.

Cultivated blueberry bushes are started from cuttings planted in rows in low, moist, acidic soil. The plants blossom in May, and the berries ripen from mid-June through early August. Originally the berries were picked by hand, and many still are, but the more modern method employs a mechanical blueberry picker that straddles the rows and shakes the fruit from the bushes. Before cultivation many people in the Pines used a system they called "knocking." Knocking was accomplished by strategically placing a basket under the bush and hitting the trunk with a one-foot club or rubber hose, resulting in most of the berries, falling into the basket.

SPHAGNUM MOSS

Sphagnum moss is a plant that grows in low-lying bogs and cedar swamps throughout the Pine Barrens. Sphagnum moss gathering, though not an organized, large-scale Barrens industry, brought in supplemental income for many residents of the Pinelands during the late 19th and early 20th centuries. Because of its amazing capacity to absorb water—up to 22 times its own weight—sphagnum moss became a product in demand by florists and nurseries. For many years florists used sphagnum moss at the base of floral arrangements to keep flowers moist during shipping. Nurseries used sphagnum moss during the cultivation of plants requiring a constant supply of water around their roots. Native Americans reportedly used the moss to heal sores and as diaper material for their babies. Sphagnum moss was also widely used during World War I in army hospitals as an absorbent filler for surgical dressings. In the Pine Barrens, pinecones, laurel, mistletoe, and holly were also collected by locals and sold to florists for their decorative value, especially around the Christmas season.

THE PINEYS

For many generations self-reliant individuals who lived in the Pines found a way to support themselves and their families by living off the land. These individuals, often referred to as Pineys, were a hardy bunch who through hard work and resourcefulness managed to stay on even after most of the major industries of the Pine Barrens had failed or moved away. Depending largely on the cranberry and blueberry business for income, most Pineys also farmed a bit, hunted, and gathered sphagnum moss, pinecones, and other products in demand by florists and nurseries. They lived simple lives deep in the forest and required little in the way of modern conveniences.

Unfortunately, these individuals and their lifestyle were brought into disrepute by exaggerated, distorted publicity in the early 1900s.

In 1913, Elizabeth Kite, a psychological researcher working for the Vineland Training School for Feeble-minded Boys and Girls, undertook a two-year study of a group of Pine Barrens residents who were in need of public assistance. The completed report, entitled *The Pineys*, told a story of generations of families who were criminal, illiterate, incestuous, mentally deficient, immoral, and a general burden to society. When the report was presented to the then governor of New Jersey, James Fielder, he made a special trip to the Pines. On his return he called a news conference and stated that the Pine Barrens should somehow be segregated from the rest of the state for the safety and welfare of the state at large. He said the people who lived in the Pines were a serious menace as they so often produced offspring who eventually would rely on public assistance. At about the same time, Dr. Henry Goddard—Ms. Kite's supervisor—published a book entitled *The Kallikak Family*. Extrapolating information from Ms. Kite's genealogical charts, Dr. Goddard invented a family he called the Kallikaks. This invented family, all descendants from Martin Kallikak and a nameless imbecile barmaid he impregnated and never married, were supposedly responsible for generations of morons, prostitutes, epileptics, and drunks. Goddard, whose work was an attempt to prove that heredity was the sole cause of mental deficiency as well as all the rest of society's ills, was later discredited.

Unfortunately, the impact of the negative publicity of the Kite report and its aftermath created a terrible stigma for the people of the Pine Barrens. Ms. Kite had focused on only a small group of people living in the Pines, yet her study was somehow generalized in the public consciousness to include everyone who lived there. Although many attempted to fend off this indictment of all the people of the Pines, the term Piney eventually came to represent a group of antisocial characters who were dim-witted, degenerate, and incestuous. Even though there were and are residents of the Pines who live in poverty and squalor, most of its citizens are descendants of noble families who worked at the bog iron furnaces, glass houses, and paper mills of years gone by. Because they loved the land of their forefathers, they carried on through difficult times and managed to eke out a living even after the industries had failed.

Today, other than those few families that make a living from cranberry and blueberry farming, few people who live in the Pines live entirely off the land. Most enjoy modern conveniences and live like everyone else. Yet the Piney myth continues. Perhaps this is not an entirely bad thing as it adds to the mystique of the Pines. Today many who make their homes in the Pine Barrens consider being called a Piney the ultimate compliment.

WATER, MUNITIONS, AND JETPORTS

It seems the New Jersey Pine Barrens, with all of its natural resources, has always attracted speculators and promoters, the story of Joseph Wharton being one example. In the late 19th century, wealthy Philadelphia industrialist-financier Wharton quietly went about the Pines acquiring a number of abandoned towns, ponds, and woodlands until he had accumulated over 100,000 acres of prime New Jersey real estate. His plan was to dam the many Pine Barrens rivers and pump the fresh water of the Pines to the city of Philadelphia. The undertaking was blocked, however, when the New Jersey legislature heard of the plan and enacted a measure that prevented the export of water from the state. Ironically, though Wharton had planned to exploit the resources of the region, his acquisition eventually led to their preservation when the Wharton tract was purchased by the state in the mid-1950s and designated a state forest.

In the waning days of World War I, owners of two munitions companies, contracting with the federal government, spent millions of taxpayer dollars constructing two huge shell loading plant-depots in the New Jersey Pines. Near the plants these companies also built large towns for the plants' workers. These plants and towns were in existence for less than one year when the armistice put an end to the need for increased artillery ammunition production.

One of the most ambitious plans for the use of the Pines came in the 1960s, when a study—largely paid for by the federal government—proposed the building of a city of 250,000 people and a supersonic jetport four times as large as Newark, LaGuardia, and Kennedy airports combined. This project, publicized in 1964, united a number of conservationists, farmers, hunters, and others who, realizing the threat to the Pinelands, began to work together on preservation efforts.

Those efforts finally came to fruition in the late 1970s with the establishment of the federal Pinelands National Reserve and the corroborating state legislation, the Pinelands Protection Act. The New Jersey Pine Barrens, with its 1.1 million acres of protected land, is now a place that is quickly returning to its natural state, leaving little behind of its illustrious industrial past.

REFERENCES

Atkins, George F. 1976. *Historic Atsion Village*. Indian Mills, NJ: Indian Mills Historical Society.

Baer, Christopher T., Coxey, William J., and Schopp, Paul W. 1994. *The Trail of the Blue Comet: A History of the Jersey Central's New Jersey Southern Division*. Palmyra, NJ: The West Jersey Chapter, National Railway Historical Society.

Boyd, Howard. 1991. *A Field Guide to the Pine Barrens of New Jersey*. Medford, NJ: Plexus Publishing, Inc.

Boyer, Charles. 1962. *Old Inns and Taverns in West Jersey*. Camden, NJ: Camden County Historical Society.

Cresson, Jack. "Prehistory and Batsto's Environs." *Batsto Citizens Gazette*, Fall/Winter 1996.

DeCou, George. "The Indian Reservation." *Mt. Holly Herald*, April 15, 1932.

DeCou, George. "Trails and Old Roads." *Mt. Holly Herald*, November 25, 1932.

Fowler, Michael, and Herbert, William A. 1976. *Papertown of the Pine Barrens: Harrisville, New Jersey*. Eatontown, NJ: Environmental Education Publishing Service.

Goddard, Henry, H. 1916. *The Kallikak Family: A Study in the Heredity of Feeblemindedness*. New York: The MacMillan Co.

Kraft, Herbert C. 2001. *The Lenape-Delaware Heritage: 10,000 B.C. to A.D. 2000*. Lenape Books.

McPhee, John. 1967. *The Pine Barrens*. New York: Farrar, Straus and Giroux.

Mountford, Kent. 2002. *Closed Sea: From the Manasquan to the Mullica, A History of the Barnegat Bay*. Harvey Cedars, NJ: Down the Shore Publishing.

Pearce, John E. 2000. *Heart of the Pines: Ghostly Voices of the Pine Barrens*. Hammonton, NJ: Batsto Citizens Committee.

Pierce, Arthur, D. 1957. *Iron in the Pines: The Story of New Jersey's Ghost Towns and Bog Iron*. New Brunswick, NJ: Rutgers University Press.

Regensburg, Richard. 1978. "Evidence of Indian Settlement Patterns in the Pine Barrens." *Natural and Cultural Resources of the New Jersey Pine Barrens*. Pomona, NJ: Stockton State College.

Stansfield, Charles A. 1983. *A Geography of New Jersey: The City in the Garden*. New Brunswick, NJ: Rutgers University Press.

Starkey, Albert J., Jr. 1962. "The Bog Ore and Bog Iron Industry of South Jersey." *The Bulletin*, Vol. 7, No. 1.

Stinton, John W., and Masino, Geraldine. 1978. "A Barren Landscape: A Stable Society of People and Resources of the Pine Barrens in the Nineteenth Century." *Natural and Cultural Resources of the New Jersey Pine Barrens*. Pomona, NJ: Stockton State College.

Wilson, Budd. 1978. "The Pine Barrens Glass Industry." *Natural and Cultural Resources of the New Jersey Pine Barrens*. Pomona, NJ: Stockton State College.

Wilson, J. G. "Not So Barren Barrens Provided a Living for Many." *Batsto Citizens Gazette*, Spring/Summer 1984.

Atsion and Hampton

where iron, cotton, and cranberries ruled

Atsion and Hampton

ATSION

OVERVIEW AND WALKING TOUR

On the shores of Atsion Lake off Route 206 in Shamong Township stand the remains of a once vibrant and historically significant village. Little is left to mark the prominence of this once thriving industrial center, but enough remains to tell its story. In 1766 Charles Read dammed the Atsion River and erected an ironworks there that operated successfully for a number of years. Around the forge and later a furnace grew a village that included 19 homes for workers, a dwelling house for the manager, barns and stables, a gristmill, two sawmills, a company store, and a church. By 1820 the ironworks, entangled in foreclosure proceedings, was in a neglected and dilapidated condition. The furnace and forge were shut down, and the property was put up for sale. With no work to be had, the villagers moved away, and Atsion soon became a ghost town. In 1824 Samuel Richards, who had acquired the ironworks in 1819, reopened the forge and furnace and reestablished the town. Under Richards's leadership the town reached its highest prominence. The manor house built by Richards in 1826 still stands, as does the company store and community church.

Not long after Richards's death in 1842, the Atsion Ironworks shut down as a result of the discovery of a better grade of iron in Pennsylvania. There was an effort to establish a paper mill on the site, but though the factory was built, evidence suggests it never opened. By 1871 Maurice Raleigh, a wealthy Philadelphian, had acquired the Atsion tract. Raleigh enlarged the paper mill and opened it as a cotton mill. During his tenure, Raleigh built a school, restored the church, and opened several new shops. The cotton mill ran successfully until Raleigh's death in 1882.

27

getting to Atsion

From the West
Take Route 70 East to Route 206 South. Drive about 10 miles south on Route 206 until you reach the Atsion ranger station on your left.

From the South
Take Route 30 West to Route 206 North (just above Hammonton). Follow Route 206 North for approximately 7.5 miles. The Atsion ranger station will be on your right.

From the North via the New Jersey Turnpike
Take exit 7 to Route 206 South. Follow to the Red Lion Circle (where Route 206 intersects Route 70). Drive about 10 miles south from the Red Lion Circle on Route 206 until you reach the Atsion ranger station on your left.

From the North via the Garden State Parkway
Take the Garden State Parkway to exit 88. Take Route 70 West to Route 206 South. Drive about 10 miles south on Route 206 until you reach the Atsion ranger station on your left.

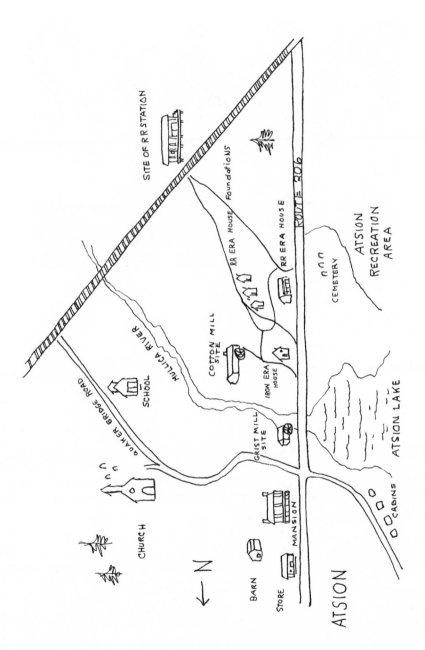

Atsion site map. (*Drawn by Berminna Solem*)

Atsion store, 1923.
(*Photo by William Cole, courtesy of Budd Wilson*)

After Raleigh's death his heirs made an attempt to establish a planned community on the Atsion tract. This too failed, and only a few lots on the north side of the lake were sold. In 1892 Joseph Wharton bought the town and used the old mill as a sorting and packing house for the cranberries he grew in surrounding bogs. In 1955 the state of New Jersey bought the property as part of the Wharton Tract purchase and soon developed a recreation center there.

With the site map, it should be easy to explore what remains of the old village of Atsion. A good place to start your tour is at the ranger station, located in the old company store.

Built by Samuel Richards in 1827, the store was restored when the state took possession of the property. The store had been a vital part of an old company town and the place where all the village folk came to find out what was going on and to purchase their basic necessities. For many years the Atsion store housed a post office. It also sold food, medicine, farm tools and equipment, cloth and sewing supplies, animal grain, livestock, and whiskey. Oftentimes local folks would barter at the store for those things not raised at home. They would bring in butter, eggs, milk, peas, peaches, apples, strawberries, grapes, and potatoes, and in turn would receive credit for needed supplies.

During Raleigh's time, the store's inventory expanded to include boots, shoes, hats, shawls, jewelry, and cutlery. When Wharton owned the property, there was a candy-counter that sold gumdrops, candy bananas, Tootsie Rolls, and sourballs. Behind the counter were bolts of multicolored yard goods to make new clothes or couch cov- ers. There were white lima beans and dried red beans in big barrels, as well as feed for chickens, cows, and horses.

On top of the store was a belfry with a bell that rang to call the men to work or to warn of some calamity. Beginning in 1900, a ship- ment of oil arrived each month by rail from the Standard Oil Company to fill a pump that stood in front of the store. The store closed its doors in 1946, a victim of the gasoline scarcity during World War II.

After visiting the store, follow the map to the nearby mansion. The Richards mansion, built in 1826, is an example of rural Greek Revival architecture. The mansion, which had no central heating system, was used by the Richards family in the spring and summer

The Atsion store, shown in 2004,
is now used as an office for the state forest service.
(*Photo by Gordon Stull*)

A view of the north side of the Atsion mansion before state restoration.
(*Photo courtesy of Budd Wilson*)

months. When the weather grew cold, the Richards family would return to their Arch Street residence in Philadelphia.

. The exterior of the mansion was renovated by the state in the early 1960s. Although there were plans to renovate the inside of the mansion, as of this writing it has not occurred.

On the south side of the mansion is a wide veranda. When New Jersey purchased the property, this veranda also extended to the westerly side of the mansion. Because the veranda extension was known not to have existed originally (during the Richards era), it was removed during the 1960s renovation.

During the Richards era, many large social functions took place in the Atsion mansion. When guests arrived, they were driven to the carriage entrance on the north side of the mansion. They entered the house through a wide hallway that connected with a spacious dining room on one side and two well-proportioned parlors on the other. The parlors could be opened to form one large room for dancing. An elegant stairway led to the second floor, which held four bedrooms for the family's use. A narrow, steep stairway led to the third floor,

Another view of the Atsion mansion before state restoration.
(Photo courtesy of Burlington County Library)

which held four smaller bedrooms used by the household servants. The kitchen was located in the basement and included an eight-foot-wide, open-hearth fireplace. A milk and meat room, which by design was dark and cool, was located near the kitchen. A smaller kitchen and serving room were located on the first floor. A covered service entrance on the eastern side opened into the basement kitchen and first floor.

Leave the mansion, cross Quaker Bridge Road, and walk toward the highway. A short distance into the woods stood the large village gristmill, built in the last quarter of the 18th century. All that remains are a few moss-covered stones and the remnants of the raceway that powered the mill. In the early years the gristmill served an important function in the rural village; it was the place where wheat was ground into flour and corn into meal. The Atsion gristmill, which was still standing in 1890, was hit by lightning sometime later and burned to the ground.

Leave the gristmill ruins, return to Quaker Bridge Road, and proceed in a northerly direction. There you'll find a large concrete barn

Wharton barn in early 20th century.
(*Photo by William Cole, courtesy of Budd Wilson*)

located near the mansion and built during the Wharton years, in the early 1900s. The barn—built as a concrete structure as protection against fire—once housed horses and cows. The second floor was used to store hay and grain for the animals.

After a short distance on Quaker Bridge Road, you will pass a hunt club and an old house located to the rear of the club. Although it is likely the old house was originally a part of the Atsion village, it is now privately owned, as is the hunt club. During the iron era, the workers' houses were located in this area. After passing the hunt club, go a short distance and look for a small white clapboard church and cemetery on the left side of the road.

The church was built in 1828 by Samuel Richards to be used by all Christian denominations. Soon after the church was built, Richards turned the deed over to a board of trustees to ensure that his wishes for the multidenominational use of this church would be followed. During the years it has been used by Presbyterians, Methodists, Episcopalians, and during Raleigh's tenure, as a "Free

Wharton barn, 2004.
(*Photo by Gordon Stull*)

Union" church. Today the church is called the Grace Bible Baptist Church, and services are still held here every Sunday morning.

Next to the church is a cemetery where many 19th and 20th century villagers of Atsion are buried. Across Route 206, in the picnic area by Atsion Lake, is another cemetery called the "Catholic cemetery" because many of those buried there had Irish names. Although few burial stones remain to tell the story, archaeologists who have examined the cemetery tell us that there are some 60 graves spread over an area of about 100 square feet.

Leave the church area, return to Quaker Bridge Road, and proceed a short distance in an easterly direction until you reach a building on the right side. This is the site of a school built by Maurice Raleigh in 1872. The current structure was built in 1916 and used as a school until 1922 and later as a private residence. At the time of the original construction, free public education had just come into existence in New Jersey. Prior to this time, children of the village received little if any education, although children of wealthy families received education at private schools.

Atsion church, 2004.
(*Photo by Gordon Stull*)

When this school, Public School 94, first opened in 1872, it provided education for students from the first through fifth grades. Teachers, who usually boarded with the parents of the children in the village, made $20 a month and were responsible for teaching all grades. Important duties at home and at work in the local industries often kept the village children from attending school regularly.

To continue your exploration of the old village, take Quaker Bridge Road back to Route 206. At the highway, turn left, go across the dam, and turn left into the first dirt road. Following the road straight back, you will pass a bungalow on your right. This cottage is believed to be the oldest building in Atsion, probably dating back to the early iron days. Continuing a short distance, you will come to the ruins of the cotton mill. Built in 1852 as a paper mill, the main part of the two-storied building is 60 feet long and 50 feet wide.

The old furnace sat nearby and probably used the existing raceway to power its bellows. Several large balls of black slag can be found in the woods behind the cotton mill ruins and raceway, evidence that the furnace was once located nearby.

During the cotton years, about 170 workers at the mill produced over 500 pounds of yarn per week. The cotton mill closed soon after

Atsion school, 2004.
(*Photo by Gordon Stull*)

Raleigh's death, but after Joseph Wharton purchased the property, it was reopened as a cranberry sorting and packing plant. For years the Atsion railroad depot shipped cranberries as well as cotton to New York and Philadelphia. The old factory was used until the cranberry factory closed down in the 1940s. In 1977 the building was set on fire by arsonists and burned to the ground.

Proceed south on the dirt road located near the slab-sheathed bungalow toward the site of a fenced-in, weathered house (close to Route 206). This typical Victorian frame structure, built during the cotton years, was a double house used by two families. On a dirt road between the cotton mill ruins and the road where the fenced-in double house stands are the remains of three double houses that were similar in appearance to the one that still stands.

Continuing on this road in an easterly direction, you will cross railroad tracks. The clearing on the northeast side of the track was where the Atsion Railroad Depot once stood. The Raritan and Delaware Bay Railroad first built a line through the town in 1861, receiving right-of-way in 1862. The rail line through Atsion was

Atsion cotton mill, 1923.
(*Photo by Arthur Pierce, courtesy of Budd Wilson*)

Railroad era home, 2004.
(*Photo by Gordon Stull*)

connected to New York and north by ferry from Port Monmouth and south by boat across the Delaware Bay. A spur track went from Atsion to Atco, where it connected with a rail line that ran from Camden to Atlantic City. In later years the rail line became the Central Railroad of New Jersey, colloquially referred to as "the Jersey Central." During those years a number of trains, carrying both freight and passengers, ran through Atsion on a daily basis. Although freight trains ran on the existing line as late as 1978, the Atsion station was retired in 1949.

A Deeper Look

Atsion, now a sleepy little hamlet in Shamong Township, bears little resemblance to the vibrant industrial village of days gone by. Once a successful ironworks and subsequently a productive cotton mill, Atsion also had several failed ventures to round out its colorful past. During the Wharton years, the town hosted a cranberry farm and packing plant. Today Atsion is part of a state forest and a recreational park visited by those largely interested in its bountiful natural attractions. Nearby, the deteriorating village with its once stately mansion stands silent watch, unable to inform the infrequent visitor of its grand history.

In the days when this land was still inhabited by the Lenape Indians, the river we now call the Mullica was then named the Atsayunk. Originating 10 miles to the west near the town of Berlin, this river, with its potential water power and rich beds of bog iron, was what first attracted the interest of Charles Read.

Read, who was called by some the Benjamin Franklin of New Jersey, was a man of many interests and talents. Born in Philadelphia to a father who was once mayor of the city, Charles Read was educated both there and in England. As a young man he joined the British Navy and was soon sent to Antigua, in the West Indies, where he met his wife, Alice Thibou. After returning to Philadelphia some years later, Read settled his family in Burlington, New Jersey.

Read's political career alone would have been enough to keep most men busy for a lifetime. He was involved in the legislative, executive, and judicial branches of colonial New Jersey government and was no minor player in any of these arenas. As secretary of the Province of New Jersey, he was second in command to the governor. A longtime member of the Assembly, Read also served for a time as Assembly leader. During his years in the Assembly, he served as commissioner of Indian Affairs and was involved in the establishment of the Brotherton Indian Reservation. In later years he was a prominent member of Council of the Province and in this role served as an advisor to the governor. He was also a judge of the New Jersey Supreme Court and served for a short time as chief justice. To round out his public career, he served as commander of the Burlington Militia with the rank of colonel.

Charles Read was no idler when it came to cultural and community affairs. He founded the first library in his hometown of Burlington and was involved in the establishment of the Queens College.

Aside from his public life, Read was also quite busy with his private business ventures. As a land promoter and speculator, he bought and sold over 35,000 acres in his lifetime. He owned several plantations, including Sharon in Springfield Township and Breezy Ridge near Mt. Holly, and was very interested in innovative farming practices, maintaining voluminous notes on farming methods of the day. He was also interested in the timber business and dammed several streams on his lands where he operated sawmills. As part of his business ventures, he also invested in a fishery on the Delaware River near Trenton.

Not withstanding his many interests and activities, Charles Read is best known for his involvement in the New Jersey bog iron industry, which he began when he was 51 years old. Noting the large quantities of bog iron in the swamps on some of his land, Read decided to open a string of ironworks. Beginning in 1765, and in quick succession thereafter, he built the Taunton, Etna (also spelled Aetna), Batsto, and Atsion ironworks. Between 1766 and 1768, Read, who was investing large amounts of his own capital in the ambitious ironworks venture, soon began advertising for partners to share the financial burden. After erecting a forge at Atsion in 1766, Read took on two partners, David Ogden and Lawrence Saltar.

Pig iron made at Batsto was carted over dirt roads for further processing at the Atsion forge. The forge flourished for several years, but Read, who owned the controlling interest, was experiencing serious financial and personal difficulties that adversely affected the Atsion Ironworks operation.

Although no slaves were used at Atsion, Read utilized both slave and indentured servant labor at his other ironworks. Because indentured servants often ran away, manpower was frequently in short supply, which resulted in temporary shutdowns of the ironworks. Overindulgence in alcohol by workers contributed to delinquency and low production, which plagued Read's business interests even further. The liquor problem became so pervasive that Read eventually used his influence to pass legislation prohibiting the sale of liquor to any employee of an ironworks within a four-mile range of the plant. The only exemption to this law allowed the owner of an ironworks to provide liquor to his workers as he deemed appropriate.

During this period, Read's wife passed away, and Read himself was experiencing serious health problems, at one point being bedridden for the better part of a year. Along with his bereavement, health, and labor problems, he was in serious financial straits. He had overextended himself with his numerous enterprises and needed an infusion of cash just to stay afloat. In 1770 he advertised his share of the Atsion Ironworks in a Pennsylvania journal, but no buyers readily appeared. In 1773 he finally sold his share of the ironworks to Henry Drinker and Abel James. Soon after, David Ogden sold his share of the ironworks to Lawrence Saltar, who remained at the village as manager.

With creditors pressing, Charles Read secretly left for Antigua in an attempt to gain some much-needed cash by settling his wife's estate. Before leaving the area, he turned his remaining assets over to trustees for assignment, though he did not resign from several of his public offices. Little is known of his whereabouts and dealings after his departure for Antigua, although it was later learned that he had returned to America within the year, opening a small shop in the frontier town of Martinsburg, North Carolina. Without family or friends to comfort him, Read, who had contributed so much to his new country, died indigent and alone on December 27, 1774. It was a sad end for such an accomplished and prominent man.

Soon after Read's departure from the business, Lawrence Saltar and Henry Drinker built a furnace at Atsion in 1774, freeing themselves from their dependence on Batsto. At about this time, Drinker's older brother, John, bought a small share of the ironworks.

During the period of the Revolutionary War, the Drinkers—Quakers who were opposed to the war—shut down the furnace. Although the furnace was under the Drinkers' control, the forge was not. Lawrence Saltar continued to operate the forge and in 1776 contributed to the war effort by supplying the Pennsylvania Navy with iron products.

After the war years, with the furnace back in blast, the Atsion Ironworks prospered. Soon there was a gristmill, three sawmills, a furnace, and a forge in concurrent operation. In 1798 a post office was established in the town, another sign of its success and prominence. Wood stoves were among the products of the ironworks, and several of them found their way to Congress Hall in Philadelphia.

In 1784 Abel James sold his share of the business to Henry Drinker. In 1794 the furnace burned down, resulting in costly repairs and the beginning of more serious troubles for the ironworks. During this period Lawrence Saltar died, and his share of the business passed to his heirs. Henry Drinker and the Saltar heirs did not get along and were continually in conflict over management issues. By 1804 Henry, now tired of the feuding, advertised the property for sale. The sale listing described the property as over 20,000 acres of land, 19 houses for workers, a dwelling house, barn, stables, store, gristmill, two sawmills, and the furnace and forge. The whole estate was valued at $15,000, and Henry Drinker, who owned ten-sixteenths of the property, was asking $12,000 for his share. The property was finally sold at sheriff sale in 1805. Jacob Downing, Henry Drinker's son-in-law, bought the estate, with Henry continuing as 50-percent owner of the property. Under Downing's management the ironworks prospered for a number of years, but by 1817 Downing was in financial trouble and had mortgaged a section of the estate. In 1819 he had defaulted on his mortgage, and the Bank of North America took over his share of the ironworks, promptly selling it to Samuel Richards. Richards, the son of William Richards, ironmaster at Batsto, had also acquired interest in two other ironworks, at Weymouth and Martha.

Having obtained a contract with the city of Philadelphia to make sewer pipes, Samuel Richards kept the furnace at Atsion in blast until the contract was satisfied. Then in February 1820, he put the property up for sale. All the furnace and forge workers, as well as the colliers and lumbermen who supported the ironworks, were out of work and soon moved their families out of the town. Neglected and deserted, Atsion quickly became a ghost town.

Even though it looked as if the lights had gone out forever in Atsion, the old furnace was back in blast four years later. Not able to find a buyer for his property, Richards bought out Henry Drinker's one-half share and reestablished the Atsion Ironworks and village, serving as its ironmaster.

Samuel Richards was said to be handsome, imposing, and dynamic. It appeared he had the golden touch when it came to business matters, even surpassing his famous father. During his early years, Samuel worked in the Philadelphia family store. In 1796 he purchased land in Pleasant Mills that included several sawmills. Richards soon established a mill there for reclaiming wool from used and worn fabrics. By 1801 he had purchased a large gristmill and sawmill called the White Clay Creek Mills, located in Delaware. He married for the first time at the age of 28. His first wife, Mary Smith Morgan, was the daughter of a wealthy shipping magnate. They had eight children, though five died in childhood. Mary died in 1820, and two years later Samuel married Anna Maria Witherspoon, a wealthy widow from New York. Samuel was 53 and Anna 39 when the two married. Together they had three children, including one who died in childhood.

In 1826 Richards built his mansion at Atsion. He and his family spent the warmer months at Atsion, returning to Philadelphia in the winter. The Richards family reportedly entertained lavishly in their 13-room Atsion villa. Carriages would pull visitors up to a north-side portico, where they would enter the mansion through a wide center hallway on the first floor. On one side of the hallway were two parlors that opened to create one large ballroom for dancing. On the other side of the hallway was a spacious dining room. The kitchen, where the food was prepared, was in the basement.

In 1827 Richards built a company store. The store was a vital part of the village and provided the furnace workers with all the necessities of life. The store sold food, liquor, medicine, livestock, stoves, cloth, sewing supplies, farm equipment, and animal grain. In 1827 coffee sold for 16 cents a pound, eggs for 11 cents a pound, and rye whiskey for 37 cents a gallon. Oftentimes staples raised at home by the local folks were bartered in return for store items. Meantime in 1832 the post office, which had been moved temporarily in 1815 to Washington—a settlement approximately 10 miles east of Atsion—was returned to Atsion and located in the store. In 1828 Richards built the church, whose deed he soon turned over to a group of trustees.

Shortly after reestablishing the ironworks, Richards rebuilt the furnace and forge. With his family connections at Batsto, he was able to use Batsto Landing on the Mullica River to ship his products to New York. Those products going to Philadelphia were carted by wagon to the Lumberton Wharf on the Rancocas River.

Under Richards's leadership, Atsion knew its greatest prosperity. By 1834 there were 100 men working there, with a reported 600–700 people dependent on the ironworks for their sustenance.

Samuel Richards died in 1842, leaving Atsion to his two children with his second wife, Anna Maria. His daughter Maria received the northern half of the tract, and his son William the southern acres. William Richards had little interest in Atsion and spent much of his time on his 150-acre farm on Atsion Road. Maria married in 1849, and her husband, William Walton Fleming, took over some management of Atsion. Unfortunately, by the time Walton—as the family called Maria's husband—entered the picture, the iron industry was collapsing in New Jersey. Walton, who also owned the Fleming Cobalt and Nickel Works in Camden, built a paper mill at Atsion in 1852. The paper mill venture failed (many believe it never actually opened), and by September 1854 Fleming was in debt for more than $500,000. He soon fled the country without telling his many creditors—one of which was his father—or his family of his whereabouts. Undaunted and forgiving, Maria located him in Brussels, Belgium, one year later. After paying off Walton's father, who had pressed criminal charges against him for a bad debt, Maria joined her husband in Europe. Maria's mother soon joined the Flemings in Brussels, and there the family lived until their deaths.

Maria's share of the Atsion property was soon advertised for sale. By this time the Raritan and Delaware Bay Railroad had built a line through the town, considered an important drawing card in the sale of the property.

By 1862 the property had passed into the hands of Colonel William Patterson. Patterson changed the name of the town to Fruitland and subdivided the property into farm plots. In or around 1871, after selling only a few lots, Patterson was in bankruptcy.

In May 1871 Maurice Raleigh bought the property for $48,200. He enlarged Fleming's paper mill in order to establish a cotton mill on the site. The town that had been renamed Atsion was once more back in business. Raleigh built carpenter and blacksmith shops, restored the church, and built a school for the children of the village. By 1880, 300 people lived in Atsion.

In 1881 a "colored delegation" visited Atsion with the idea of purchasing the entire estate for the purpose of establishing a "colored colony" there. Raleigh's asking price was steep—$1.3 million (almost 3 times what he had paid for it)—and nothing came of the proposed plan.

In January 1882 Raleigh died, and his heirs formed the Raleigh Land and Improvement Company, with plans to once more subdivide the land and establish a planned community. The tract was subdivided into one-acre plots that sold for $25 each. The new town, now called Raleigh, was advertised as having pure air and good water and as being free of malaria. Only a few lots sold, on the north side of the lake.

In 1892 Joseph Wharton bought the entire Atsion tract. Foiled by the New Jersey legislature in his attempt to pump water out of the Pines for sale to Philadelphia, he turned to farming. Cranberry bogs were soon constructed on the land, and the old cotton mill was turned into a sorting and packing house. The harvested berries were shipped to markets in Philadelphia and New York through the Atsion train depot. Before the advent of the refrigerator, ice blocks were used to keep food fresh in warm weather, and the Atsion Ice House—located on the south side of the lake—was also a good

ATSION COTTON MILL AND BLACKSMITH SHOP

(*Illustrated by Berminna Solem*)

source of income for the town residents. When the lake froze, block-sized squares were sawed through and hauled into the icehouse for storage until the summer months. The cranberry bogs and sorting and packing plant were in operation until sometime in the 1940s. In 1892 Andrew Etheridge was appointed the caretaker of the estate and also became responsible for the management of the store. Upon his death, his son-in-law, Leeson Small, took over the job.

In 1955 the state of New Jersey purchased Atsion as part of the Wharton Tract purchase. Today, Atsion Lake is a popular recreational center for campers, picnickers, and swimmers. Most of what is left of the historic old town stays closed and bolted up, slowly deteriorating as it surrenders to the elements.

HAMPTON

OVERVIEW AND WALKING/DRIVING TOUR

A short distance north of the Atsion ranger station on Route 206 is a dirt road that heads east to the former industrial village of Hampton Furnace, later called Hampton Park. During the late 18th and early 19th centuries, Hampton was an ironworks village with a large mansion house, furnace, forge, gristmill, and many workers' dwellings. In the latter part of the 19th century, Hampton became a cranberry village with a four-story packing and sorting house at its core. Ponds that had once served the furnace and forge were turned into cranberry bogs, and on the site of the ironworks village stood the houses where pickers lived during the harvest season.

Although little remains to mark the iron years, those who look closely will see the chunks of iron slag that fleck the road, charcoal leaching through the road bank, and remnants of the old ponds and raceways. Though subtle, these remains clearly mark the location of the ironworks, which has now been almost totally reclaimed by the forest.

Most of what remains at Hampton are the foundations of buildings from the cranberry era. Foundations of the cranberry packing house and managers' residences are clearly visible. Foundations of the other structures are less obvious but can be located, especially after a controlled burn of the tall grasses of the village. Such burnings are regularly performed as part of the state of New Jersey's forest fire management plan.

History tells us that on the road to Hampton, Andrew Rider, owner of the Hampton Cranberry Bogs, his daughter, his brother, and another passenger were ambushed in 1916 by a group of bandits with designs on the $4,000 cash payroll the Riders were carrying to the village. Although the Rider party was able to escape with the payroll intact, Andrew, his daughter, and the passenger were wounded, and Andrew's brother, Henry, was killed. After the attack the gang of robbers fled into the woods. Fortunately, a neighbor had noticed a strange car in the vicinity and was able to furnish police with enough information to identify and eventually capture most of the gang.

After traveling approximately 2.3 miles, you will pass the ruins of a house on your left side. The ruins, located 100 feet in from the road

getting to Hampton

From Atsion

Travel north on Route 206, passing the Atsion ranger station. After approximately 0.1 mile, turn right onto a dirt road heading into the woods and travel approximately three miles to Hampton. Be sure to check your rearview mirror and to signal early when making the turn because traffic moves very quickly on Route 206.

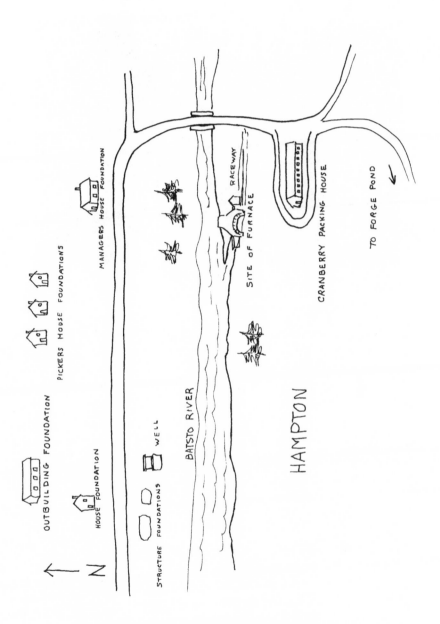

Hampton site map. (*Drawn by Berminna Solem*)

Ruins of house on Hampton Road, 2004.
(*Photo by Gordon Stull*)

(and close to a former cranberry bog), are likely those of a cranberry-era dwelling.

Proceed on to Hampton, which is easily identified by a large, open grassy area to the left. This is the former site of the Hampton village. If the grass is low, use the map to locate the foundations of six dwellings; if the grass is high, walk with caution as there are depressed areas and well holes within the village site.

Across from the village are the remnants of several buildings and a circular well. The road down to the river is currently a popular put-in spot for canoeists and kayakers paddling the upper Batsto River.

After visiting the village, use the map to locate the cranberry sorting and packing house ruins. As you cross the bridge, look to your left. What is now a cedar swamp was once the furnace pond. On your right as you cross the bridge, you will see a smaller pond that connects with the raceway that ran past the furnace and powered its waterwheel. Walking down in the area next to the raceway, you will find a large mound of iron slag, an indicator that the furnace stood close by.

In its day, the cranberry sorting and packing house in Hampton was one of the largest buildings in the area. It was four stories high, 150

Remains of Walk Bridge at Hampton, 2004.
(*Photo by Gordon Stull*)

feet long, and 60 feet wide. The factory housed a gasoline-powered elevator that moved the berries between floors.

To visit the site of the Hampton Forge, follow the road in front of the packing house to the right, traveling south. Drive or walk two-tenths of a mile to a bridge that crosses the Skit Branch, a tributary of the Batsto River. On the northwest side of the river is a large mound of iron slag, indicating the forge stood nearby. Across the road from the mound of slag was the forge pond, later a cranberry bog, and now a cedar swamp filled with sphagnum moss. Sphagnum moss was once an important local crop, gathered by many people living in the Pine Barrens for sale to florists and nurserymen.

A DEEPER LOOK

Once called Hampton Furnace and then Hampton Park, this lonely, woodland clearing deep in Wharton State Forest was a major center for two important Pine Barrens industries.

In the early spring of 1795, Clayton Earl and Richard Stockton built Hampton Furnace on the Batsto River on the site of a former sawmill. Earl—not a newcomer to the iron industry, having built Hanover Furnace in 1791—sold his share of Hampton to William

Ruins of Hampton cranberry sorting and packing house, 2004.
(*Photo by Gordon Stull*)

Lane and John Godfrey within a month of its construction. Lane and Godfrey soon sold their share to two brothers, George and William Ashbridge, who also purchased Stockton's one-half share in the furnace complex. The Ashbridge brothers operated the ironworks together until 1810, when George sold his one-half interest to William. About this time William had two forges constructed on the Hampton property. Hampton Forge was located just around the bend (approximately two-tenths of a mile) from the furnace site on a tributary of the Batsto River. The other, called the Lower Forge or Washington Forge, was located several miles below the furnace site on the Batsto River.

Kettles, wagon axles, sledgehammers, and skillets were some of the products made at the Hampton ironworks. The finished goods were transported to the Lumberton Wharf on the Rancocas River, then shipped by boat downstream to Philadelphia.

After William Ashbridge's death, the ironworks property was put up for sale. The advertisement listing the sale described the property as having 20,000 acres of land, a large mansion house, a furnace, two forges, a gristmill, a stable for four teams of horses, and a number of dwelling houses for workers. The ironworks was sold to Samuel Richards at a public auction held in Philadelphia on February 3, 1825. What the advertisement did not mention was the dilapidated condition of the ironworks complex. Ashbridge, who often leased or rented his ironworks to others, had not kept the property in good repair, and by the time Richards bought the property, the furnace was nonfunctioning and in ruins. As Richards owned Atsion (located three miles from Hampton) by this point, it can be assumed that he was well aware of the poor condition of the ironworks at the time of the purchase.

In 1828, Gordon's "Map of New Jersey" showed both Hampton Furnace and Hampton Forge in ruins. But in 1829, Samuel Richards rebuilt Hampton Forge, and he operated it until his death in 1842. Forge records also indicate that Richards's successors kept it running until 1850. Lower Forge, also known as Washington Forge, operated until about the same time.

Today, all that remains of the Hampton Furnace and Forge ironworks are several large chunks of iron slag and the remnants of the raceways and ponds that powered the waterwheels. It is said that during the cranberry years, a furnace wheel was found in the bottom of the raceway near the packing house. Although attempts were made to raise the wheel from its muddy bed, it apparently was so heavy that the workers gave up, leaving it where it had been found. As far as anyone knows, this last remnant of a long-gone age is still there, hidden and forgotten in the muddy banks of the old raceway.

In the latter 19th and early 20th centuries, Andrew Rider, former president of Rider College, and his partner Charles Wilkerson operated cranberry bogs and a sorting and packing plant at Hampton. During the cranberry years, the village was referred to as Hampton Park.

The bogs at Hampton Park covered the areas that previously comprised the ponds of Hampton Furnace and Hampton Forge. Hampton Bog No. 1, located on the old furnace pond, was one-half mile across at its widest point and extended almost three miles north and south on the Batsto River. Bog No. 2, just east of Bog No. 1, straddled the Skit branch, a tributary of the Batsto River.

During the cranberry years, there were two residences at Hampton Park. In one house lived David Kell, the manager of the Hampton Cranberry Bogs, and his family. When Kell retired, his son-in-law, John Wells, took over as manager and moved his family to Hampton Park. Along with the two residences were three two-storied picker houses. In the early years, before 1930, pickers stayed the whole picking season—September through October—at Hampton Park. In later years pickers did not live at Hampton Park but instead were trucked in daily from Camden and Philadelphia.

The cranberry sorting and packing plant at Hampton was one of the largest buildings in the area, measuring 150 feet long by 60 feet wide and standing four stories high. There was a gasoline-operated elevator in the building that transported the berries between floors. After being sorted and packed, the berries were stored in boxes until the Thanksgiving and Christmas holidays. They were then taken to Riders Siding, one-half mile away, for shipment by rail to New York and Philadelphia.

During the Rider years, cranberries were picked using a large wooden scoop with sharp wooden teeth. Pickers were given chits for each container of berries picked, and these chits were exchanged for cash at the end of each week. This well-known payroll practice inadvertently led to the death of Henry Rider, Andrew's brother, on the payday of October 5, 1916.

On this particular payday Andrew Rider, his daughter Elsie Smathers, his brother Henry, and a mechanic named Charles Rigby had picked up $4,000 in cash from a bank in Hammonton. Elsie was driving, her uncle was in the front seat with her, and her father and Charles Rigby were seated in the rear. On their way to the bogs to pay the workers, they passed a car with an out-of-state license plate parked at the Atsion store. The passengers, two men and a woman, were laughing and seemed to be having a good time. Although Rider and his party took little notice of the vehicle, automobiles were uncommon in the area at the time, and a suspicious neighbor noted the license plate number.

Turning onto Hampton Road on the way to the bogs, Andrew's car soon approached a small bridge. In an interview printed in the

Batsto Citizens Gazette in 1974, Elsie Smathers (later Hinch) recalled that suddenly 10 or 11 men came out of the woods (other accounts of this incident mention 8 bandits). Some of the men were dressed in women's clothes, and all were masked. Elsie, at first believing it was some kind of Halloween joke, stopped the car. Her father, realizing the danger, urged her to drive on. As soon as she restarted the car, a number of shots were fired at the passengers by the bandits. Rider, who was armed, handed his pistol to Rigby, who began returning the fire. Elsie floored the gas pedal and drove as quickly as she could toward the bogs as the bandits dispersed into the surrounding woods. During the drive she discovered that her uncle Henry had been seriously injured from a gunshot wound in his neck. Although she tried to stop the bleeding, Henry bled to death by the time they reached the bogs two miles away. Elsie, who had done a remarkable job getting her passengers to safety, had been shot twice, and her father and Rigby had each taken four bullets. When they reached the bogs with the $4,000 payroll intact, a worker was dispatched on a motorcycle to Hammonton to contact the police. Medical personnel were also contacted, but it was three hours from the time of the shooting before help reached the injured parties. When the doctor finally arrived, he pronounced Henry Rider dead. After treating the others, the doctor had them taken to Jefferson Hospital in Philadelphia, where all three made a full recovery.

By the time the police arrived, the bandits had escaped. The local villager who had noted the license number of the unidentified car gave the information to the police, who were able to quickly track down the owner. As the story goes, the owner of the vehicle had been paid to take three of the gang members to Atsion on the day of the incident. His two friends had gone along for the ride. None of these passengers were aware of the robbery or why they were driving to Atsion. The other gang members had arrived in the area by train and had spent the night in the woods. The gang leader, it seems, was a former cranberry picker who was aware of Rider's practice of bringing large amounts of cash to the bogs at the end of the week.

Even though all the bandits were identified, only five were ever actually located. One was caught and convicted in Mt. Holly and then taken to Trenton, where he was electrocuted. Another had fled to Italy, where he was captured and imprisoned for life. A third was killed in a gang fight in Newark, while a fourth was captured in a Pennsylvania town where he was living under an assumed name. Another, who had fled to South America and later to Spain and Italy, was found 15 years later serving a prison sentence in California. None of the other Hampton bandits were ever apprehended.

The cranberry bogs at Hampton operated for a number of years after the shooting incident. When Rider and his partner Charles Wilkerson left the business, Robert Clayburger, Wilkerson's son-in-law, took over operation at the bogs. By the time the state purchased Hampton, Clayburger's son Charles and his son-in-law Robert Goodrich were in possession of the property.

ATSION AND HAMPTON SIDE TRIPS

ATSION LAKE RECREATIONAL CENTER

To extend your visit at Atsion, you may want to visit the Atsion Lake Recreational Center. The center features a lake for swimming, a sandy beach, a playground, barbecue pits, picnic areas, nature trails, and boat rentals and launch. There is a concession stand in summer that sells soft drinks and lunch fare. Swimming is permitted from Memorial Day to Labor Day, and lifeguards are on duty during this period. There are nine cabins in the park on the north shore of the lake that can be rented from April to October. The cozy cabins all have kitchens, bathrooms, fireplaces, and electricity and range in size from those sleeping four people to those providing accommodations for eight. The rental cost will vary depending on the size of the cabin. Cabin permits are available at the Atsion ranger station, as are permits for camping in the Wharton State Forest. For further information on obtaining camping permits or to make arrangement for a cabin rental, call the Atsion ranger station at 609-268-0444.

Atsion Lake Recreation Center.
(*Photo by Gordon Stull*)

PADDLING THE MULLICA RIVER

To enjoy a paddle on the Mullica River (or other nearby rivers), contact Adams Canoe Rental at 609-268-0189. Adams Canoe Rental is located on Atsion Road on the north side of the lake.

If you are interested in doing your own boat launch and shuttle, a good starting point is the Mullica River access area located near the cotton mill ruins. If paddling all the way to Pleasant Mills (where you will find a canoe access area on Route 542 across from the Pleasant Mills Church), consider an overnight stop at the Mullica River campsite. The paddle trip from Atsion to Pleasant Mills takes approximately six to seven hours and may be too long for novices. Obtain a camping permit from the Atsion ranger station if you decide to overnight at the campsite.

PIC-A-LILLI INN

For a local culinary and cultural experience, visit the Pic-A-Lilli Inn. This longtime family-owned restaurant and tavern has a color-ful history, including visits by Gene Autry and Will Rogers (there are pictures on the wall to prove it). A historical summary of the Inn is on the back of the menu, and the employees are always willing to share a story or two about its past. The Inn has a bar and dining room, where lunch and dinner are served daily. It is located on Route 206 less than a mile north of the Atsion ranger station.

REFERENCES

Brumbaugh, G. Edwin. "Historical Background of Atsion and Richards' Mansion." *Batsto Citizen Gazette*, Spring/Summer 1981.

Dwier-Kirby, Lois. "Ironworks in the Pine Barrens." *Batsto Citizens Gazette*, Spring/Summer 1990.

Ewing, Sarah W. R. 1979. *Atsion: A Town of Four Faces*. Batsto, NJ: Batsto Citizens Committee.

Ewing, Sarah W. R. "Atsion Was Self Sustaining." *Batsto Citizens Gazette*, Spring/Summer 1979.

Ewing, Sarah W. R. "Atsion's General Store Vital Part of the Village." *Batsto Citizens Gazette*, Spring/Summer 1979.

Ewing, Sarah W. R. "Samuel Richards' Mansion Unchanged Through Years." *Batsto Citizens Gazette*, Spring/Summer 1979.

Ewing, Sarah W. R. "Once There Was a Park in the Pine Barrens." *Batsto Citizens Gazette*, Spring/Summer 1983.

McMahon, William. 1973. *South Jersey Towns*. New Brunswick, NJ: Rutgers University Press.

Pearce, John E. 2000. *Heart of the Pines: Ghostly Voices of the Pine Barrens*. Hammonton, NJ: Batsto Citizens Committee.

Pierce, Arthur D. 1964. *Family Empire in Jersey Iron: The Richards Enterprises in the Pine Barrens*. New Brunswick, NJ: Rutgers University Press.

Pierce, Arthur, D. 1957. *Iron in the Pines: The Story of New Jersey's Ghost Towns and Bog Iron*. New Brunswick, NJ: Rutgers University Press.

Wilson, J. G. "Survivor Recalls Harrowing Day at Hampton." *Batsto Citizens Gazette*, Spring 1974.

Woodward, Carl R. 1941. *Ploughs and Politicks: Charles Read of New Jersey and His Notes on Agriculture*. New Brunswick, NJ: Rutgers University Press.

old tuckerton
stage road

Old Tuckerton Stage Road

OVERVIEW AND DRIVING TOUR

Old Tuckerton Stage Road, once an Indian migration trail to the seashore and later called the Road to Little Egg Harbor, has carried many generations of wayfarers through the Pine forests to the coast. The first Europeans settling in Little Egg Harbor followed the old path on horseback and by foot. As more settlers moved into the area, the trail was widened and improved to accommodate the wagons that brought the needed supplies. Eventually, as the popularity and prosperity of the seaport grew, a stage line began making regular runs from the ferry at Coopers Point in Camden straight through the Pine Barrens to Little Egg Harbor. In 1791, George Washington designated Little Egg Harbor as a port of entry for the United States. Being the third-largest port of entry in the country (after Philadelphia and New York), Little Egg Harbor was a place of considerable commerce and much prosperity in the late 18th and early 19th centuries. The principal village in Little Egg Harbor was initially called Clam Town or Middle of the Shore and named Tuckerton in 1798. Soon thereafter the Stage Road to Camden became known as the Tuckerton Stage Road.

Today, with the exception of a few detours, this road can, as in times past, be traveled directly to Tuckerton from Shamong Township, providing you with much the same experience as those who traveled it several centuries ago. Traveling through two state forests, much of the time on rutted dirt roads, the journeyer with a little imagination can transport himself back to an earlier time. Although traveling by car is certainly faster than by horse or horse-drawn carriage, when traveling the back roads of the Pines, don't expect to drive more than 15 miles an hour. Also be aware that several sections of the Old Tuckerton Stage Road are through lowland areas that may be flooded after heavy rains. Traveling in the deep

61

getting to
Tuckerton Stage Road

From the West
From the Marlton Circle (where Route 70 intersects Route 73), take 70 East to the first traffic light. Make a right onto Maple Avenue and proceed to the next light. At the light make a left onto Main Street. After two more lights, the road will curve to the left and become Tuckerton Road. Drive through five more lights. After the fifth light (Jackson Road), look for Atsion Road, a turnoff on your right. Turn onto Atsion Road and proceed for five miles until you reach the intersection of Jackson Road and Atsion Road, the suggested starting point of the Tuckerton Stage Road driving tour.

From the South and East
Drive to the intersection of Route 30 and Route 206/54 just above Hammonton. Take Route 206 North for approximately 7.2 miles. Immediately after passing Atsion Lake on your left, make a left turn onto Atsion Road. Proceed 4.5 miles to the intersection of Jackson Road and Atsion Road, the suggested starting point of the Tuckerton Stage Road driving tour.

From the North via the New Jersey Turnpike
Take exit 7 to Route 206 South. Follow to the Red Lion Circle (where Route 206 intersects Route 70). After the circle, drive to the third light (at mile marker 13) and make a right onto Tuckerton Road. Proceed to the next crossroads and make a left turn onto Oakshade Road. Drive 2.3 miles, passing two stop signs, until you reach the intersection of Jackson (Oakshade) Road and Atsion Road, the suggested starting point of the Tuckerton Stage Road driving tour.

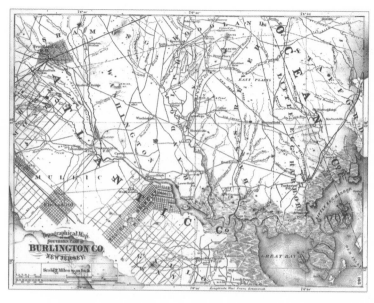

The Tuckerton Stage Road, beginning in Shamong and ending in Tuckerton, is shown on this F. W. Beers Map from *State Atlas of New Jersey*. *(Map courtesy of Steve Eichinger)*

woods is generally safe, but you should be prepared (see "Avoiding Mishaps in the Backwoods" in Chapter 1) and mindful of the amount of remaining daylight. It is best not to travel deep in the Pines at night as one wrong turn can result in your becoming seriously lost.

The Tuckerton Stage Road began in Camden, traveled through Ellisburg and Marlton, and then coursed through Medford Township. Before you begin the journey to Tuckerton on the old stage road, it is important to understand that in Medford, the current Tuckerton Road splits into two separate routes. After passing the crossroads at Jackson Road in Medford, Atsion Road diverges from Tuckerton Road in a southerly direction. Both the current Atsion Road and the current Tuckerton Road were referred to as the Tuckerton Stage Road, one taking a more northerly route and the other taking a more southerly route. To take the northerly stage road route, continue on Tuckerton Road past the crossroads at Stokes Road and across Route 206. Tuckerton Road, then becomes a dirt road that connects with

Carranza Road, eventually diverging to the right onto another dirt road through Wharton State Forest. To take the more southerly stage road route, follow Atsion Road when it splits from Tuckerton Road. Continuing on Atsion Road, cross Route 206 in Atsion and head straight into Wharton State Forest. The northerly and southerly routes reconnect when they enter the deserted village of Washington and then travel on as one road to Little Egg Harbor. The wayfarer is welcome to take either road on the journey to Tuckerton; however, the driving tour outlined here will take travelers to the shore on the southerly route and guide them back on the northerly route. Time constraints may prohibit traveling both of these dirt roads in the same day.

To travel the southerly route, begin the journey at the junction of Jackson and Atsion roads. At this intersection there once stood a hotel, built by Manasses Dellett in 1880. An earlier tavern built by John Piper stood on the opposite corner. Piper's tavern was in operation until 1853 and is known as the place where the public sale of the Brotherton Indian Reservation lands occurred. Brotherton, the first and only Indian reservation in New Jersey, contained 3,044 acres and was founded in 1758 and disbanded in 1802. Although irregular in shape, the largest section of the reservation stood between the boundaries of Tuckerton and Atsion Roads and Route 206 and Jackson/Oak Shade Road.

Leaving the intersection and driving approximately three miles, you will come to the former site of the Indian King Tavern, built by Ephraim Cline in 1795. The tavern sat on the west side of the road leading to the Goshen Campsite and fronted onto Atsion Road. The tavern, which operated until the mid-1800s, was frequented by the workmen of the nearby Atsion Ironworks and by the Indians of the Brotherton Reservation.

Leaving the tavern site, travel in a southerly direction until you reach the village of Atsion. Atsion, established by Charles Read in 1766, was initially the site of an ironworks and later a cotton mill. Crossing Route 206, head directly into the woods; this dirt road, now known as Quaker Bridge Road, begins to turn in a more southeasterly direction. After traveling several miles, over the old Jersey Central rail line and past an abandoned cranberry bog, look for a dirt

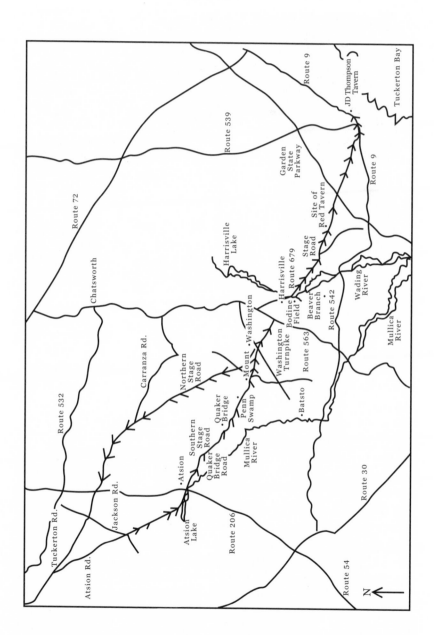

Tuckerton Stage Road tour map.

Tuckerton Stage Road in Wharton State Forest.
(*Photo by Gordon Stull*)

road leading to the right and a sign indicating that this is the way to the Mullica River campsite. Originally this was the road to Batsto and the main thoroughfare between the two ironworks. In the early years, wagons loaded with pig iron traveled on this road bound for the forge at Atsion. Today the road is a footpath that leads to a remote campsite that may be entered only by river travel or by foot. Continue on Quaker Bridge Road and travel for several more miles on the old stage road until reaching the Batsto River and the site of the famous Quaker Bridge. In 1772 a group of Quakers built a bridge over this stream after several members of their traveling parties had drowned here on their way to an annual meeting in Little Egg Harbor. Today this site is often used by outfitters as a put-in spot for canoe and kayak trips down the Batsto River.

On the slight rise on the east side of the river, a stage tavern once stood, built in 1808 by Arthur Thompson. Weary travelers, having spent many hours riding along the desolate stage road, were always happy to see the inviting lights of the Quaker Bridge Tavern. Local storytellers speak of an incident occurring one cold and stormy night when a stage driver, seeing the lights of the tavern in the distance, urged his horses on in hopes of a speedier arrival at the warm and dry dwelling at Quaker Bridge. Suddenly, out of nowhere, as the story goes, a large white stag appeared in the middle of the road. Frightened, the horses reared and refused to move forward. The driver, fastening the reins to the stage, jumped to the ground with his rifle in hand. When he reached the spot where the white stag had been standing, he saw that the bridge leading over the Batsto River had been washed away by the storm. Shaken, the driver returned to the stage knowing full well that without the appearance of the white stag, the coach and all of his passengers would have surely plunged into the river.

Penned by a young Philadelphia woman on her way to the most popular shore resort of the day, another story tells of the difficulty of early-19th-century stage travel and the joy of finally arriving safe and sound at a warm and cozy tavern. On a damp June morning in 1809, Sarah Thompson left Philadelphia with her mother and brother for the overnight journey to the shore resort of Tuckerton. Sarah and her

Quaker Bridge.
(*Photo by Gordon Stull*)

family, along with six other passengers, crammed themselves into a stagecoach that Sarah described as having "the appearance of an old Jersey wagon such as they go to market in." Sarah further described the journey in her diary, telling how after a short stopover in Haddonfield, her party headed out in a thunderstorm. After a harrowing ride through the Pines in a leaky stagecoach, the group finally arrived at Quaker Bridge, where they were to spend the night. "Arrived safe through all our troubles at Quaker Bridge, had a very good supper with clams in abundance, good coffee and very good beds. Landlady very kind. Charles complained of the rats, said they bit his ear, could not discover any mark; he must of dreamt it, swears he did not. Started next morning at daylight, a very pleasant ride after the rain."

At the small settlement of Quaker Bridge were three dwellings. The cellar hole of one of these, and quite possibly that of the tavern, stands between the junction of the road that swings northwesterly, running along the banks of the Batsto River, and the second road, which leads to High Crossing. The third road, leading in a southeasterly direction, was the main stage road to Little Egg Harbor.

Continuing on the Tuckerton Stage Road in a southeasterly direction, approximately two miles from Quaker Bridge, you will come to a significant bend in the road. This bend marks the beginning of Penn Swamp and a forest of dense cedar trees. In the bygone days this swampy area would have presented a challenge for stages and other forms of conveyance on their way to the coast. Today the road is generally passable except after very rainy weather or deep snow. Township records indicate that people once lived in this area, as three births occurred here in 1853–1854. The fathers of these children, all listed as laborers, may have been woodcutters or colliers living in the area on a temporary basis.

Just beyond the swamp is a fork in the road, with the right road going to Batsto and the left onward to Little Egg Harbor. Take the left fork and continue onward about one mile, until coming to a wide clearing and intersection. At this intersection was once the small settlement of Mount and another stage tavern operated by Jonathan Cramer in the early to mid-1800s. Leah Blackman wrote in *Old Times* of stopping at Mount on a trip with her father in 1829. Leah

Horseback riders on the Tuckerton Stage Road.
(*Photo by Gordon Stull*)

wrote that they had risen at 2:00 A.M. on a cold January day to begin the journey from Little Egg Harbor to Philadelphia. Traveling by horse and in a wagon covered with hay, 12-year-old Leah was wrapped in a homemade woolen coverlet trying to stay warm. Despite these efforts she reports that by the time they reached Mount her toes were so cold and numb that they bothered her for the next two to three years. Having traveled 15 miles from Little Egg Harbor, Leah and her father reached Mount just as the sun was rising. Entering the tavern, she was shown into a sitting room where a roaring fire of pitch pine knots in an ample fireplace allowed her to warm her feet. Leah's account of her wagon trip to Philadelphia offers a clear view of the rigors of 19th-century travel and the importance of the taverns in the life of those who made the journey.

Today, on the northwest corner of the intersection at Mount, you will find a cellar hole and some scattered bricks. This is probably the site of the old tavern. Across the road are the remains of another dwelling and a bricked well. It is known that the Coleman family lived at Mount for a number of years and raised 11 children there.

Crossroads at Mount, 2004.
(*Photo by Gordon Stull*)

Today Mount is a lonely place in the midst of nowhere, but 150 years ago it was a busy waypoint with visitors coming and going at all hours.

Leaving Mount, the stage road continues in a southeasterly direction. After several miles you will reach the deserted settlement of Washington, where the northerly and southerly routes of the stage road reconnect. At this junction another dirt road, known as the Washington Turnpike, crosses Tuckerton Stage Road. The Washington Turnpike, built by Joseph Wharton for his private use after he acquired the property in 1873, runs straight to Batsto.

The small community of Washington was the site of a famous Pine Barrens tavern built in 1773 by Nicholas Sooy. Sooy's Tavern, later called the Washington Tavern, was a busy stagecoach stop and an important township center. Centrally located, it was frequented by many of the local people who lived in the nearby furnace towns. It was the site of many town meetings and the place sergeants from the Continental Army went to find much-needed recruits. Later, when Wharton purchased this property at Washington, he cleared the woods and began to raise cattle on the land. The remains of a stone cattle

Ruins of a barn and pit silo at Washington, 2004.
(*Photo by Gordon Stull*)

barn and pit silo can be seen when one first enters the settlement. Across the Stage Road from the ruins are the cellar holes of two dwellings. The largest cellar hole was the site of Public School 3001. Behind the cellar holes are the remnants of an apple orchard that is reported to have held over 300 trees. Approximately 700 feet down that same side of the road is another cellar hole, believed to be the ruins of the Sooy family home. The tavern was located approximately three-tenths of a mile southeast of the barn ruins. Old maps tell us that it was located at the intersection of the Tuckerton Stage Road and the Speedwell-Green Bank Road. Today the crossing of two rarely used dirt roads, this intersection was once a major stage junction where travelers from near and far often stopped for rest and refreshment.

Leaving Washington, the dirt road continues another two miles before it intersects with a paved road, Route 563/Green Bank-Chatsworth Road. The old stage road would have continued directly across the highway, where it would shortly traverse the Wading River. Because a bridge no longer exists there, it is necessary for today's travelers to detour around this area. Turning left onto Route 563, travel approximately one mile to the fork of Routes 563 and 679. Make a sharp right onto Route 679/Chatsworth-New Gretna Road and proceed 1.7 miles to the Harrisville Paper Mill ruins. You will pass Harrisville Lake shortly before reaching the turnoff at Harrisville. At Harrisville there will be a sign directing you to Bodine Field. After turning right onto the dirt road, make a quick left and follow the road for one mile. Turn right at the next Bodine Field sign, heading directly toward the Wading River. After parking, walk to the beach area and turn right, then walk approximately 220 feet to the large cellar hole with scattered brick around its edges. This was the site of Bodine's Tavern. It is believed that the old stage road ran directly in front of the tavern. On days when the water is low, you can see six of the bridge pilings where the old stage road crossed over the Wading River.

Bodine's was another important tavern built around the time of the Revolutionary War. The open field next to the tavern was the site where local men would meet four times a year for military training. Early reports indicate that much more drinking than training occurred during these military practice sessions. This site where men from Martha and other nearby villages practiced military maneuvers is now a state campground.

After crossing the Wading River, the Tuckerton Stage Road crossed the meadow in a direct line to Little Egg Harbor. To follow the path of the stage road, turn right onto the dirt road after leaving Bodine Field. The stage road ran directly parallel with this road, running past Beaver Branch on its right. Beaver Branch was once an important river wharf called the Landing or Charcoal Landing during the early iron and paper years. After passing the Landing, the stage road ran directly through the woods, and after crossing Beaver Run it began to follow the course of Route 679, heading in a southeasterly direction. As the dirt road dead-ends at Beaver Branch, the traveler following Tuckerton Stage Road today will have to detour around this section, returning to Harrisville and making a right onto Route 679.

Approximately 3.5 miles from Harrisville and shortly after passing Timber Lake Campground on Route 679, make a left turn onto stage road. This is the original path of the stage road through Bass River

Beaver Branch, the former site of Charcoal Landing, 2004.
(Photo by Gordon Stull)

State Forest, leading into Tuckerton. After about 1.7 miles, you will pass Pilgram Lake Campground. The depression in the ground in front of the campground sign marks the cellar hole of the last stage tavern on the route. Named French's after its original owner and later called Bass River Tavern, it was known colloquially as the Red Tavern because of its color. Drive another 1.2 miles, passing the entrance to Lake Absegami and Bass River State Park. After 4 more miles, the road will intersect Route 9 in West Tuckerton.

The original stage road made a left at this point and traveled approximately 1.5 more miles to downtown Tuckerton. After 1828, many journeys on the Tuckerton Stage Road ended and began at the J. D. Thompson Tavern. Thompson was famous for owning the first stage line that made the journey by stage to Philadelphia from Tuckerton in one day. Today the beautiful, refurbished J. D. Thompson Inn is a bed and breakfast operated by Joseph and Gloria Gartner. The Inn is the perfect place to end your journey down the old stage road and to spend a few days if you have the time.

After enjoying a side trip to the Tuckerton Seaport Museum or a ride out on Great Bay Boulevard to see the Tuckerton Shell Mound

Lake Absegami.
(*Photo by Gordon Stull*)

J. D. Thompson Inn, 2003.
(*Photo by Gordon Stull*)

and the Crab Island Fish Factory, the traveler with enough time can do a return trip taking the more northerly stage route. The trip to Tuckerton from Shamong Township is approximately thirty miles when traveling the course of the old Tuckerton Stage Road. When using the northerly route, the course will require at least ten miles on dirt road through deep forest. This should be taken into consideration when deciding on a return trip.

If you decide to travel the stage road back to Shamong Township, you should retrace your steps to Washington. Staying on the same dirt road, you will cross the Washington Turnpike and head in a northwesterly direction this time in order to take the more northerly route of the stage road. After traveling seven miles through the forest, you will reach High Crossing, the old Jersey Central Railroad stop. After you proceed another 1.5 miles through the woods, Carranza Road will intersect Tuckerton Stage Road. If you turn right here and go a short distance, you will find the Carranza Memorial. Aviator Emilio Carranza, known during the early days of flight as the "Mexican Lindbergh," plunged to his death near here on his way back to Mexico from a goodwill flight to New York City. Every July an annual ceremony held at the memorial commemorates Carranza's journey and untimely end.

To continue on the stage road, turn left after reaching Carranza Road (for several miles Carranza Road follows the course of the old stage road). After about 1.5 miles you will come to the site of the former Hampton Gate settlement and Hampton Gate Tavern. The site of the settlement can be easily located as it stands near the sign indicating one is leaving or entering Wharton State Forest. It is said the tavern stood at the base of "the stone hills," which were once mined for building stone. Continuing on Carranza Road, you will see a dirt road on the left about one mile past Hampton Gate. This is where the stage road turned toward Flyatt. Make a left onto the dirt road, and you are now on Tuckerton Road heading toward Marlton. Proceed several miles, passing the crossroads at a place once called Oriental, and shortly thereafter you will reach Route 206. After crossing Route 206, travel to the next crossroads at Oakshade Road. This was the site of Flyatt, a settlement founded by three deserters of Washington's Army and the site of the Half Moon and Seven Stars

Tuckerton Shell Mound, 2003.
(*Photo by Gordon Stull*)

Tavern, another stage stop in the early and mid-19th century. The old stage road would continue down Tuckerton Road through Marlton and then to Ellisburg to the Cooper's Point Ferry in Camden for travel across the river to Philadelphia. Stage travelers needing a rest stop in Marlton found their way to Swain's Tavern (also known as the Rising Sun Tavern and later the Marlton Inn Tavern). In Ellisburg, stage travelers could refresh themselves at the Bush Tavern (later the Waterford Hotel), opened by Isaac Ellis sometime between 1773 and 1780 and operated by the Ellis family for a number of years.

A DEEPER LOOK

The Road to Little Egg Harbor—today known as Tuckerton Road—has gone through many changes. Beginning in Camden and traveling in an almost direct line to Little Egg Harbor, it was initially an Indian summer migration path. The native Lenni-Lenape, who lived near the Delaware River, had probably been using the trail for centuries. Each summer, those who lived near the Delaware would pack up their belongings and head to the seashore to join with other tribes who made the sea coast their permanent home. There they would share in the abundant bounty of the seashore, feasting on shellfish, terrapin, bird eggs, fish, and fowl. The Indians left unmistakable evidence of their presence in the hummocks and shell beds still extant on the tidal marshes surrounding Great Bay. One surviving example is the well-known Tuckerton Shell Mound, located off Great Bay Boulevard (Seven Bridges Road) in Tuckerton. The Tuckerton Shell Mound, believed to be about 1,500 years old, is a huge accumulation of quahog (clam) shells, with lesser amounts of oyster and conch shells. The mound covers about one-tenth of an acre laterally and rises about 10 feet above the tidal meadow. Ongoing research by archaeologists indicates that the shell deposits extend as much as 14 feet below the present marsh meadow. The area is believed to have been used as a shell refuse for Indians who lived nearby, and the mounds may have been used by them as a landmark for navigation purposes.

The first European reported to have used the old Indian path to Little Egg Harbor was Henry Jacob Falkinburg. Falkinburg had originally settled on Burlington Island (an island located in the Delaware River near Burlington City) in 1655, when it was a Dutch settlement. He was a linguist who had learned the Lenape language. Known widely as an Indian interpreter, Falkinburg, who seemed to have enjoyed the confidences of both the Europeans and the Indians, was successful in negotiating important land deals for the settlers. When the settlement was taken over by the English, Falkinburg was forced to leave Burlington. Aware of the abundance of resources to be found at the seashore, he followed the old Indian path to the coast. After arriving in Little Egg Harbor, Falkinburg made his first home in a cave. Shortly thereafter, in 1698, he bought 800 acres of land from the Lenape Indians and with his family, settled permanently in the area.

Soon other European settlers joined Falkinburg in settling Little Egg Harbor. It was not long before family and friends of these early settlers were enjoying summer vacations at the coast. In 1709 the Little Egg Harbor Meeting House was built to serve as a place of worship for the many Quakers who had settled permanently in the area. Soon thereafter an annual meeting was established there, and

The Friends Meeting House in Little Egg Harbor (now Tuckerton) was built in 1709 and rebuilt in 1863.
(*Photo by Gordon Stull*)

Quakers from upper Burlington County, Gloucester County (now Atlantic), and even Philadelphia would join their brethren at Little Egg Harbor to worship for five days every June. A great many young Quakers making this summer journey found opportunities to enjoy the environs and to make new friends. Skipping out on meetings became the norm, and soon the young Quakers were spending wonderful summer days joining old and new friends at beach parties.

In 1765 Reuben Tucker established a "house of entertainment" on Short Beach. This island, once located off the tip of Long Beach Island, was eventually known as Tucker's Beach and later Tucker's Island. Reuben provided food, drink, entertainment, and boarding to the many sea travelers who found their way to his beachfront property. Soon young Quakers were regularly sailing out to Tucker's Beach instead of attending meeting. The older members of the fellowship, disturbed by the scandalous behavior of their young people, continually and often unsuccessfully tried to return them to services. The young people always seemed to find a way to outwit their elders

Gravestone at Friends Meeting House in Little Egg Harbor (now Tuckerton).
(Photo by Gordon Stull)

and to continue to enjoy themselves at their beach festivities. The breach between the elders and the young people became so serious that a conference was held to discuss the problem. Finding no solution to the dilemma, the elders decided to discontinue the annual meetings. By the end of the 18th century, the Quaker summer meetings in Little Egg Harbor had become a thing of the past.

Reuben Tucker's tavern and boarding house continued to prosper, providing a place of entertainment for locals and other summer visitors. After Reuben's death in 1815, his wife took over the management of the resort and ran it successfully for another 30 years. In 1854 the tavern burned down and was not rebuilt. In the late 1870s there were attempts to revive the resort with the building of several new hotels. The resort was renamed Sea Haven, and soon guests were flocking to the island by paddle wheel steamer. This revitalization was short lived, however, as the railroad never made it to Sea Haven. Rail travel to other shore resort areas eventually starved Sea Haven of its business, and the deserted hotels fell to ruin. By the 1920s the island had begun to erode, and after a fierce storm in 1927, the island's lighthouse fell into the sea. In 1933 the lifesaving station closed and the island was quickly deserted. Soon afterward Tucker's Island was totally submerged beneath the sea. There are reports today that Tucker's Island has begun to rise again and that the sand-bar that can be seen off the tip of Long Beach Island at Holgate Beach is the beginning of its resurrection.

As more and more people began to travel to the Little Egg Harbor area, the old Indian trail was gradually improved into a crude road-way for wagon and stage travel. In 1789 the Burlington Court of Common Pleas (Little Egg Harbor was then a part of Burlington County) authorized the Burlington County Overseers of the Highways to clear out the road for public use. This road began at the "Keith Line" (the dividing point between East and West Jersey) in West Creek and ran in a northwesterly direction through Tuckerton and Bass River and across the Wading River one mile south of the town that would later be known as Harrisville. It continued through Washington, Mount, and Quaker Bridge, and finally reached Atsion.

What was referred to as the Tuckerton Stage Road was in some locations actually two different roads. After leaving Marlton, the Tuckerton Stage Road (now Tuckerton Road) crossed Taunton Road in Medford Township. Soon after the next crossroads at Jackson Road, the Atsion Road (the secondary stage road) diverged from the Tuckerton Stage Road in a more southerly direction, heading through Atsion and Quaker Bridge and, after rejoining the more northerly route in Washington, on to Little Egg Harbor.

As the traffic increased on the stage line, taverns began to spring up along the road from Little Egg Harbor to Camden. Some of the most important to travelers were those that were found in the less populated areas of the Pine Barrens. Riding on stages in all types of weather on rutty dirt roads was not the most comfortable experience, and travelers were always happy to see the lights of the taverns in the distance as their coaches drew near.

One of the better-known stagecoach stops on the southerly route was at Quaker Bridge, approximately four miles from Atsion and a favorite stopping place for Quakers on their way to annual meeting. For many years, Quakers traveling on horseback on the old Indian trail to Little Egg Harbor would be forced to ford the Batsto River as part of their journey. This proved a hazardous situation, and on several occasions those making the crossing drowned. In 1772 a group of Quakers from Little Egg Harbor and upper Burlington County met on the banks of the river and constructed a bridge across the stream. From that time on, the bridge and surrounding area came to be known as Quaker Bridge. In 1808 Nicholas Sooy (owner and proprietor of the Washington tavern) sold the land at Quaker Bridge to his son-in-law, Arthur Thompson, and his daughter Elizabeth for $2,400. Thompson soon built a tavern on the site, and it received its first license in 1809. The tavern was known as Thompson's and was a popular place for the local population as well as stagecoach travelers. Those who worked in the nearby iron furnace towns of Atsion and Batsto often frequented the tavern for weddings and other socials events. For many years it was a local election headquarters and a place where town meetings were held. Ten years after the purchase of the property, Arthur died at the age of 46. Elizabeth Thompson carried on after her husband's death and continued to run the tavern until 1836. From 1837 to 1852, the tavern was run by a number of different individuals. Because it is known that the property was sold to Samuel Richards in 1832, it can be assumed that from that time forward the tavern site was leased. The last recorded year of operation of the Quaker Bridge Tavern was 1857.

Another noteworthy event to have occurred at Quaker Bridge was the discovery of a rare and inconspicuous plant called *Schiza pusilla* (curly-grass fern). This plant find was so significant that it brought botanists to the area from as far away as Europe. The Curly-grass Fern was found within 50 feet of the bridge by a group of botanists traveling in the area in 1808. A 1910 report of the New Jersey State Museum states the botanists were lodging at the tavern at Quaker Bridge when they made their discovery. The author of the report states that the Quaker Bridge Tavern furnished one of the few available stopping places for those interested in the study of the flora and fauna of the Pines. For a time the area was the only known location of plants that were later found to have a wider distribution. Eventually the Curly-grass Fern was found near Toms River, in Pleasant Mills, and in 27 other locations scattered throughout the Pines Barrens.

The next tavern located on the old stage road was found at a place referred to as the "Mount" (why this name was chosen is not clear, as the elevation is scarcely higher than the surrounding area). In 1839 Jonathan Cramer opened a tavern on the property and likely operated it for another 20 years. Town meetings were held at the Mount Tavern from 1843 to 1846. In a letter petitioning for the change of the stage mail route in 1846, it was proposed that a post office be opened at the Mount Tavern, though this never occurred. The last proprietor of the Mount Tavern appears to have been Shreve Wills, under whose ownership it served as a polling place for Washington Township.

In addition to the tavern, there was one other dwelling located at Mount. Richard and Hannah Coleman reportedly raised eleven children at the small settlement, staying long after the tavern closed in the 1860s. Although the Mount had few permanent residents, it was a busy place during its heyday, catering to stage travelers as well as to locals from nearby villages.

The next tavern on the stage route to Little Egg Harbor was probably the earliest and best known of all the area's watering holes. Two miles southeast of Mount was the village of Washington and the tavern built by Nicholas Sooy in 1773. Here during the war years, military recruiters attempted to enlist the men from the surrounding communities of Speedwell, Atsion, Hampton, Batsto, and Martha. Sooy's Tavern was also used as a "mustering," or training, area for the local militia. Being centrally located, the tavern became a favorite meeting spot for the locals to celebrate weddings and to enjoy good food and camaraderie. It is reported that the famous Pine Barrens highway robber, Joe Mulliner, was once riding by Sooy's when a wedding was about to take place. Seeing the bride crying outside the tavern, Mulliner asked the young woman what could be wrong on her wedding day. She replied that she did not love the intended groom and did not wish to marry him. Mulliner, who was known as a lady's man, is reported to have run the groom off the premises at gunpoint, saving the day for the young woman.

Town meetings were held at Sooy's for 11 years, from 1809 to 1819. Soon after the death of George Washington, Sooy, in honor of his late president and victorious commander, renamed his tavern

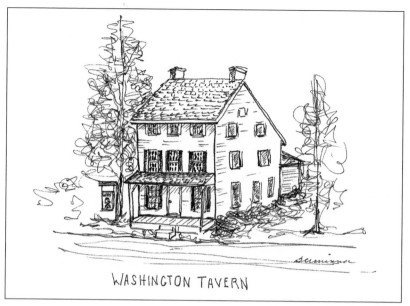

WASHINGTON TAVERN

(*Illustrated by Berminna Solem*)

Washington. Reportedly, a large sign with a crude representation of Washington hung in front of the tavern for many years, and under Washington's portrait were printed the words "Our Country Must Be Free."

Nicholas and Sarah Sooy raised thirteen children in Washington. A settlement grew up around the tavern, and soon Public School 3001 was built to educate the children of the expanding community. When Nicholas died in 1822, his son, Paul Sears Sooy, ran the tavern for a number of years. Like most of the other stage taverns, Sooy's closed its doors sometime in the 1860s.

When Joseph Wharton purchased Washington and the surrounding lands in the late 1800s, he established a cattle ranch near the site of the old tavern. Here he built a large barn and pit silo, the remains of which are still visible.

Further down the stage road, nestled on the east bank where the stages crossed the Wading River, stood a tavern owned and operated by John Bodine. John, who was a French Huguenot, bought his land in 1791 and soon thereafter built a tavern on the site. The tavern, which was located approximately nine miles from Tuckerton, was often the first and last stop on the stage route. Bodine's Tavern was frequented by many late-18th-century locals who worked at Martha's Furnace and the nearby Wading River Forge and Slitting Mill.

The Landing (also called Charcoal Landing), located approximately 0.5 mile south of the tavern, was an important river wharf where products from the furnace, forge, and later the McCartyville Paper Mill were loaded on small transports for shipment downriver to Leeks Wharf. Here they were reloaded onto coastal vessels headed for New York, Philadelphia, and other cities. Teamsters who carried these goods to and from the river wharf also were frequent patrons of Bodine's Tavern.

The open land near Bodine's was used for "Training Days"—military drills that every able-bodied male over age 18 was expected to attend three or four times a year. Martha's Diary—a diary maintained by a clerk at the Furnace from 1808 to 1815—offers insight into the daily life of the furnace workers and reports that these drills were often a raucous affair. Usually located near a tavern, the mandatory mustering of the troops offered an opportunity for men to forget about the difficulties of their daily life and enjoy themselves. Even the officers took part and, according to Martha's Diary, were often too drunk to command.

Bodine's, like the other taverns, also served as a polling place and location for town meetings. After John Bodine died, his widow Ann and son John ran the tavern until 1840, when it is believed to have closed.

The Hampton Gate Tavern, another well-known tavern on the northerly stage route, was located on what is now the Carranza Road, near the sign indicating one has entered the Wharton State Forest. The tavern was located at the base of what was known in early deeds as "the stone hills." The hills, unique for their presence in otherwise flat terrain, were mined for building stone. It is believed that the Hampton Gate Tavern, a large stone structure, was built from the stone taken from these nearby hills. David Cavileer, who had purchased the tract in 1812, was the first known proprietor of the tavern. The name Hampton Gate referred to a gated road near the tavern that led to Hampton Furnace. Cavileer maintained the tavern until his death in 1824. He left his entire estate to his wife, Mary, with the provision it would pass on to "his friend" Mary Smith and her descendants upon Mary Cavileer's death. One of Mary Smith's children, David Cavileer Smith, was, however, to receive a larger share than his siblings, including 200 acres of land and a house and barn. One can only wonder about the relationship between David and Mary Smith and her child who bore his name. Cavileer's widow continued to run the tavern after his death. In later years, the tavern was known as the J. Smith Hotel, possibly run by a descendant of Mary Smith.

In 1836 a charter was granted to the Camden and Egg Harbor Railroad with authorized capital of $200,000 for the purpose of building a railroad route from Camden to Tuckerton with stops at Quaker Bridge and McCartyville (later Harrisville). The project, which was supported by local businessmen such as William McCarty, Jesse Evans, and Samuel Richards, never got beyond the planning stages. With the collapse of the iron industry in the mid-1800s, many of the company towns of the Pines became deserted. Soon the railroads, which had bypassed many of the towns of the Pine Barrens, became the preferred mode of travel, and the stage runs became obsolete. Because of these combined factors, the old taverns along the stage routes were forced to close.

An Indian reservation, located in what is now Shamong Township, was situated between the two routes of the Tuckerton Stage Road. In 1754 John Brainerd, a Presbyterian missionary who ministered to the Indians living in West Jersey, was attempting to raise money to purchase a large tract of land for the Indians' use. Simultaneously, a group of Quakers in Burlington had formed an association called the New Jersey Association for Helping Indians for the same purpose. These plans were abandoned, however, when it was learned that the New Jersey legislature was considering purchasing a large tract of land for the exclusive use of all Indians living south of the Raritan River. On August 29, 1758, a tract of 3,044 acres was purchased for this purpose from Benjamin Springer. The land, which was then a part of upper Evesham Township (now Shamong), eventually became known as Indian Mills. Initially the reservation was called Edgepillock, named after a group of Indians who lived in the area. A stream (now called Springer's Brook) that runs through Indian Mills also bore this name. Soon the name was changed to Brotherton by then governor of New Jersey, Francis Bernard. After the tract was purchased, approximately 100 Indians of several tribes and clans made their way to the reservation. The title to the reservation was to be held in trust for the Indians by the West Jersey Proprietors.

Although the Brotherton Reservation was established initially as a homestead for Christian Indians, it was later opened to all Indians living south of the Raritan River, regardless of their religion. Many Indians, however, refused this invitation as they were distrustful of the colonists and afraid of being concentrated in one place, where they might be confined and killed.

On the Brotherton lands were a cedar swamp and a sawmill. The land was considered suitable for hunting and was conveniently situated for fishing off the seacoast. John Brainerd came to live at Brotherton in 1759 and was named superintendent of the reservation in 1762. In 1760 he built a log meetinghouse and later a school, blacksmith shop, gristmill, and trading post. No intoxicating beverages could be sold on the reservation. During Brainerd's tenure he tried to "civilize" the Indians by teaching them agriculture and skills to run the sawmill and gristmill. Soon traditional Indian skills like hunting practices and pottery making were forgotten. Brainerd continued to work at Brotherton until 1768, when he moved to Mt. Holly to accept a new post. The reservation, which had not prospered under Brainerd's supervision, deteriorated further after his departure. Herbert Kraft, in *The Delaware-Lenape Indian Heritage*, suggests that Brotherton failed because the land was not sufficiently productive for growing crops and because colonists who lived in surrounding areas harassed the Indians. Trees on the reservation were continually cut down, and cattle belonging to the neighboring whites grazed on Brotherton lands. Visitors to the reservation in 1777 found the Indians to be living in poverty and near starvation.

In 1801 the Brotherton Reservation Indians received an invitation from their kin living at New Stockbridge, New York, "To pack up their mat and come eat out of their dish." The Brotherton Indians, upon receiving this invitation, petitioned the New Jersey legislature to sell the reservation lands so they could use the pro-ceeds to join their relatives in New York. The legislature agreed, and the governor appointed three commissioners to divide up the land into lots of no more than 100 acres each. The public sale was held at Piper's Corner, at the junction of Jackson and Atsion roads. There were 32 buyers, and the land sold for between $2 and $5 an acre. Proceeds of the sale were given to the Indians for the purchase of clothing, farm equipment, household furnishings, and land on which to build homes in their new location. Some portion of the sale monies was kept by the state and invested in U.S. Securities on behalf of the Indians. The last of the Brotherton Indians left for New York in 1802. It is reported that only 12 wagons were needed to carry all of the Indians' household goods. The elderly people of the reservation rode in the wagons while the young men and women of the reservation walked beside them all the way to New York. Twenty years later the Indians from the Brotherton Reservation, who were planning another move, petitioned the state for the money that had been invested for them. The Indians, who were forwarded $3,551.23 from their remaining investment, moved to Green Bay, Wisconsin, where their descendants live to this day.

Archaeological work done on the site of the Brotherton Reservation has revealed extensive evidence of land use by Native Americans dating back to the Middle Woodland period (100 B.C. to 900 A.D.). It is ironic that long before the Brotherton Reservation was created, aboriginal populations inhabited the very land on which it was established.

OLD TUCKERTON STAGE ROAD SIDE TRIPS

GREAT BAY BOULEVARD (SEVEN BRIDGES ROAD) TO TUCKERTON SHELL MOUND

To take a side trip on Seven Bridges Road, turn onto Great Bay Boulevard (right turn off Route 9 just before the Tuckerton Seaport entrance). After traveling several miles, look for a small island or hummock in the marsh on the right side (just before the first bridge). On this island of shells, called the Tuckerton Shell Mound, stand several red cedars. The Tuckerton Shell Mound is believed to be 1,500 years old and was a shell refuse for the Lenape Indians and their ancestors who lived here and for those who visited the area during summer migrations. The shell mound is 10 feet high and covers one-tenth of an acre; the shell deposits reportedly extend some 14 feet below the marsh. For historical and archaeological reasons, access to the shell mound is not permitted.

As you drive down Seven Bridges Road, you will notice a large structure on an island off to your right in Great Bay. This is the now abandoned Crab Island Fish Factory. Built in the 1930s, the factory operated until the early 1970s, when the species of fish (Menhaden, or Moss Bunker) processed there became seriously depleted. During its peak years (1952–1955), the fish factory processed 200 million Menhaden and employed 100 workers. The products made at the fish factory included fish oil used in cosmetics and paint additives and fishmeal for fertilizer and animal feed.

To look for Tucker's Island, travel to the end of the road, park, and walk to the beach. By looking toward the left, off the tip of Long Beach Island, you will see the sandbar that has begun to form, which many believe is the beginning of the resurgence of Tucker's Island. To hear the story of Tucker's Island in song, pick up the CD *Tucker's Island Rises Again*, by New Jersey troubadour Valerie Vaughn. The CD can be purchased at the Tuckerton Seaport Museum gift shop.

Returning from the point and after crossing the last bridge, look for First Bridge Marina on the left. The folks at First Bridge Marina (609-296-1888) offer kayak ecotours of Great Bay and also provide a free kayak launch for those who want to go it alone.

TUCKERTON SEAPORT MUSEUM

To learn more about Tuckerton and Tucker's Island, visit the Tuckerton Seaport Museum (609-296-8868) on Route 9. The museum is located on a 40-acre site along the bank of Tuckerton Creek. This recreated Maritime village offers exhibits, displays, and demonstrations that highlight various seaport traditions, such as boat

Crab Island Fish Factory.
(*Photo by Gordon Stull*)

building and decoy carving. *Life on the Edge*, a permanent exhibit at the museum, focuses on the habitat in and around the estuary of the Mullica River and Great Bay.

ABSEGAMI LAKE AND BASS RIVER STATE FOREST

Bass River State Forest (609-296-1114) is a state preserve encompassing over 18,000 acres and includes Lake Absegami, a 67-acre lake that is open for swimming and boating during the summer season. At the lake are picnic tables, a playground, and a food concession that is open during the summer months. The forest has 186 campsites with showers, laundry, and restroom facilities. There are 10 miles of hiking trails within the forest, including an entrance to the 50-mile-long Batona hiking trail.

REFERENCES

Beck, Henry Charlton. 1936. *Forgotten Towns of Southern New Jersey*. New Brunswick, NJ: Rutgers University Press.

Blackman, Leah. 2000. *Old Times: Country Life in Little Egg Harbor 50 Years Ago* (written in 1880). Tuckerton, NJ: Tuckerton Historical Society.

Boyer, Charles S. 1962. *Old Inns and Taverns in West Jersey*. Camden, NJ: Camden County Historical Society.

Buchholz, Margaret Thomas. 1999. *Shore Chronicle: Diaries and Travelers' Tales from the Jersey Shore 1764–1955*. Harvey Cedars, NJ: Down the Shore Press.

Cresson, Jack. "Brotherton Reservation." *Batsto Citizens Gazette*, Winter/Spring 1997.

De Cou, George. 1949. *The Historic Rancocas*. Moorestown, NJ: The News Chronicle (printer).

Eichinger, Steve. "The Stage Road." *Bass River Gazette* (a newsletter from the Bass River Community Library History Committee and the Great John Mathis Foundation), January–June 2002.

Ewing, Sarah. "Old Tuckerton Road Linked Pine Barrens Towns." *Batsto Citizens Gazette*, Spring/Summer 1980.

Flemming, George. 2005. *Brotherton*. Medford, NJ: Plexus Publishing, Inc.

Flemming, George. "The Gate: Popular Old Tuckerton Road Tavern." *Batsto Citizens Gazette*, Spring/Summer 1990.

Kraft, Herbert C. 2001. *The Lenape-Delaware Indian Heritage: 10,000 B.C. to A.D. 2000*. Lenape Books.

McMahon, William. 1980. *Pine Barrens Legends and Lore*. Moorestown, NJ: Middle Atlantic Press.

Mountford, Kent. 2002. *Closed Sea: From the Manasquan to the Mullica: A History of the Barnegat Bay*. Harvey Cedars, NJ: Down the Shore Publishing.

Mounier, R. Alan. 2003. *Looking Beneath the Surface: The Story of Archaeology in New Jersey*. New Brunswick, NJ: Rutgers University Press.

O'Leary, Terry. 2000. *Ecotour Trail Guide to Great Bay Boulevard*. Tuckerton, NJ: Tuckerton Seaport.

Pearce, John E. 2000. *Heart of the Pines: Ghostly Voices of the Pine Barrens*. Hammonton, NJ: Batsto Citizens Committee.

Peterson, Robert A. 1998. *Patriots, Pirates, and Pineys: Sixty Who Shaped New Jersey*. Medford, NJ: Plexus Publishing, Inc.

Pierce, Arthur, D. 1964. *Family Empire in Jersey Iron: The Richards Enterprises in the Pine Barrens*. New Brunswick, NJ: Rutgers University Press.

Pierce, Arthur, D. 1957. *Iron in the Pines: The Story of New Jersey's Ghost Towns and Bog Iron*. New Brunswick, NJ: Rutgers University Press.

Wilson, J. G. "Discovery of the Curly Fern Was Clouded by Controversy." *The Batsto Citizens Gazette*, Summer/Fall 1980.

Harrisville
and Martha

industry deep in the pines

Harrisville and Martha

HARRISVILLE

OVERVIEW AND WALKING TOUR

Adjacent to a beautiful lake on Route 679 (a spur of Route 563) 12 miles south of Chatsworth and eight miles northwest of New Gretna stand the ruins of one of the most intriguing forgotten towns of the Pine Barrens. The town, first called McCartyville, later became known as Harrisia, and finally, as it is known today, Harrisville. Once the site of a forge and slitting mill built in 1795 by Issac Potts, Harrisville's real glory lies in its 60 years as a paper mill company town.

Today's paper mill ruins, often missed by passing motorists, are an astonishing sight when stumbled on for the first time. Appearing much older than they actually are, the ruins of the old stone paper mill, with its crumbling brick arches over now dry canals, resemble ancient aqueducts. Most surprising to the first-time visitor is that a flourishing industrial community once existed in this remote and natural setting. In actuality, Harrisville was in the center of an industrial area in the 18th and 19th centuries. The company towns of Martha, Speedwell, Atsion, Hampton, and Batsto, which surrounded Harrisville, were some of the most productive bog-iron furnaces in the state. Not far to the east lay Tuckerton, the third officially established port of entry in the United States and a flourishing foreign trade center.

When you enter the town of Harrisville, look for the green fencing that encloses the paper mill ruins. The fencing was erected by the state in 1975 in an attempt to prevent further vandalism of the remaining ruins as well as to protect the public from injury in case of collapsing walls. State forest rangers have recently cleared away much of the overgrowth inside the fencing, allowing the visitor a good view of the paper mill ruins. Those ignoring the "keep out"

95

gettinǥ to Harrisville

From the West
Take Route 70 East to Red Lion Circle (where Route 70 intersects Route 206). Take Route 206 South to the second light.
Turn left onto Route 532 East, passing the crossroads in
Tabernacle (approximately 1.2 miles). From the Tabernacle
crossroads, drive approximately 9.7 miles to Route 563. Turn
right and proceed on Route 563 South for 9.8 miles, at which
point the road will fork. Bear left onto Route 679 and proceed
1.7 miles, passing Harrisville Lake on your left. Shortly after the
lake, look for a sign on your right marked Bodine Field. Turn
right at the Bodine Field sign and park.

From the East
Take Route 30 West to Route 542 (just outside Hammonton).
Turn right onto Route 542 and drive 11 miles to Route 563.
Turn left onto Route 563 North and proceed 5.4 miles to the
Route 679 intersection. Turn right onto Route 679 and drive
1.7 miles, passing Harrisville Lake on your left. Shortly after the
lake, look for a sign on your right marked Bodine Field. Turn
right at the Bodine Field sign and park.

From the South via the Garden State Parkway
Take the Garden State Parkway North to exit 50 (New Gretna)
for Route 9 North and follow to the Route 679 (Maple Avenue)
intersection. Turn left onto Route 679 and proceed 6.7 miles to
Harrisville. Turn left onto the dirt road marked Bodine Field
and park.

From the North via the Garden State Parkway
Take the Garden State Parkway South to exit 52 (New Gretna).
Turn right at the stop sign onto East Greenbush Road (CR
654). Make a left at the next stop sign onto Stage Road. Stay to
your right and continue on Stage Road as you pass through the
next two forks in the road. Continue on Stage Road until it
intersects with Route 679. Turn right onto Route 679 and drive
3.3 miles to Harrisville. Turn left onto the dirt road marked
Bodine Field and park.

signs and venturing inside the fenced areas should be prepared for steep fines if caught trespassing by forest rangers.

To take a walking tour of the ruins, first locate Main Street on the site map. As you walk down Main Street and explore the ruins, try to imagine a time when this was a prosperous community and home to 75 residents. Then as now, the focus of the town was the paper mill. For 60 years the workers of this mill made heavy brown butcher paper, in high demand for many years. During much of the 19th century, Harrisville thrived and was considered a model and modern community. As in most communities of the day, the town included a company store; a gristmill and a sawmill; a blacksmith shop; a school, which served as a church on Sunday; and a number of tenant buildings. There were several mansions inhabited by the owners of the town, along with outbuildings for their carriages and animals.

To get your bearings, stand on the crossroads of the two dirt roads with your back to Route 679 and with the paper mill ruins to your right. Directly in front of you was once the south end of Main Street. Turning around and looking straight ahead, try to envision the road extending across the highway and heading into what are now woodlands. During the heyday of Harrisville, Route 679 did not exist, so try to block this from your mind as you attempt to envision the layout of the town. If you go across the highway, continuing on a straight course, you will locate the remnants of North Main Street. After locating the road, begin to look for the remains of the sawmill and gristmill on your left and the cellar holes of the two Harris mansions and company store on your right. While looking for the ruins, you will notice thick grapevines that twist themselves throughout the Catalpa and other "exotic" trees originally planted by Harrisville residents. (The presence of nonindigenous plants is a good clue when you are looking for the remains of old towns.) The gristmill ruins are quite noticeable, and the remains of the brick archway over the now dry tailrace (the lower millrace) present the onlooker with a good photo opportunity. Although not much remains of the two mansions and store, the cellar holes of these dwellings are easily located.

The two mansions built for the Harris brothers were lavish and modern and contained the amenities of inside plumbing, gas lighting, exquisite furnishings, and in many rooms, black walnut paneling. The

Ruins of the gristmill at Harrisville 2003.
(*Photo by Gordon Stull*)

Howard Harris mansion (the larger, with 15 rooms) had a veranda extending the full length of the north side. The veranda, decorated with Victorian gingerbread, had two porch swings. Richard—who lived with Howard and his family—maintained a garden with a large number of rare and imported plants and shrubs. Behind the mansion were an apple orchard and a lane that led across the canal to the horse and carriage barns.

A second mansion, built for Benjamin Harris, was smaller, with 11 rooms, but considered just as grand, with all the modern conveniences. There are reports that Benjamin and his family occupied the mansion even after his business ownership ended in 1857. This mansion is often referred to as the Broome mansion because Mahlon Broome, a manager at the paper mill, and his family resided there after Benjamin Harris's departure.

The Harrisville company store was located close to the road and between the two mansions. The store was constructed of New Jersey sandstone and stood two stories high. In 1862 a post office was established in the town and run from the company store. Richard Harris managed the store and was also the postmaster.

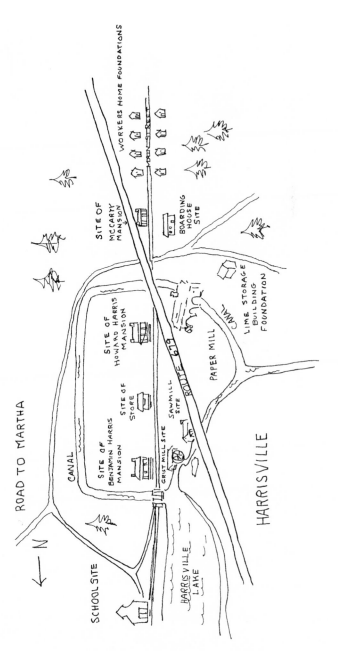

Harrisville site map. (*Drawn by Berminna Solem*)

The footbridge across the millrace connected outbuildings with the Harris mansions.
(*Photo courtesy of the Howard Feyl Collection*)

Standing directly opposite the store was the sawmill, which for the period was considered small as it supplied only the lumber needed for the village. A few yards away stood the gristmill—also known as the feed mill—which, like the paper mill, stood three stories high.

Other important landmarks, such as the quadrangle raceway system, are clearly noted on the site map and will help you locate the foundations of the noted structures. After locating the ruins on North Main Street, go back across the highway and attempt to remain on the original main street. Once you get on the dirt road across the highway, look for the flowing artesian well. The well piping is embedded in a stone foundation and is tucked in a corner outside the green fencing.

The paper mill ruins are located within the green fencing behind the artesian well. The main part of the mill was built of New Jersey sandstone and was originally covered with whitewashed stucco. The original mill structure was constructed by McCarty in 1835 and "upgraded" after a fire, in 1847. The largest wall of the factory (and the largest wall still standing today) was the west wall of the central portion of the main mill. This section of the mill was three stories

Harrisville Paper Mill ruins, 2003.
(*Photo by Gordon Stull*)

high and 122 feet long. The raceway that cut through the central portion of the mill first brought rushing water to the turbines, then flowed out through the (still standing) brick archways.

After viewing the paper mill ruins, head in a southerly direction, remaining on the original Main Street. After passing the crossroads, you will begin to notice a wide-open area on your right where you will see a large cellar hole. This was the location of the boarding house and in later years a two-family workers' home. A little further, on your left, surrounded by trees and overgrowth, are the remains of the McCarty mansion. When Richard Harris first moved to Harrisville in 1856, he resided in the old McCarty homestead. This home, though large in comparison with the tenant homes, actually resembled a large country farmhouse. Richard, who was a lifelong bachelor, moved in with his brother Howard's family as soon as the larger mansion was completed. The McCarty home was later turned into a double tenant house for the mill workers.

Continuing on the same southerly route, on both sides of the street you'll find the cellar holes of the workers' homes. These are

This view of Main Street after a fire in 1914 shows
the company store on the left and the gristmill on the right.
(*Photo courtesy of the Howard Feyl Collection*)

quite small, especially when compared with the cellar holes of the
owners' mansions.

As a late-19th-century town, Harrisville was unique. For example,
in about 1875, ornamental gas street lanterns were installed on its
main street. Main Street was also lined with white picket fencing
broken only by gates leading to the front door of each home. Each
worker was entitled to a small tenant home and an acre of land on
which to raise vegetables and grow fruit trees. Throughout the village, wild huckleberries, raspberries, and strawberries grew in profusion. If you were a single man, the boardinghouse served
home-cooked meals in its dining room.

As was the fate of numerous other lost towns of the New Jersey
Pine Barrens, the paper mill eventually failed. Deprived of their
means of earning a living, the residents of Harrisville moved on. Fire
and vandals took away much of what remained. What is left today
offers only a glimpse of what was once a flourishing and vibrant
industrial community.

A DEEPER LOOK

Although paper put Harrisville on the map, it was initially the site of an iron forge and slitting mill. In 1795, Issac Potts, a well-known Philadelphia iron baron, erected the Wading River Forge and Slitting Mill. Potts's forge and slitting mill were built 1.5 miles south of the furnace town of Martha, which he had established in 1793. Pig iron produced at Martha was brought to the forge for further processing. Machine-made nails, a new invention, were the main product of the slitting mill. Potts sold the property within several years, and the forge and slitting mill passed through the hands of several owners, including Samuel Richards, son of William Richards, the ironmaster of Batsto.

In 1832 William McCarty, a Philadelphia merchant and book-seller, and several associates purchased the property. Probably aware that the bog iron industry was on its way out, the new owners decided to erect a paper mill. Papermaking production was just getting off the ground in the 1830s, and by 1834 there were 29 other paper mills in the state. Previously paper was made by hand using linen and cotton, relatively scarce materials. McCarty had discovered a formula for papermaking that used salt hay, which could be found in abundance along the Wading River and in nearby bay areas. Other ingredients in McCarty's recipe for paper included old ropes, rags, paper scraps, and burlap bagging material.

Nineteenth-century papermaking began with the cutting up of all the raw materials and the "melting" of the materials into a pulp mixture. The process involved the sorting, cleaning, and shredding of the fibrous raw materials and then the cooking, washing, and bleaching of the resulting pulp. A thin mat of pulp would then be spread out and dried. The final step involved rolling, coating, and then cutting the finished product into the sizes ordered by the customer. Women working at the mill were given the job of sorting and cleaning the raw materials that entered the plant. Considered "light work," it was also a very disagreeable job as dust and dirt from the old rags and other material filled the air.

After constructing the paper mill, McCarty and his partners established a small town, soon to be known as McCartyville, which provided homes for the people who would work in the mill. In addition to a number of tenant homes, there was a company store, gristmill and sawmill, blacksmith, carpenter and machine shops, and a boardinghouse. Because the plant needed significant waterpower to run the mill's turbines, a long canal was hand dug to divert water from the pond. The canal was lined with sandstone to prevent erosion and was seven feet deep in most places. A large country house was built across from the boardinghouse and served as an estate for William McCarty. It was here that McCarty entertained many of his influential and literary friends from Philadelphia.

One wealthy and prestigious friend, Henry Carey, eventually became a partner in and president of what was by 1834 known as the Wading River Manufacturing and Canal Company. Carey, who appeared to have a major influence on McCarty, was a well-known and respected economist who had written several books, including *The Principals of Political Economics*. Although Henry Carey had no formal education, he was considered one of the most knowledgeable men of his era. He was the son of Matthew Carey, a wealthy Philadelphia publisher. As a partner in his father's business, Henry had contact with the great literary men of the time and hosted many of the city's intellectuals in his Walnut Street mansion during his regular Sunday night soirees.

Under Carey's leadership, the mill, which produced butcher paper, bonnet boards (visors or rims of bonnets), and binder boards (the cardboard backing used for book jackets), increased both production and profits. By 1836 the mill was producing nearly a ton of paper a day. The company's real estate holdings by now encompassed 5,000 acres and included a 550-acre farm, which produced much of the food for the community. The company also owned a schooner that was used to transport goods—barged down the Wading River—to New York and Philadelphia. By 1837 the company store alone yielded a $3,000 annual profit, and the paper mill cleared $10,000.

During this period, McCarty was also experimenting with silk production. The worms were to be raised in mulberry trees, and these trees were planted throughout the town. However, this interesting venture was never developed into a full-blown commercial enterprise.

Although the Wading River Manufacturing and Canal Company was considered one of the largest and most successful paper mills in the state, in 1846 the firm defaulted on a $50,000 loan, and collateral property was seized and sold at sheriff's sale.

McCarty, not ready to let go of his dream, was able to buy back one-quarter interest of what was left of the company. Shortly thereafter, however, a fire struck the paper mill, and much of the factory was destroyed. Discouraged, McCarty sold his interest and returned to Philadelphia to live out his remaining years in retirement.

In 1851, Richard Harris, then 32, and his brother William, 28, entered an agreement of sale with the new owners to buy 300 acres of the town. The purchase included the paper mill, gristmill, sawmill, tenant houses, store, and mansion. The Harris brothers, who had previously worked in McCarty's paper mill, were well-to-do gentlemen from Philadelphia. They were members of a wealthy and prominent family who lived in a Locust Street mansion that still stands as property of the University of Pennsylvania. Eventually four of the Harris brothers—Richard, Benjamin, William, and Howard—as well as their father, John, would become involved in the family business. Although William and Richard signed an agreement of sale in May 1851, untoward circumstances prevented them from taking possession of the paper mill and the surrounding properties until November 1856. After gaining possession, the Harris brothers soon changed the name of the town first to Harrisia and later to Harrisville. They also began a series of improvements, including enlarging the paper mill and canal and modernizing some aspects of the papermaking process.

In 1866, in an attempt to find iron-free water that would not rust out the wrought-iron boilers used in the papermaking process, an artesian well was dug. At one point during the drilling, iron-free water flowed from the well, but the driller, not satisfied, decided to dig further. Unfortunately, the final result of these efforts was a low-volume flow of iron-rich water. Frustrated, the well-driller abandoned the project, and the well continued to bring forth water impregnated with iron, as it does to this day. Modern geologists tell us that if the well driller had drilled only 30 feet more, he would have found the pure water he sought.

Another improvement undertaken by the Harris brothers made the paper mill town the talk of the Pine Barrens. Around 1875 ornamental gas lanterns were installed on the main street and gas lighting was installed in parts of the paper mill and Harris mansions. A gas generator was located in an unusual octagonal building near the main mill. (The remains of this gas plant cannot be located today because they lie directly beneath Route 679.) The Harrisville gas lanterns could be seen for miles and were considered a modern and remarkable innovation by those living in nearby towns.

For many years, products of the paper mill were taken by wagon to "the Landing" several miles out of town and were barged down the Wading River where they were eventually taken by schooners to the markets of New York and Philadelphia. In 1861 the Raritan and Delaware Bay Railroad built a line through the Pine Barrens and erected the Harris rail station 11 miles north of the town. In the high production days, especially after the Civil War, when paper was in great demand, mule-driven wagons brought the paper mill products to the rail depot daily, returning with goods for the company store.

In 1865 Richard Harris incorporated the business with a capital stock of $500,000. Richard served as the overseer of the plant and the town, while three of his brothers worked from Philadelphia and New York, where the firm owned stores that distributed products from the paper mill. Eventually Howard, the youngest brother, moved with his family into Harrisville.

Soon the community grew to 75 people, with half the population being comprised of children under 14 years of age. Each tenant home was made of wood and most often contained four rooms and a half-cellar. The homes generally included a front room, a lean-to kitchen, and two bedrooms on the second floor. Each house had a privy; there was no indoor plumbing installed in the workers' homes. Every man who worked in the mill was entitled to occupy a rent-free tenant home, which included one acre of ground behind the house where the family could raise vegetables. In the front yards were a variety of fruit trees (apple, pear, and peach), and strawberries, raspberries, and huckleberries grew wild throughout the town. White picket fences surrounded each home, with a gate opening at each front door. Provisions that could not be grown could be purchased at the company store. There was a public school that all children under 18 were free to attend. An 1876 population data report, however, indicates that although 40 children were eligible to attend school, only 24 students took advantage of the opportunity to enroll. The same report indicates that $350 was appropriated to run the school that year and that the teacher made $40 a month. On Sundays the school, which reportedly could comfortably seat 100 students, served as a church for the community.

For recreation, fairs and picnics were often held in the community. A softball team was formed, and the boys of Harrisville often played against teams from nearby towns. Work hours were long and included 12-hour shifts from 6 A.M. to 6 P.M. daily. At the age of 17, local residents could apply to work in the mill. The pay was $1.25 per day, which was exclusive of the free housing offered to each worker. In times of celebration, sickness, or death, the Harrises' horses and vehicles were at the whole community's disposal. By the standards of the day, Harrisville was a very modern and pleasant community in which to live and work.

Richard Harris remained at the helm of his paper mill for all but the last four years the family owned the town. Other partners, including three of his brothers and his father, were owners for varying lengths of time. Howard, the youngest brother, became involved in the firm in 1866 and stayed until the business closed in 1891. Howard was said to be fun loving and jovial, especially in comparison to the older Harris brothers, who were considered stern and serious. Despite these differences, all the Harris brothers were widely admired and respected.

Although Harrisville prospered throughout the 1860s, the 1870s brought hard times. Between 1870 and 1878, John Harris, the patriarch of the family, three of the Harris brothers, as well as three of the sisters, passed away. The full weight of managing the firm fell on Howard and Richard. While Howard traveled to New York and Philadelphia to oversee the family stores, Richard stayed at home and managed the mill. Eventually John W. Harris III and Richard C. Harris, Howard's two sons, would join the family firm and help with its management.

Other problems began to plague the firm, including the lack of diversity of the plant, its location far from the mainstream, and the age of the equipment. With butcher paper as its only product, the value and utility of the company diminished. Other, more modern paper mills were able to produce a larger variety and better grades of paper. Much of Harrisville's paper processing equipment was outdated, and the location of the plant in the middle of the New Jersey Pine Barrens—far from major population centers and avenues to transportation—added to the mounting difficulties. By 1887 the company's financial problems came to a head. In need of new capital, Richard obtained a $20,000 mortgage from Maria Robbins, a family acquaintance. A second mortgage for a lesser amount was obtained from John Pratt. The company was then reincorporated with a capital stock of $100,000 as an exclusively Harris family operation.

Within two years Maria Robbins started foreclosure proceedings for default of the mortgage loan. On February 28, 1891, at a sheriff's sale, Maria Robbins, the only bidder, purchased the entire estate for $10,000. In the years that followed, the property changed hands several times, but on July 16, 1896, perhaps the

Abandoned Harrisville Paper Mill prior to fire in 1914.
(Photo coutesy of the Howard Feyl Collection)

Harrisville Paper Mill after the fire of 1914.
(*Photo courtesy of the Howard Feyl Collection*)

most historically significant transaction occurred when Harrisville was purchased at a sheriff's sale by Joseph Wharton, a Philadelphia financier. By this time the paper mill had been closed for many years, and most residents had moved away. Harrisville was becoming a ghost town, and junk men and vandals soon made off with much of what was left that had any value.

The town stood deserted for many years until after Wharton's death in 1909, when Camp Lyon, a Y.M.C.A. boys' camp, was established there. With the old Harrisville schoolhouse serving as its headquarters, Camp Lyon was set up on the west shore of the lake in the spring of 1910. The camp was in operation for three summers and was preparing for its fourth season when in April 1914 a forest fire ravaged the entire town and surrounding woodlands. The fire, which was of suspicious origin, destroyed the mill and other town buildings and put an end to any possible resurgence of Harrisville. In 1954, Harrisville was purchased as part of the Wharton Tract by the state of New Jersey and became part of its forest system.

MARTHA

OVERVIEW AND WALKING/DRIVING TOUR

Directly off Route 679, across from the Harrisville paper mill ruins, is a dirt road that heads east to the old iron town of Martha (see the site map of Harrisville). Although today it is a quiet, wooded area with infrequent visitors, in its heyday Martha Furnace employed 60 men and had a population of 400 people. The furnace made pig iron and cast iron products such as stoves and hollowware (skillets, kettles, etc.). In the town stood a mansion house, 40 or 50 workers' homes, and a gristmill, sawmill, stamping mill, school, and infirmary. A furnace diary, which also noted the daily happenings of the villagers, was maintained at Martha from 180 to 1815. The "Martha Furnace Diary and Journal," found in a safe at the Harrisville paper mill, offers the reader an interesting glimpse of the daily life of villagers living in a 19th-century iron furnace town.

Following excavation of the Martha furnace in the late 1960s, state archaeologists covered the remains with dirt and fenced in the ruins. Next to the fenced-in ruins is the remnant of the race-way that once powered the large waterwheel that kept the furnace in blast. Nearby stands what remains of the dam that created a pond nearly two miles long. Across from the furnace ruins are some scattered bricks and the cellar hole of the large mansion home. Within the village site, thick grapevines can be found twisting and climbing through the nonindigenous trees planted long ago by the residents of Martha. On the road between the mansion and ruins are leftover chunks of black and blue-green iron slag (the remains of the iron smelting process), a scant reminder of a village of 400 people who once called this remote woodland area home.

Along the way to Martha, about one mile from Harrisville, is a beautiful overlook and beach next to the Oswego River. Often employed as a rest stop for kayakers and canoers, this remote beach is also used by locals for picnicking and swimming in summer months. Once you have reached Martha, you will see the high green fencing that encloses the earth-covered furnace ruins. Running east to west past the furnace ruins is the well-known Batona Trail. The

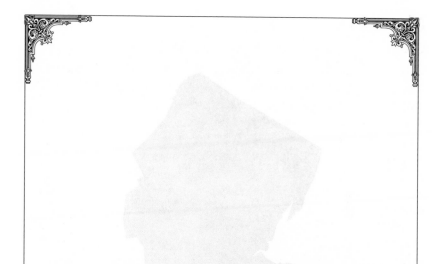

getting to martha

From Harrisville
To visit Martha, turn onto the dirt road located across the highway from the Harrisville ruins. After driving 1.5 miles, you will reach the town center at an intersection of dirt roads.

Budd Wilson at excavated site of the Martha Furnace, 1968.
(*Photo courtesy of Budd Wilson*)

Batona, a 50-mile marked trail running through the Pine Barrens, is recognizable by the pink blazes painted intermittently on trees along its path.

After exploring the village site, continue on the Martha road, heading in a northerly direction. Within approximately a quarter of a mile you will reach Calico Ridge, a lovely overlook—particularly spectacular in early June, when the mountain laurel is in bloom. Cellar hole depressions and winding grapevines indicate Calico Ridge was once a home site for some of the workers employed by Martha Furnace.

To locate the village of Calico, the elusive suburb of Martha where many of its workers reportedly lived, return to the furnace site and follow the dirt road marked as the Batona Trail in an easterly direction. It is better to walk rather than drive to Calico because the road can be impassable by car due to water holes and deep, mud-filled potholes. Shortly after leaving the furnace site, look for depressions in

Martha Furnace site during 1968 excavation.
(*Photo courtesy of Budd Wilson*)

the ground along the road. These are likely the cellar holes of the homes lived in by the furnace workers.

After nine-tenths of a mile, the Batona Trail will veer off to the right. Follow the Batona Trail for another three-tenths of a mile after making the right turn. You will know you have reached Calico when you locate, on a rise to your right, the cellar hole of the Ellis Adams farmstead. Made famous by Henry Charlton Beck in *Forgotten Towns of Southern New Jersey*, the Ellis Adams farmstead was located by Beck and a few old-timers who were searching for the lost town in the 1930s. Located near Beaver Run, the farmstead ruins found by Beck included a sandstone chimney. While the foundation of the house is still clearly visible today, the chimney has long since disappeared. Beck, who was often vague about the whereabouts of the forgotten towns he wrote about, indicated Calico was four miles northeast of the village of Martha. Budd Wilson, archaeologist and noted local historian, is confident that the Adams farmstead was actually less than 1.5 miles from Martha Furnace.

A DEEPER LOOK

About 100 yards south of Harrisville Lake is a dirt road that intersects with Route 679 and heads east to the site of the forgotten iron furnace town of Martha. In this desolate place frequented today mainly by hunters, hikers, and naturalists, was a 19th-century industrial village. Excavated during the summer of 1968 by New Jersey archaeologist Budd Wilson, the furnace ruins have been covered with a large mound of earth to protect them from vandals and the elements. The ruins are surrounded by high green fencing as a further deterrent to trespassers. Across the road from the furnace ruins, easily located by the nonindigenous trees standing nearby, is the cellar hole of the ironmaster's mansion. The home of Jesse Evans, who was manager of Martha Furnace for almost a half century, was a grand manor house and the place where villagers could go for a meal or a helping hand.

The furnace base was located in a depression next to a raceway that powered the waterwheel and bellows. Beyond the furnace was the dam, which backed up the river water to make a pond almost two miles long. Surrounding the furnace were a half dozen structures associated with the making of iron. Nearby stood a gristmill, a sawmill, and a stamping mill, where large pieces of bog ore were crushed into sizes small enough to feed the furnace. Strung along the roads leading to and from the town were 40 to 50 workers' homes. In the village was an orchard of 600 apple trees and 150 peach trees. Just down the road stood the school, which doubled as a Quaker meetinghouse on Sundays. In the town was a hospital (infirmary), where villagers could recuperate from illness or injury.

During its heyday, Martha produced 750 tons of iron castings annually and employed nearly 60 men. Aside from pig iron (long narrow bars of iron that required further processing by a forge), Martha Furnace produced cast iron products such as stoves, firebacks, sash weights, kettles, skillets, and cannon wheels.

In 1741, on the site of what was later to be known as Martha, Gervis Pharo built and operated the Swago Sawmill. Built on the Swago (the name later corrupted to Oswego) Branch of the Wading River, the tract also included a gristmill and probably a small settlement of mill workers and their families. By 1765 the tract was owned

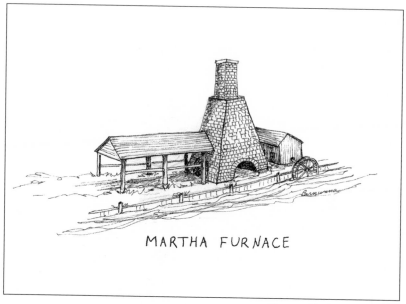

MARTHA FURNACE

(Illustrated by Berminna Solem)

and operated by two Springfield Township Quakers, Samuel Hough and William Newbold. In 1793 Isaac Potts, a Pennsylvania Quaker, purchased the tract from Hough and Newbold. Potts, who had run a gristmill at Valley Forge, Pennsylvania, from 1768 through the years of the Revolution, was also involved in the iron industry in his home state. After Potts purchased the Swago tract, he immediately erected an iron furnace and changed the name of the settlement to Martha, naming it after his wife. The Martha Furnace went into blast for the first time on September 29, 1793. In less than three years, a sizable town had grown up around the furnace.

In 1795 Potts built the Wading River Forge and Slitting Mill several miles away, near the site of the Harrisville Paper Mill. Pig iron from Martha was transported to the forge to be made into wrought iron products. The slitting mill, whose main product was nails, also produced wagon wheel rims.

Potts, who never lived at Martha, soon wearied of the project, and he put the furnace and town up for sale in 1796. In 1800 the Martha tract finally sold to John Paul, Charles Shoemaker, George Ashbridge, and Morris Robeson, four partners who formed the Martha Furnace Company. The four partners did not hold on to the Martha property for long, advertising it for sale once again in 1805. An advertisement in the *Trenton Federalist* on November 4, 1805, describes the Martha Furnace complex as having 15,000 acres of land and a charcoal blast furnace in good repair. Located in the town was also a gristmill, a sawmill, a stamping mill, a mansion house, and a number of tenement homes sufficient to house all the workers. Nearby stood a thriving apple and peach orchard as well as sufficient ore beds and timber to fire the furnace.

In 1808 Samuel Richards and his cousin Joseph Ball purchased the Martha tract, and George Ashridge's heirs retained a one-quarter interest in the enterprise. Samuel Richards would later purchase the furnace towns of Atsion, Hampton, and Weymouth. Joseph Ball was a former manager of Batsto Furnace during John Cox's ownership.

Richards and Ball did not live at Martha. They retained Jesse Evans, the previous manager, to oversee the complex. Evans, who may have been in a management role at Martha as early as 1800, was definitely there by 1806. Evans would manage the ironworks for 40 years, becoming well respected in the community and prominent in the township government of Washington (the township in which Martha was located) for a number of years. From as early as 1802, when Washington Township was first formed, Jesse Evans was elected to a succession of posts, including justice of the peace, member of the township committee, judge of elections, and chosen freeholder.

Jesse Evans was born in 1770 in Old Evesham Township—probably in the Lumberton area—and married for the first time in 1795. His wife, Lucy Ann Kellum, became a Quaker when she was 45 years old and after the Evanses had settled in Martha. In a memorial to Lucy Ann written after her death, it is noted that she had struggled with a nicotine addiction in her early years. The "Memorial Concerning Lucy Ann Evans, deceased," read and approved by the Mt. Holly Society of Friends on March 10, 1881, states, "Prior to becoming a Friend, she was on the gay walks of life. She had long indulged in the habit of using snuff, but about the forty-fifth year of her age, she felt it a duty required of her to abandon the practice." Confining herself to her room for some weeks, Lucy Ann went cold turkey and was able to break the nicotine habit. Only after being completely cured did she feel right about joining the Society of Friends.

After joining the Society of Friends in 1814, Lucy Ann soon took on a prominent role, eventually becoming an elder. Lucy Ann was highly regarded in the Society and was considered a tireless humanitarian who often did good works in helping those less fortunate than herself. There is no evidence that her husband was a member of the Society of Friends, though we do know that Jesse Evans attended meetings with Lucy Ann from time to time.

Jesse and Lucy Ann took four young children into their home after the death of their friend John King on March 25, 1813. King, an occasional carter (a person who transported goods to and from the village) and the owner of the Half Moon and Seven Stars Tavern, had designated his friends Jesse Evans and Joseph Doran as court-appointed guardians of his children. Jesse and Lucy Ann took King's four youngest children: John (less than a year old), Lucy (about two years old), Margaret (four years old), and Mary (five years old).

In 1834 Lucy Ann Evans died at the age of 65. Two years later Jesse married his adopted daughter Lucy Ann King. He was 66 at the time, and she was 25. Even though marrying a woman who had been an adopted daughter from the age of two would surely raise eyebrows today, it appears that no one was disturbed about Jesse's choice of a second bride. He was continually reelected to township posts and managed Martha for Samuel Richards until 1841. Jesse and the second Lucy Ann had five children together, the last being born when he was 77.

Little remains at Martha today to tell us the town's story. The important find of the Martha Diary and Journal, written by two or more clerks at Martha Furnace between 1808 and 1815, provides us with valuable information about the day-to-day happenings of this village. The diary not only gives us information regarding the management of the ironworks but also reveals intimate details of the daily life of the villagers. We learn from reading the diary that when the furnace went out of blast every winter, it was a cause for great celebration among the workers. Drinking was common among the village men, and a great deal of time was spent in the nearby taverns.

Through the diary, we hear about "training days," when all village men under 18 were to report for military drills. These "training days," held three or four times a year and generally conducted near taverns, appear to have been little more than a pretense, with many of the participants—including the officers—returning to the village drunk.

The diary also tells us that a school existed at Martha as early as 1810. Apparently, disruptive behavior was not tolerated at the school as the diary notes that the Lanning children were expelled on April 28, 1810, for fighting.

It seems that stray dogs roamed the town, and poor old Peggy the cow was found dead in the woods after being noted as missing. Village scandals included the time "Wm. Mick's widow arrived here in pursuit of J. Mick, who she says has knocked her up."

The diary talks about the village's births, deaths, illnesses, weddings, house raisings, and quilting parties. We learn there was a colony of "free Negroes" living in Martha and that there was a marching or choral group called the Sons and Daughters of Thunder. All in all, the diary paints a picture of a village filled with colorful characters living meaningful, busy lives.

The Martha Diary and Journal was an important find, not only for what it tells us about the history of Martha, but also because it provides a rare glimpse into the daily life of an early-19th-century iron town. Reportedly found in an office safe at Harrisville before fire destroyed the town in 1914, the original diary is now at the Eleutherian Mills Historical Library in Greenville, Delaware.

In 1841, Samuel Richards, who by this time owned the Martha tract outright, sold the property to Jesse Evans for $10,000. The furnace was still in blast at the time of the sale, but the decline of the iron industry had already begun. As was the case with all the other iron furnaces in South Jersey, Martha went out of business by the mid-1800s, when anthracite (coal) and a better grade of iron were found in Pennsylvania.

Jesse stayed on at Martha for a few more years, operating an extensive charcoal manufacturing business. In 1847 he, Lucy Ann, and their five children moved to Medford Township, where Jesse died two years later.

Prior to his death, Jesse sold the Martha tract to Frances Chetwood, who was then president of the Raritan and Delaware Bay Railroad. The Raritan and Delaware Bay Railroad had at one time planned to build a rail route through Martha and Harrisville. When surveyors found the route impractical, they instead built the rail through Chatsworth and Atsion, dooming Martha for all time.

There are reports that Chetwood attempted to start a brickworks at Martha, but such a project appears never to have gotten off the ground. Sometime between 1860 and 1863, Chetwood sold most of the Martha tract (19,000 acres) to Amory Edwards, a land speculator. Edwards was able to resell a large part of the property, probably becoming one of the few to make a profit from Pine Barrens real estate. By 1896 Joseph Wharton had purchased the town of Harrisville and a large part of the Martha tract. As part of the Wharton Tract purchase, the state of New Jersey took possession of the property in the mid-1950s.

HARRISVILLE AND MARTHA SIDE TRIPS
HARRISVILLE AND OSWEGO LAKES

After exploring the Harrisville ruins, stop off at Harrisville Lake for a bathroom break (there is an outhouse across from the pond) and a picnic lunch. While at the lake, check out what may be the ruins of the Wading River Forge and Slitting Mill just south of the outhouse. Although many people swim at Harrisville Lake, swimming is prohibited (according to state law) because lifeguards are unavailable.

Oswego Lake, an even more remote piney lake, is just up the road and is the beginning of a four-hour canoe/kayak trip that travels down the Oswego River and ends at Harrisville Lake. There are several canoe/kayak rentals in the area, including Belhaven Canoe Rentals (800-445-0953), Micks Canoe Rental (609-726-1380), and Pine Barrens Canoe Kayak Rentals (800-732-0793), that can assist you with this river excursion.

Oswego Lake.
(*Photo by Gordon Stull*)

To get to Oswego Lake from Harrisville, take Route 679 North, passing Harrisville Pond on your right. Drive approximately 1.4 miles to where Route 679 joins Route 563. Continuing north on Route 563, drive another 2.8 miles. Look for Lake Oswego Road and turn right. Continue on Lake Oswego Road, passing the Rutgers University Agricultural Research Station on your left and a number of cranberry bogs on both sides of the road. After traveling 3 miles, look for a sign on your right indicating you have entered Penn State Forest. Turn right at the sign for the Oswego Lake parking lot. There are seven picnic tables, two outhouses, and ample beach areas for sunbathing along the edge of the lake. Canoeing and kayaking are permitted activities at Oswego Lake, but swimming is prohibited (though many people ignore the ban).

As part of the 1960s supersonic jetport proposal, Lake Oswego was to be filled in and turned into the main airplane runway. Imagine how different the scene would be today if this proposal had ever come to fruition!

Hike to Ogden Nash's Cabin

To hike to what has been known for many years in Piney lore as the ruins of literary great Ogden Nash's Pine Barrens cabin, walk 1.75 miles from Martha heading in a northerly direction. After traveling this distance, you will reach a small bridge that crosses Bucks Run. Immediately after crossing the bridge, look for a firebreak on the right side. Follow the firebreak for a little more than a half mile through the woods to reach the cabin ruins. Located on a pond with a beaver lodge, the cabin must have once been a cozy get-away. Unfortunately, today the site is often used as a backwoods drinking spot, and bottles and trash litter the surrounding area.

Although it is fun to think that Ogden Nash once used this cabin as a writing retreat, it appears to be a myth. The author of this book, in an attempt to verify the legend, contacted the granddaughter of Ogden Nash, who after consultation with other family members insisted that the writer never owned or rented a cabin in the New Jersey Pine Barrens.

References

Baer, Christopher T., Coxey, William J., and Schopp, Paul W. 1994. *The Trail of the Blue Comet: A History of the Jersey Central's New Jersey Southern Division.* Palmyra, NJ: The West Jersey Chapter, National Railway Historical Society.

Beck, Henry Charlton. 1936. *Forgotten Towns of Southern Jersey.* New Brunswick, NJ: Rutgers University Press.

Bisbee, Henry H., and Colesar, Rebecca Bisbee. 1976. *Martha: The Complete Furnace Diary and Journal 1808–1815.* Burlington, NJ: Henry Bisbee, Publisher.

Dellomo, Angelo N., Jr. "Carey Was Key Figure In Harrisville Venture." *Batsto Citizens Gazette,* Spring/Summer 1982.

Dellomo, Angelo N., Jr. 1977. *Harrisville: A Journey Down the Sugar Sand Roads of Yesteryear.* Atlantic City, NJ: Angelo Publishing Company.

Ewing, Sarah W. R. "Closing Martha Furnace Created Problems for Many." *Batsto Citizens Gazette,* Winter 1975.

Fowler, Michael, and Herbert, William A. 1976. *Papertown of the Pine Barrens: Harrisville, New Jersey.* Eatontown, NJ: Environmental Education Publishing Service.

Fowler, Michael. "Rural Industrial Communities in the Pinelands." *Batsto Citizens Gazette*, Spring/Summer 1984.

McMahon, William. 1973. *South Jersey Towns*. New Brunswick, NJ: Rutgers University Press.

Moore, Harvey. 1943. *An Old Jersey Furnace*. Baltimore, MD: Newth-Morris Printing Co.

Pearce, John E. 2000. *Heart of the Pines: Ghostly Voices of the Pine Barrens*. Hammonton, NJ: Batsto Citizens Committee.

Peterson, Robert A. 1998. *Patriots, Pirates, and Pineys: Sixty Who Shaped New Jersey*. Medford, NJ: Plexus Publishing, Inc.

Pierce, Arthur D. 1957. *Iron in the Pines: The Story of New Jersey's Ghost Towns and Bog Iron*. New Brunswick, NJ: Rutgers University Press.

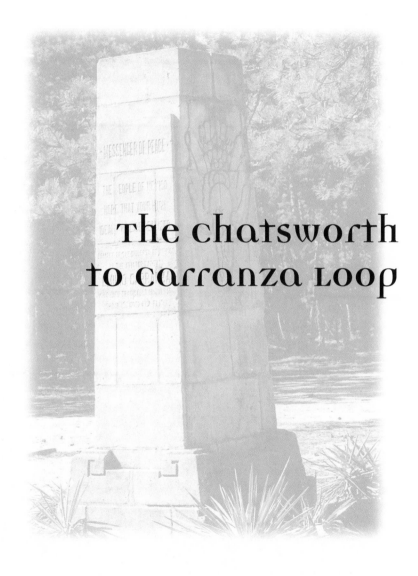

the chatsworth
to carranza loop

The Chatsworth to Carranza Loop

OVERVIEW AND DRIVING/BIKING TOUR

Chatsworth, called the Capital of the Pines by John McPhee in *The Pine Barrens*, sits in the middle of the Pinelands' most critical ecological region. Surrounded by deep forests on all sides, this town can feel like an oasis to those passing through the area.

First settled in the late 1700s, the little village was originally known as Shamong, an Indian name meaning "Place of the Horn." In 1893 the town's name was changed to Chatsworth after the Chatsworth Club, a private, 8,000-acre resort built on the shores of the town's old forge pond.

Now a quiet and remote locale, Chatsworth and the surrounding area were once the focus of many enterprising entrepreneurs looking to exploit the rich resources of the region.

Exploration of the Chatsworth to Carranza Loop is easily done by bicycle because of the flat terrain of the area and the marked bike path on all but the dirt roads outlined in the self-guided tour. Riding a bike is a great way to experience the Pines for those with the stamina to handle the ride, but the tour can also be done by car. When biking on dirt roads in the Pine Barrens, it is best to use a mountain or hybrid-style bicycle fitted with puncture-proof tires (to avoid tire perforation by briars) because of the soft "sugar sand" found in some areas.

For those interested in doing the tour by bicycle, a good starting point is the top of Apple Pie Hill. Starting at this point (if all sites along the way are visited), the mileage of the recommended tour is 16.5 miles. If this option is selected, an additional vehicle will need to be waiting at the end of the route because the ride will not terminate at the starting point. For those willing to add an additional 4.5 miles of riding through the woods, there is a passable bike route leading directly back to Apple Pie Hill from the Carranza Memorial.

getting to apple pie hill

From the West
Take Route 70 East to the Red Lion Circle (where Route 206 intersects Route 70). Take Route 206 South to the second light. Turn left onto Route 532 East, passing the crossroads in Tabernacle (approximately 1.2 miles). From the Tabernacle crossroads, drive approximately 8.3 miles to Ringler Avenue and turn right. Ringler will be on your right side and is marked by two brick posts on each side of the road. Drive two miles to the top of Apple Pie Hill.

From the South
Take Route 30 (White Horse Pike) to the intersection with Route 206 (just above Hammonton). Take Route 206 North approximately 15 miles to Route 532 East. Turn right onto Route 532 East, crossing the Tabernacle intersection (Tabernacle Town Hall will be on your left and Russo's Farm Market on your right). From the Tabernacle intersection, drive approximately 8.3 miles to Ringler Avenue and turn right. Ringler will be on your right side and is marked by two brick posts on either side of the road. Drive two miles to the top of Apple Pie Hill.

From the North via the New Jersey Turnpike
Drive south on the New Jersey Turnpike to exit 7. Take Route 206 South through the Red Lion Circle (where Route 206 intersects Route 70) to the second light. Turn left onto Route 532 East, passing the crossroads in Tabernacle (approximately 1.2 miles). From the Tabernacle crossroads, drive approximately 8.3 miles to Ringler Avenue and turn right. Ringler will be on your right side and is marked by two brick posts on each side of the road. Drive two miles to the top of Apple Pie Hill.

From the North via the Garden State Parkway
Take the Garden State Parkway to exit 63. Take 72 West to Route 563. Turn left onto Route 563 and follow until it intersects with Route 532 in Chatsworth (approximately 3.7 miles). Turn right onto Route 532 West and drive 1.4 miles to Ringler Avenue. Turn left and drive two miles to the top of Apple Pie Hill.

To begin the Chatsworth to Carranza Loop, drive to the cross-roads of Route 532 and Carranza Road in Tabernacle. From this intersection continue on Route 532 east and travel 4.6 miles to where the road intersects with Moores Meadow Road. One mile south on Moores Meadow Road is the Birches Cranberry farm and a packing and sorting house built in 1890. The sorting and packing house, which is still in use today, can be toured by appointment. For more information call Maryann Thompson at 609-859-9701. From Moores Meadow Road on Route 532 travel 1.2 miles to where the road begins to bend to the right. Shortly after the bend you will see a hunting club on your right and White Horse Road on your left. On White Horse Road and other nearby dirt roads leading off

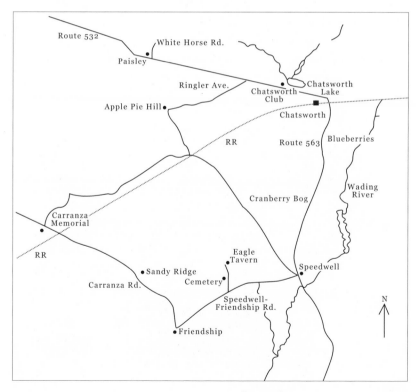

Chatsworth to Carranza Loop tour map.

the highway are the scant remains of the notorious land scheme development of Paisley. At the height of the deception, buyers visiting their new "homesteads" found little more then a mattress factory and a few dilapidated homes on dirt roads.

After passing White Horse Road, drive two miles east on Route 532 to Ringler Avenue and make a right turn. Stay on this road for two miles, until you reach the top of Apple Pie Hill, the highest point in the New Jersey Pine Barrens at 208 feet above sea level.

In 1911–1912, Dr. William White built the Pine Crest Sanatorium at Apple Pie Hill. White dug a 70-foot well and pumped out water that he sold as a cure-all to those visiting his rest home and bottling plant. The Pine Crest bottling plant was built on the east slope of the hill, and the remains of this structure are still clearly visible. A dirt road passes in front of the bottling plant and leads directly to the site of the Harris Railroad Station (renamed the Pine Crest Station in 1923). On the strip from the top of the hill down to the railroad, White laid out a number of five-acre home sites. As was the case in most Pine Barrens land development schemes, few lots were ever sold.

Ruins of the Pine Crest bottling plant.
(*Photo by Gordon Stull*)

Apple Pie Hill, with its high elevation and minimal light pollution, is a great place to observe the night sky. Don't expect to be alone, though, when there are important astronomical events occurring. Several years ago the Leonid meteor shower brought a crowd of nearly 300 people to the crest of the hill.

On leaving Apple Pie Hill, return to Route 532 via Ringler Avenue. Turn right on Route 532 and travel 0.8 miles to Chatsworth Lake, which is located on the north side of the highway.

In 1893, a wealthy New York family that owned land in the area built a hotel on the lake. The hotel was eventually incorporated as the Chatsworth Club and became an exclusive winter resort for 600 of its members. Club members hailed from the wealthy and privileged classes of New York and Philadelphia and included a former vice president of the United States. An Italian Prince, who had married into the family that owned the land, built a private lakeside villa that became known by the Chatsworth locals as the "Princess House."

Today, all that remains of the Princess House and Chatsworth Club properties are a cellar hole, part of a chimney, and some scattered bricks that can be found in the woods on the north side of the lake about 100 feet from the road.

Chatsworth Club.
(Photo courtesy of the Burlington County Library)

Guests in front of the Chatsworth Club.
(*Photo courtesy of the Burlington County Library*)

The property around the lake has recently been purchased by the New Jersey Conservation Foundation and will shortly be open for public use. For information on how to gain access to this property, call 908-234-1225 or go to its Web site at www.njconservation.org.

On the other side of the highway and across from the lake near the existing dam, Union Forge once stood. Built in 1800 the forge made bar iron from the pig iron brought in from the nearby Speedwell Furnace.

After leaving the lake area, drive a little more than half a mile to the center of Chatsworth, at the crossroads of Routes 532 and 563. On your right, near where the firehouse stands today, once stood the Chatsworth Railroad Station, where visitors would arrive to be transported by horse and buggy to the Chatsworth Club. The Chatsworth station, first established as the Shamong depot in 1862, was renamed in 1893. New stations were built in 1876 and 1897. The last railroad station built in Chatsworth was sold in 1952 and is now a private home that stands at the end of First Street, one block west of Buzby's General Store.

Continuing on the Chatsworth to Carranza Loop tour, turn right onto Route 563. Shortly after turning right you will see the restored White Horse Inn (also called the Shamong Hotel) on your left. Built in the second quarter of the 19th century, the White Horse Inn was once part of the Chatsworth Club estate. Workmen brought in to build the Chatsworth Club and Princess House boarded at the Inn. In later years the Inn served as a private residence for the Stevenson family and today is owned by Woodland Township. Volunteers have raised funds to refurbish the building, and currently there are plans to use it as a community center.

After passing the White Horse Inn, you will see Buzby's General Store on your right. Built in 1865 by Neil Wade, the building was acquired by Willis Buzby and his wife Myrtle in 1895. Willis—known locally as the King of the Pineys—and Myrtle ran a general store at this location until 1939. After Willis's death, his son Jack took over management of the store until the mid-1960s. After Jack Buzby's death, the store had a series of owners. The store was eventually closed and the building sold to pay overdue taxes. After remaining closed and vacant for seven years, it was bought by Marilyn Schmidt,

White Horse Inn.
(*Photo by Gordon Stull*)

who restored the building and now operates a gift shop that special-
izes in Pinelands books, arts, and crafts. Marilyn, who also writes and
publishes books about the Pine Barrens, is always interested in dis-
cussing the history and culture of the area with her shop's patrons.

Buzby's General Store.
(*Photo by Gordon Stull*)

Leaving the center of town, continue south on Route 563. After
about 1.5 miles, you will see a boarded-up shack on your left surrounded by fields of blueberry bushes. After another 1.5 miles you will
see cranberry bogs on both sides of the highway. About a mile from
the cranberry bogs, you will come to Speedwell-Friendship Road. As
you make a right onto this road, look down into the ravine on your
left side to see the last remaining section of the Speedwell Furnace
wall. (The site of the Speedwell Furnace is today on property owned
by the Lee family and should not be entered without the family's permission.) To the right of the furnace site are the remains of the spill-
way, while across Route 563 is a swamp—all that remains of
Speedwell Lake, the once significant body of water that powered the
Speedwell Iron Furnace.

Author standing by Speedwell Furnace ruins.
(Photo by Gordon Stull)

Speedwell, originally the site of a sawmill owned by Benjamin Randolph, eventually became an iron furnace town replete with furnace buildings, a sawmill, workers' houses, a school, and several larger homes for the manager and owner.

Benjamin Randolph, who built Speedwell Furnace in 1784, lived at Speedwell intermittently. In his early years, Randolph was a highly skilled cabinetmaker and devout patriot who was friendly with both George Washington and Thomas Jefferson. In 1776 Jefferson commissioned Randolph to make him a desk, on which Jefferson eventually penned the Declaration of Independence.

In 1868 the Speedwell property passed into the hands of Stephen Lee, who changed its use from industrial to agricultural. Lee developed bogs and began to cultivate cranberries. The Lee family continues to grow cranberries on their land to this day.

Leaving Speedwell and continuing on Speedwell-Friendship Road, travel 1.2 miles until you reach a dirt crossroads. This was another of the old stage roads and began at Coopers Ferry (now Camden). The road, known as the Washington-Speedwell Road, connected in Washington with the Tuckerton Stage Road, which headed to the shore resort of Tuckerton. Make a right on Washington-Speedwell Road and travel two-tenths of a mile until you reach a small, fenced cemetery on your left. Once the site of a much larger cemetery, this lonely little burial ground is marked by only two tombstones today.

Traveling three-tenths of a mile further, you will reach the site of the Eagle Tavern. The tavern site, once a busy way station, is today a depression in the ground on a rise next to an isolated dirt road marked with signage noting its former prominence. Built in 1795, the tavern provided refreshment for over a half century to tired stage travelers and to the workers of the Speedwell Furnace.

Returning to the Speedwell-Friendship Road, go right and travel a little over a mile to reach the ghost town of Friendship. The ruins that exist at Friendship today are the remains of a cranberry village founded in 1869. The village consisted of a large cranberry sorting and packing house, a one-room schoolhouse, a store, a bright red barn, a large home for the manager's family, six or seven homes for foremen, and several Quonset hut-style buildings for the seasonal pickers. The map detailing the location of the ruins will help you to find all of the foundations and cellar holes that currently exist at the site. The Friendship School has been removed from its original site and restored by the Tabernacle Historical Society and is now standing next to the Lenape Regional Transitional High School, near the crossroads of Route 532 and Carranza Road in Tabernacle.

Descendants of the Alloway family (who lived for many years in Friendship) have erected an 8-ton granite monument to commemorate where their family members laid out one of the first blueberry fields in New Jersey. To visit the monument, drive in a southerly direction on the Hawkins-Friendship Road (a dirt road that runs through the town) for 1.2 miles. Make a left onto another dirt road and go 0.2 mile. The monument and the foundations of three structures are in the clearing to the left of the dirt road.

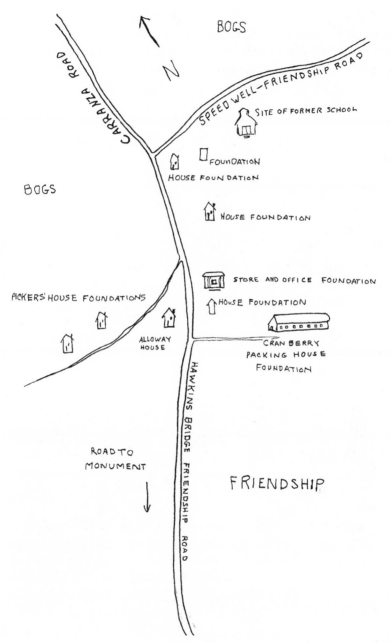

Friendship site map. (*Drawn by Berminna Solem*)

To continue the Chatsworth to Carranza Loop tour, return to the town of Friendship and turn left on what appears to be a continuation of the Speedwell-Friendship Road. Actually you will now be on Carranza Road heading in a northwest direction. The former settlement of Sandy Ridge, a cranberry farm owned by the Wharton Estate, is located eight-tenths of a mile from Friendship. After crossing a small bridge, look to the right to observe the abandoned Sandy Ridge cranberry bogs. Shortly after the bridge is a dirt road leading off to the left. The foundations and cellar holes of Sandy Ridge begin here and can be located by using the 1929 Sandy Ridge survey map included in this chapter. The Sandy Ridge cranberry bogs operated until 1941, at which time the houses of the settlement were also abandoned.

Travel another two miles and cross the old Jersey Central Railroad tracks. Continuing in a northwest direction on Carranza Road you will soon see a sign and a pink tree blaze indicating you have just passed a Batona Trail crossing. Immediately after this crossing, look for a clearing on the left side of the road. Within the clearing is a monument erected in honor of Emilio Carranza, a Mexican aviator who crashed his plane near here in 1928 while returning from a

Friendship school in Tabernacle, 2004.
(*Photo by Gordon Stull*)

Ruins of the Friendship cranberry sorting and packing house, 2003.
(*Photo by Gordon Stull*)

Ruins of house in Friendship, 2003.
(*Photo by Gordon Stull*)

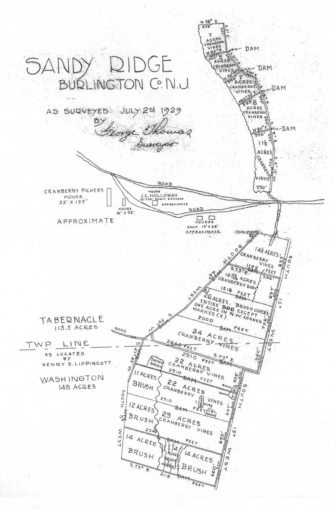

Survey map of Sandy Ridge, 1929.
(Map courtesy of the New Jersey State Archives)

goodwill flight to Washington and New York. Every year on the Saturday closest to July 12 (the day Carranza crashed), the Mt. Holly American Legion organizes a service in remembrance of this heroic Mexican pilot.

Carranza Memorial, 2003.
(*Photo by Gordon Stull*)

There are several routes through the woods that can be used to travel back to Apple Pie Hill. The longer distance requires a return to Speedwell by the road just taken. Immediately before the Route 563 and Speedwell-Friendship Road intersection is a dirt road leading to the left that will take the traveler directly north to Apple Pie Hill. The road is well maintained and can be traveled easily by bike or car. The hill is a little less than four miles from Speedwell.

A second route—manageable by four-wheel-drive vehicle and mountain bike only—can be reached by taking the dirt road across from the Carranza Memorial. Although this is a more direct route through the woods, it is a more difficult road to maneuver due to the many small bumps and the sandy texture of the dirt road. Also, after a period of heavy precipitation, the many potholes on this road may be filled with water several feet deep. To take this route to Apple Pie Hill, turn onto the dirt road across from the Carranza Memorial. Follow this road approximately one mile after passing the campsite. Make a right turn onto an intersecting dirt road and follow it for approximately one mile, bearing left at the first fork. At the next fork in the road, shortly thereafter, bear to your right. Proceed for approximately 1.3 miles until you reach the railroad tracks. Turn left and travel one-tenth of a mile to a crossroads. Turn left and proceed one mile. Turn left at the dead end to complete the final climb to the top of Apple Pie Hill.

A DEEPER LOOK

Tucked away between the Wharton and Brendan T. Byrne State Forests is the small town of Chatsworth. Known as the Capital of the Pines, Chatsworth (once known as Shamong) was settled in the late 1700s by lumbermen eager to harvest the dense pine and cedar forests of the region. By 1820 settlers from what would become Ocean County moved in and began to farm the land. Established in 1862, the town soon grew to support a church, two stores, a school, a wheelwright and blacksmith shop, 20 homes, and a population of nearly 400. The railroad came through in 1862, and shortly thereafter a depot was built; Chatsworth had become a railroad town.

Chatsworth was also the site of a fascinating local land development scheme that brought titled members of society to the area. As of 1863 Joseph D. Beers, a wealthy New York land broker, had amassed thousands of acres in the Chatsworth area. Beers never thought to develop his land holdings in Chatsworth, but his great-grandchildren, who had inherited the property by the early 1890s, decided it would serve as a premier private hunting park for their many wealthy friends and relations. In 1893 the Beers heirs established the Chatsworth Park Company—named for the famous country estate of the Duke of Devonshire—and built a hotel on what had once been an iron forge pond. The pond was turned into an ornamental lake, and soon the hotel was filled to capacity with New York and Philadelphia society folk, including Vanderbilts, Astors, and Drexels. The hotel became the site of many exclusive parties given by the Beerses' heirs, several of whom had married into European royalty. One of these aristocrats, Prince Mario Ruspoli, a diplomat attached to the Italian embassy, built a private villa for his family on Chatsworth Lake. The villa, a Queen Ann-style cottage, was soon known by the locals as the "Princess House," and here Prince Ruspoli's son, Constantino, was born.

By the late 1890s Prince Ruspoli had been reassigned to Belgium, and soon the social life at the Chatsworth resort diminished. The year 1900, however, saw a revival of the 8,000-acre resort as 600 of the friends of the Beers heirs formed the Chatsworth Club. The president of the exclusive club was Levi Parsons Morton, a wealthy banker and former vice president of the United States under Benjamin Harrison. Management at the Chatsworth Club converted the hotel into a clubhouse, and the three-storied Tudor manor house soon became an exclusive winter getaway for its members. Boardwalks and stables were built on the grounds, and rustic bridges were erected to connect the small islands on the lake. The resort was organized around private hunting parties but also featured horseback riding, golf, billiards, trapshooting, tennis, and boating. A tea pagoda was built on the top of Apple Pie Hill where Chatsworth Club members could take refreshment while enjoying the spectacular view.

By 1904, perhaps due to the remoteness of the resort, the rich and famous had grown bored with Chatsworth, and the club began to fail. In an attempt to salvage their investment, the Beers heirs formed the Chatsworth Land, Title and Improvement Company with plans of turning the lake property into a lower- and middle-class bungalow community of 5,280 lots. This venture also failed, and the Chatsworth Club was sold at auction in the fall of 1907. In 1911 the Woodland Country Club was established under local management on the site of the Chatsworth Club. This undertaking was not successful, and the building soon burned down under a veil of suspicion. For many years the Princess House, still owned by an absent Prince Ruspoli, remained standing. Vandalized by hunters and moss gatherers since its abandonment, the cottage eventually burned down in the late 1930s. Ruspoli, who for years had maintained cranberry bogs under local management, disposed of his Chatsworth properties in 1940.

By the time mounted New Jersey State Trooper Budd Wilson Sr. rode into town in the early 1920s on his horse, Dynamite, the Chatsworth Club was in ruins. Wilson's first duty station was Chatsworth, and one of his jobs during those Prohibition years was to keep his eyes open for moonshiners. Another charge was to look out for deer jackers (those shooting deer out of season). Wilson once reportedly caught a New York City man with 100 deer in a refrigerated car at a local railroad siding.

Subsequently, until December 2003, the Chatsworth Club property was owned by the DeMarco family, local cranberry growers with large land holdings in the area. In late 2003 the DeMarco family sold 9,500 acres of their land—including the property around Chatsworth Lake—to the New Jersey Conservation Foundation. With the culmination of the sale, the new acquisition linked the land with five state forests: Wharton, Brendan T. Byrne, Bass River, Greenwood, and Penn State.

Across the road from the site of the Chatsworth Club once stood Union Forge, a small iron forge that made bar iron from the pig iron hauled from Speedwell Furnace. This forge, built in 1800 by William Cook, was out of business by 1843. By the time the Chatsworth Club came into existence, the site was in ruins. In the 1930s historian Charles Boyer found the site of the forge well marked by a dam and "sheeting" still in good repair. Today there is not even iron slag (generally found at most furnace and forge sites) to mark the forge's former location.

By the 1930s the famous Blue Comet, a luxury passenger train run by the Central Railroad of New Jersey, began roaring through town four times a day on its two daily round-trips from Jersey City to Atlantic City. Once, during a torrential rainstorm, the Blue Comet derailed near Chatsworth. There was no loss of life, even though early news reports suggested the casualties were enormous.

Driving to or away from Chatsworth today, with its dense surrounding woodlands, blueberry fields, and cranberry bogs, it is hard to believe the area was once the focus of many land speculation schemes. Fortunately, at least for those who love the natural beauty of this place, these plans never quite materialized or, at best, were short lived.

One of the most notorious of the Pine Barrens real estate schemes occurred in Paisley, a town about 2.5 miles west of Chatsworth's center. For four years advertisements touting Paisley as the "Magic City" ran in the Sunday *New York World* and in a promotional paper called the *Paisley Gazette*. Paisley sales offices were located in New York, Philadelphia, Washington, and Chicago. Some 14,000 acres of land, split into 13,000 lots, were being offered for sale by out-of-town land promoters for $375 an acre. In order to get sales moving, some lots were given away. Advertisements for home sites at Paisley hyped them by claiming "Your neighbors are great artists, authors, composers, medical men, and lawyers." The town was described as a manufacturing center with an academy of music, conservatories, schools, and colleges. In actuality, the town never consisted of anything more then a dozen or so houses, a ramshackle mattress factory, and a 22-room hotel called the Paisley Inn. The Inn, often depicted in a pen-and-ink drawing on the front page of the *Paisley Gazette*, was surely the most elegant structure in town and was obviously used to draw in buyers.

Although the "Magic City" never materialized as planned, promoters did manage to sell 3,100 lots, netting themselves a $250,000 profit.

On the outskirts of Chatsworth lies Apple Pie Hill, the highest point in the New Jersey Pine Barrens at 208 feet above sea level. In 1911–1912, Dr. William A. White built the Pine Crest Sanatorium at the top of this hill. He dug a well 70 feet deep and began marketing his elixir, Pine Crest Water.

Out-of-town visitors would be chauffeured to the Sanatorium after taking the train from New York or Philadelphia, and here they would lounge on the large sunporch, consuming Dr. White's tonic of Pine Crest Water and taking in the grand view and fresh Pinelands air.

In 1913 Dr. White laid out five-acre home sites on the strip of land lying between the Jersey Central Railroad and the hill, calling his new development Pine Crest Estates. As was the case with most real estate promotions in the Pine Barrens, relatively few lots were sold.

Today the only structures that remain of Dr. White's enterprise are the ruins of the bottling plant on the east slope of Apple Pie Hill and

Apple Pie Hill fire tower.
(*Photo by Gordon Stull*)

the filled-in cistern at its crest. The views are still great, especially when taken from the 60-foot fire tower that sits on the top of the hill. No one knows exactly how or when Apple Pie Hill got its name, but we do know the name dates from at least 1759, when it was used as a descriptor on survey records.

Three miles south of the town of Chatsworth, where Route 563 crosses the west branch of the Wading River, is the site of the forgotten town of Speedwell. Named after a wildflower (*Veronica virginica,* commonly called Speedwell), the town was originally the site of a sawmill and later became an iron furnace town owned by Benjamin Randolph, a Philadelphia cabinetmaker.

Randolph, who acquired his land in the Pines in 1760, was initially an absentee owner. His brother Daniel ran the sawmill while he was busy building his cabinetry business in Philadelphia. By 1767, Benjamin, who was considered a master carver, had acquired a shop at Third and Market streets called the "Sign of the Golden Eagle." (As an example of Benjamin's exceptional workmanship, a wing chair he had carved, which was passed down as a family heirloom, sold in the 1920s to the Philadelphia Museum of Art for $33,000.)

Benjamin and his wife Anna Bromwich lived over the shop. Soon they were the parents of two daughters, Mary and Anna. Even with the addition of two young children, the family must have considered their lodgings to be larger than they needed as they shortly began to take in boarders. The first boarder was Giovanni Gualdo, a widowed Italian wine merchant and musician, and his daughter Frances. Gualdo soon opened a music store and, being a talented impresario, began giving concerts. During one of his concert tours, Gualdo had such a severe mental breakdown he was confined in chains in the Pennsylvania Hospital, where he died

Wing chair made by Benjamin Randolph.
(*Photo by Gordon Stull*)

BENJAMIN RANDOLPH HOUSE

(Illustrated by Berminna Solem)

a few years later. Gualdo's daughter, Frances, now parentless, became a ward of the Randolph family.

During this pre-Revolutionary period, Randolph, a fervent nationalist, became very involved in the patriot cause. In 1774, with the American Revolution close at hand, colonists held the first Continental Congress in Philadelphia. George Washington, looking for lodging when he came to town to attend the congress, was directed to the Randolph home. In 1776, when the second Continental Congress was held in Philadelphia, Thomas Jefferson boarded with the Randolph family. During his visit Jefferson commissioned Randolph to make him a portable desk. This desk, now on display in the Smithsonian Museum of American History in Washington DC, was the one on which Jefferson wrote the Declaration of Independence.

By 1777, with the British occupying the city of Philadelphia, Randolph, who had gotten more and more involved in the patriots' cause, decided it was time to close up shop and move his family to the wilds of New Jersey. With his family safely ensconced in Speedwell, Randolph became increasingly involved in the war efforts. By June of 1778, when the British had evacuated the city, Randolph moved his family back to Philadelphia. On his return, Randolph found that his Tory neighbors, angry at his involvement with the patriots' cause, had trashed his shop and done a great deal of damage to his inventory. To add to his troubles, Randolph's wife passed away during this period, leaving him with the sole care and support of his two daughters, Anna and Mary, and his ward, Frances. Discouraged and distraught, Randolph sold his business at the end of 1778 and became involved with the merchandising business. For a brief period, he was part owner of a privateer—a privately owned trading vessel authorized by the Continental Congress to harass and prey on merchant ships owned by the British.

By 1779 Randolph had decided to sell his Pine Barrens property. He put the sawmill and his land holdings at Speedwell up for sale, but after two buyers defaulted on their deals, the Speedwell property was his once again.

In 1784, after moving his family to Burlington, Randolph, with the knowledge that large bog ore deposits existed on his property, decided to build an iron furnace at Speedwell. About this time, John Sluyter, who had been overseer of the sawmill, married Randolph's daughter Mary. They lived at Speedwell, with John managing the furnace and sawmill operations. Despite his efforts, Speedwell Furnace was never more than a moderately successful enterprise.

In 1788 Benjamin Randolph married Mary Wilkerson Fennimore, and together they moved into her Springfield Township home. It appears the marriage was not a successful one, however, as Randolf was living with his daughter and son-in-law in Speedwell by 1790. In 1791 he died, leaving the Speedwell property to his unmarried daughter Anna. For another six years John Sluyter continued to operate the Speedwell property, which he leased from his sister-in-law. Anna continued to live at the Speedwell property until 1792, when the estate was settled. After leaving Speedwell, Anna went to live with her adopted sister Frances, who had married by now and was living in Morristown. Frances had married Gabriel Ford, whose father had built the historic mansion in Morristown known as "Washington's Headquarters." Together with her adopted sister and brother-in-law, Anna lived out her life in this famous Morristown mansion.

In early 1797 the Speedwell Furnace failed. Sluyter, with his wife and children, left Speedwell forever and moved to Augusta, Georgia, to start a new life. For the next 30 or so years Anna leased the furnace property to a series of individuals, earning an average income of $500 a year.

In 1833 the aging Anna decided it was time to sell the Speedwell property. The property was purchased by Samuel Richards, the well-known and successful ironmaster of Martha, Atsion, and Weymouth Furnaces. Richards repaired the furnace, and it was soon back in blast. Unlike his other furnace enterprises, Speedwell was barely profitable, and Richards only intermittently kept it in operation. After Richards's death in 1842, the Speedwell Furnace went out of blast for the last time. The furnace complex stood vacant until 1850 when the Richards heirs sold the entire property to James McCambridge, the former owner of the nearby Eagle Tavern, for $1,750.

On August 28, 1868, McCambridge sold the Speedwell tract, along with some adjoining land he had acquired, to his brother-in-law Stephen Lee for $8,000.

Realizing the glory days of iron were over, the Lee family decided to change the use of the property from industrial to agricultural. By 1870 they had built a series of cranberry bogs on their Speedwell property. With the exception of some difficult years during the Depression, the Lee family has continued to farm the land and remains cranberry growers to this day.

Near each Pine Barrens iron town there invariably was a tavern that served as a gathering place for the local furnace workers. Speedwell was no exception, and within a mile and a half of the village was the Eagle Tavern. Located off the Speedwell-Washington stage road, the tavern also provided refreshment to travelers journeying through the area.

The first known operator of the Eagle Tavern was Gideon Pharo, who was given a tavern license for his establishment in 1798. Soon after, in 1810, Jacob Barnhart became the tavern keeper, and the way station became known as Barnhart's Tavern. After passing through the hands of several more owners, the tavern was bought by James McCambridge in 1826. It retained the name of Barnhart's Tavern for a number of years after McCambridge purchased the property, but the name was eventually changed to the Eagle Tavern. McCambridge operated the tavern until approximately 1849. Even after the tavern closed, McCambridge and his family continued to live at the tavern site.

Down the road from the tavern site is a small, fenced-in cemetery marked by several graves. One of the tombstones, still legible, indicates that a child, Charles Wills, died and was buried here in 1839. Behind the small cemetery is a clearing where the village of Eagle once stood. Excepting the clearing and small cemetery, there is no evidence suggesting that a village once existed here.

Several miles from Speedwell, at the intersection of the Speedwell and Carranza roads, is the ghost town of Friendship. Located near the site of the Friendship Sawmill, built in 1795, the property eventually passed into the hands of three Quaker brothers, who used the property for occasional hunting and berry picking. In 1868 the 1,200-acre site was developed into a cranberry village by Joshua Wills (a son of one of the brothers) and Joseph Evans (Wills's brother-in-law). After building a large cranberry packing house, a store, a school, and homes for their workers, Evans and Wills purchased another 810 acres and continued to expand the bogs on their land. Soon Friendship was considered the largest cranberry-producing operation in the area. In 1892 Wills and Evans decided to expand their operation further and purchased cranberry bogs in Medford. After Evans's death in 1909, Joshua Wills continued to produce cranberries with his former partner's heirs. In 1930 the company was incorporated as Evans and Wills Inc. Four years after the incorporation, Joshua Wills died. In 1951 the company was split between the Wills and Evans heirs. As specified by the agreement, the Evans heirs kept the Friendship bogs, and the Wills heirs kept those in Medford.

Eventually the Friendship tract passed into the hands of Andy Andrews, who sold the land to a real estate speculation company for $42 an acre. The company, Friendship Forest Lakes, never developed the land and soon sold the property to the state of New Jersey for $525 an acre, making a hefty profit.

Gravestone at Eagle Cemetery, 2003.
(*Photo by Gordon Stull*)

The Alloway family, long involved in cranberry and blueberry farming, lived for three generations in Friendship. Gladys Alloway married Tony DeMarco, a local picker boss, and together they founded the Chatsworth Cranberry Company, a business that at one time was considered the largest cranberry farm in the area. The descendants of the Alloways and DeMarcos erected a monument deep in the woods near Friendship to commemorate where members of their family set out their first blueberry field, one of the original and most productive in the area.

As is often the case when a town becomes abandoned in the Pines, arsonists burned down all existing structures in Friendship.

Today the ruins of the town are clearly visible, leading the infrequent visitor to ponder what may have once existed in this forlorn and spooky clearing in the Pines.

Less than a mile from Friendship, traveling north on Carranza Road, are the ruins of Sandy Ridge, a cranberry farm once owned by the Wharton estate. Sandy Ridge was a smaller version of Friendship, and the settlement consisted of only four residential structures and housing for the pickers. Joseph Holloway came to live in Sandy Ridge with his family in 1920. He managed the bogs for the Wharton Estate until the enterprise closed in 1941. All that remain in Sandy Ridge today are the abandoned bogs and the foundations and cellar holes of five residential structures.

Several miles north of Sandy Ridge stands a 12-foot monument with a falling Aztec eagle relief on one of its sides. The monument is a memorial to a Mexican aviator who crashed near its site on July 12, 1928. Emilio Carranza, a grand-nephew of Mexican president Venustiano often referred to as the "Mexican Lindbergh," was flying home from a goodwill flight when his plane crashed during a storm over the New Jersey Pinelands.

Emilio Carranza, just 22 at the time, had flown from Mexico City to Washington on June 11, 1928, in response to a goodwill flight made by Charles Lindbergh the previous December. Emilio's flight was planned as nonstop, but he ran into a storm over North Carolina, where he was forced to land and wait out the bad weather. After the storm, Emilio flew on to Washington, DC and a few days later went to New York City. In both cities, he was received by cheering crowds and parades in his honor. Newspapers from around the world reported on his flight, referring to him as the Mexican Lone Eagle.

On the morning of July 12, 1928, Carranza went to Roosevelt Field on Long Island, hoping to get an early start on his nonstop flight back to Mexico. When he arrived at the airfield, he was met by thunderstorms and decided to delay his flight. That evening, while waiting out the storm, Carranza received a telegram from his Mexican superior ordering him to return immediately.

At 7:18 P.M. on July 12, 1928, Carranza took off in his single-seat plane for his return flight to Mexico despite electric storms that were raging throughout the region. Sometime that night his plane crashed in the Pine Barrens at a place known as Sandy Ridge.

The next day John Carr, his wife, Marie, and his mother, May, were out berry picking when they found a part of a plane wing. Carr quickly notified the authorities, and a search party was organized to look for survivors. Carranza's body was soon found next to a dirt road near where the monument stands today. Carranza's body was removed to Buzby's General Store in Chatsworth and then taken to New York City, where it was put on a train and sent back to Mexico. When the train pulled into Mexico City, it was met by 300,000 mourners.

Carranza was considered a great hero by his countrymen, and the school children of Mexico raised the funds to build a monument in his honor. Built from stone quarried near Mexico City, the sandstone monument was cut and fitted in Mexico, then disassembled and shipped to Mt. Holly. The Mt. Holly American Legionaries, who had participated in the search for Carranza's body, took the monument pieces to the site where his body was found and there reconstructed and erected the Carranza Memorial. The inscription on the memorial, written in both Spanish and English, reads:

> MESSENGER OF PEACE
> THE PEOPLE OF MEXICO
> HOPE THAT YOUR HIGH IDEALS
> WILL BE REALIZED
> HOMAGE OF THE CHILDREN OF MEXICO
> TO THE AVIATOR CAPTAIN
> EMILIO CARRANZA
> WHO DIED TRAGICALLY ON JULY 13, 1928 ON
> HIS GOODWILL FLIGHT

One year after Carranza's death, Post 11 of the American Legion held a memorial service at the site where Carranza's body was found. A similar service was held at the same time at Carranza's gravesite in Mexico City. Each and every year since, a memorial service honoring the young aviator has been held on the Saturday closest to the crash date of July 12 at 1:00 P.M. both in Mexico City and at the Carranza Memorial in Tabernacle, New Jersey.

The ceremony, which now has incorporated a reenactment of finding Carranza's body, often draws speakers from the aviator's family as well as Mexican and American government officials. There are performances by Mexican schoolchildren and speeches by dignitaries from both far and near. For more information about this event, go to the American Legion Post 11 Web site at www.postll.org.

THE CHATSWORTH TO CARRANZA LOOP SIDE TRIPS AND EVENTS

HEDGER HOUSE

When in need of refreshment as you travel through the Chatsworth area, stop by the Hedger House, a pleasant restaurant/bar/deli located on Route 563 several miles north of the town center. This nicely renovated restaurant is believed to have been operated as a stagecoach stop on the run from Philadelphia to Barnegat Bay prior to the American Revolution.

Although now a family establishment, the Hedger House was once a rough-and-ready bar that few community outsiders dared to enter. In 1965, a stranger with a stocking over his head, brandishing a handgun, entered the bar. The robber demanded that the bartender hand over the cash register. When the bartender pleaded he was too old and weak to lift the register, the bandit pushed his way behind the bar and began to scoop out the cash. Unbeknownst to the robber, the owner's wife had slipped out of the bar and gone upstairs to the family living quarters to rouse her sleeping husband. Just as the thief was about to flee the bar, the owner arrived with a loaded double-barrel shotgun. He yelled for the masked man to halt, and when the thief turned around, the owner fired. Even though all documented reports of the incident indicate the robber was mortally wounded, piney lore has it that the owner, Al Sweet, blew the thief's head clear off his body.

Today the Hedger House is a welcoming and safe place to stop for a meal, drink, or snack. In the summer months, the establishment hosts live entertainment in the beer garden. Throughout the rest of the year, there is occasional live entertainment in the bar as well as a weekly karaoke night.

CHATSWORTH CRANBERRY FESTIVAL

On the third weekend of every October, the little town of Chatsworth plays host to a festival that often attracts over 50,000 visitors. The annual two-day Cranberry Festival, which coincides with the fall harvesting of the berries, is about everything cranberry—cranberry jams and jellies, cranberry breads and baked goods, cranberry ice cream, and much more. The festival features over 160 artists and craftsmen displaying their wares, along with many local organizations that mount exhibits and distribute information. Other activities and attractions of the festival include bus tours of a cranberry bog, live country music, and an antique auto show. Although there is no festival admission cost, there is a $5 fee for parking. The two-day event is a fundraiser organized by the Festival Committee of Chatsworth, Inc., for the purpose of restoring the White Horse Inn. To learn more about the Cranberry Festival, visit the Festival Committee of Chatsworth, Inc.'s Web site at www.cranfest.org.

HIKE THE BATONA TRAIL FROM CARRANZA MEMORIAL TO APPLE PIE HILL

To enjoy a great hike on the Batona Trail, start your walk on the dirt road leading into the campground across from the Carranza Memorial. Look for pink blazes (trail markers for the Batona Trail) on the trees after you pass the campsite. Continue to follow the pink-blazed trail as you head off the road and into the forest. It is a little over four miles to the top of Apple Pie Hill from the Carranza Memorial.

REFERENCES

Adams, John M. "Apple Pie Hill." *Batsto Citizens Gazette*, Spring/Summer 1996.

Baer, Christopher T., Coxey, William J., and Schopp, Paul W. 1994. *The Trail of the Blue Comet: A History of the Jersey Central's New Jersey Southern Division*. Palmyra, NJ: The West Jersey Chapter, National Railway Historical Society.

Beck, Henry Charlton. 1936. *Forgotten Towns of Southern New Jersey*. New Brunswick, NJ: Rutgers University Press.

Beck, Henry Charlton. 1937. *More Forgotten Towns of Southern New Jersey*. New Brunswick, NJ: Rutgers University Press.

Beck, Henry Charlton. 1956. *The Roads of Home: Lanes and Legends of New Jersey*. New Brunswick, NJ: Rutgers University Press.

Boyer, Charles S. 1931. *Early Forges and Furnaces in New Jersey*. Philadelphia: University of Pennsylvania Press.

Boyer, Charles S. 1962. *Old Inns and Taverns in West Jersey*. Camden, NJ: Camden County Historical Society.

Brown, Edward. "Stagecoaches Once Rumbled Up to the Door." *Philadelphia Inquirer*, March 8, 1981.

Daniels, Mike. "Pinelands Memorial Honors Pioneer Pilot." *Courier Post*, March 14, 2003.

Hajna, Lawrence. "Pinelands Houses Cranberry Firm Ghost Town." *Courier Post*, November 17, 2003.

McPhee, John. 1967. *The Pine Barrens*. New York: Farrar, Straus and Giroux.

Pearce, John. 2000. *Heart of the Pines: Ghostly Voices of the Pine Barrens*. Hammonton, NJ: Batsto Citizens Committee.

Pierce, Arthur D. 1964. *Family Empire in Jersey Iron: The Richards Enterprises in the Pine Barrens*. New Brunswick, NJ: Rutgers University Press.

Ruset, Ben. 2002–2003. *New Jersey Pine Barrens: Exploring the Ghost Towns of Southern New Jersey*. Retrieved from http://www.njpinebarrens.com

Schmidt, Marilyn. 2001. *A Self-Guided Tour of Chatsworth and Vicinity*. Chatsworth, NJ: Pine Barrens Press.

Wilson, Budd. "Cabinet Maker, Randolph, Developed Speedwell." *Batsto Citizens Gazette*, Spring/Summer 1982.

Wilson, Budd. "The Outfit." *Bass River Gazette* (a newsletter from the Bass River Community Library History Committee and the Great John Mathis Foundation), January–June 2002.

Wilson, J. G. "Cloudburst Wrecked Blue Comet, Flooded Batsto—Damaged Roadbed Toppled Train Near Chatsworth." *Batsto Citizens Gazette*, Spring/Summer 1983.

The forks to Hermann

The Forks to Hermann

OVERVIEW AND PADDLE/DRIVING TOUR

Not far from the Colonial village of Batsto lies a place called The Forks. Situated where the Batsto and Mullica rivers converge, this quiet and lovely area was once a thriving port and trading center. Settled in the early 1700s by Europeans seeking religious freedom, The Forks soon prospered due to its location at the head of a navigable inland river. Merchant ships regularly left Batsto Landing (now called Stone Landing) at The Forks loaded with iron products manufactured at the Batsto Iron Furnace and returned there laden with goods for the furnace community.

Due to its remoteness, the port at The Forks was a great place to unload cargo brought up the Mullica River clandestinely to avoid the hated British import tax. Smuggled goods were either taken overland by wagon to Philadelphia or sold right at the docks of The Forks.

With the advent of the American Revolution, the Continental Congress authorized privateers (private vessels given license to harass and loot enemy ships) to capture British merchant ships and to seize their vessels and cargoes. These ships and their cargoes were often auctioned off at The Forks at the house (tavern) of Richard Wescott, a wealthy local businessman and landowner. Blatantly advertised in New Jersey, New York, and Philadelphia newspapers, these auctions often brought large crowds to the Mullica River wharves. Captured goods destined for the Continental Army were stored on Rabbit Island in large warehouses protected by a military post. Near Rabbit Island was the Van Sant Shipyard, where many of the privateer vessels were built.

The end of the War of Independence brought a decline to the prosperity of The Forks. With the major ports of New York and Philadelphia in the hands of the colonists, there was little need to

getting to the forks

From the West
Take Route 73 to Route 30 East (White Horse Pike). After passing the intersection of Routes 206 and 54 near Hammonton, continue on Route 30 approximately 1.2 miles to Route 542. Make a left turn and drive 6.2 miles to the Mullica River Canoe Landing on your right.

From the South via the Garden State Parkway
Take the Garden State Parkway North to exit 50 (New Gretna) for Route 9 North. At the Gulf Gas Station, turn left onto Route 542 and continue for approximately 12.4 miles. The Mullica River Canoe Landing will be on your left shortly after Batsto Village.

From the North via the Garden State Parkway
Take the Garden State Parkway South to exit 52 (New Gretna). Turn right at the stop sign onto East Greenbush Road (CR 654). Make a left at the next stop sign onto Stage Road. After you go over two small wooden bridges, Pilgrim Lake Campground will be on your right. Bear left onto Leektown Road (CR 653). Take Leektown Road to where it intersects with Route 542. Turn right onto Route 542 and proceed for approximately 9.7 miles. The Mullica River Canoe Landing will be on your left shortly after Batsto Village.

From the North
Take Route 206 South to mile marker 3 and make a left onto CR 613. Proceed 2.4 miles to the first intersection. Turn left (a brown Batsto sign is at this intersection) and drive 0.2 mile to the "T." Turn left onto Route 693. Continue on Route 693 until the road ends (approximately 2.7 miles). Turn left onto Route 542 and proceed 3.7 miles to the Mullica River Canoe Landing on your right.

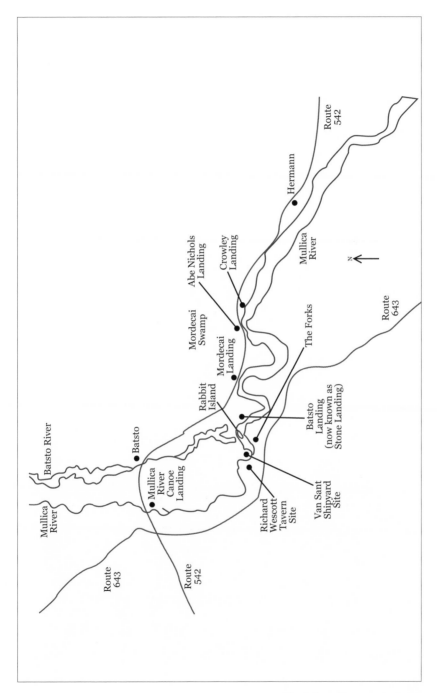

The Forks to Hermann tour map.

unload cargo at a remote wharf. By the mid-1800s, however, industries emerged that brought new life to the Mullica River basin, and once more the waterway became a vital link to the outside world.

With so much of the history connected to the river, traveling by boat from The Forks to Hermann is an excellent way to experience the outlined tour.

If you have your own canoe or kayak, a free launch site is located on Route 542, one-tenth of a mile east and across from the Pleasant Mills Church. It will take approximately an hour to paddle from the Mullica River Canoe Landing to the area of The Forks. For a small fee, you can launch your own boats from The Forks Marina (located across from the Sweetwater Fire Company on Pleasant Mills Road). Belhaven Canoe Rentals (800-445-0953), located just east of Batsto in Green Bank, rents canoes and kayaks and will launch you from the Pleasant Mills location at your request. Tell them you want to paddle to Hermann, and they will arrange to have you end your trip at their boat marina in Green Bank.

Before planning a canoe or kayak trip on the Mullica, you should be aware of the tidal nature of the river. Although it is certainly possible to paddle against the tide, it is always less strenuous when you

Boat launch ramp at The Forks Marina, 2004.
(*Photo by Gordon Stull*)

are going with the current. With a little research, you can plan your trip upriver on a slack or outgoing tide and return on an incoming one. In determining tide schedules, it is important to know that tide changes at The Forks are approximately four hours later than at the beach of Atlantic City.

At The Forks (where the Mullica and Batsto Rivers merge), use the tour map to locate the former sites of the Van Sant Shipyard, Batsto Landing, Rabbit Island, and Richard Wescott's Tavern.

Leaving the area of The Forks, you will pass several islands as you paddle upriver. The remoteness of the Mullica River made it a prime locale for smugglers and privateers to conduct business. Less patriotic and celebrated outlaws also found the area around the Mullica River, with its many secluded inlets and islands, to be an auspicious setting for a home base. Edward Teach, also known as Blackbeard the Pirate, was said to have had a hideout on one of the islands in the Mullica River and possibly to have buried treasure there. Joseph Mulliner, a well-known late-18th-century Pine Barrens outlaw, was reported to have his headquarters in Cold Spring Swamp—thought to be located deep in the woods between Crowleytown and Batsto in an area referred to as Mordecai Swamp. Local legend also has it that John Cox, owner of Batsto during the War of Independence, hid cannon balls there when the British were on their way up the Mullica in 1778 to destroy The Forks and Batsto.

Mordecai Swamp was named after Mordecai Andrews of Tuckerton, who had purchased a large parcel of land on the Mullica sometime in the first half of the 18th century. Mordecai is reported to have conducted a fairly large lumbering operation on his land, and his ship landing (referred to as Mordecai Landing to this day) was a major wharf during the 18th and early 19th centuries. Mordecai Landing was the dock used by Batsto during the early iron days. For all its early importance, Mordecai Landing is barely visible today. It is located approximately three-quarters of a mile from The Forks Marina.

Another important wharf of the early 19th century was Abe Nichols Landing, located at the bend in the river just before Crowley's Landing. Definitely more visible and certainly more

"The Forks" Batsto Landing (on right) and Rabbit Island (in background).
(Photo by Gordon Stull)

accessible than Mordecai Landing, Nichols Landing is often used today by canoe and kayak outfitters as a launching and pull-out spot.

A quarter mile from Abe Nichols Landing and a little over two miles from The Forks is Crowley's Landing. Now a boat launch and picnic area, it was once the site of an eight-pot glass house and a village of seventeen homes. Crowley's Landing is a nice place to stop for a picnic lunch. Canoes and kayaks are easily docked there, and picnic tables and public bathrooms are available. Although almost nothing remains of the old glass town, you can locate its former site by crossing the bridge over the small stream and walking toward the picnic area. After crossing the stream, you will see several mounds of dirt with bricks and pieces of colorful glass scattered on the ground. Even though little is left to identify the site, this is the location of the Civil War-era glass factory built by Samuel Crowley III.

Return to your boat and paddle another 1.4 miles downriver to reach Hermann (also known as Herman or Hermann City), once referred to as Steamboat Landing. The piling of the old wharf is still visible during a low tide.

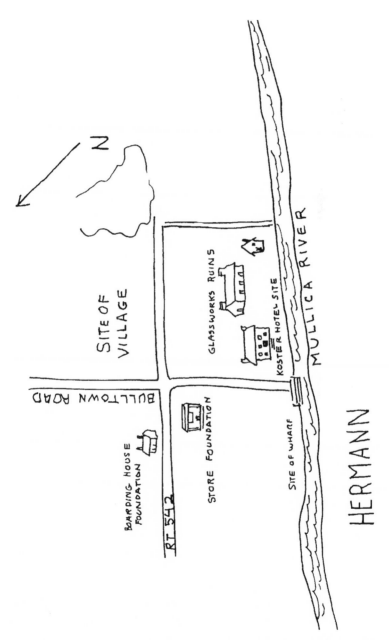

Hermann site map.
(*Drawn by Berminna Solem*)

The town of Hermann is the site of a short-lived glass factory built in 1873. It was also the location of the Hermann Hotel, built by John Sooy prior to the American Revolution. Three sailing ships, the *Jemima Harriet*, the *Argo*, and the *Mary Francis* (also known as the *Two Marys*), were reportedly sunk offshore near the hotel landing loaded with glass products when the glass factory closed its doors in 1874. The ships are underwater and covered in sand, approximately 100 feet offshore, but it is said that on a "blowout" tide, you can still see the hull of one of them.

To walk the ruins of Hermann after landing your boat, walk up the rise to an open field area where several old buttonwood (sycamore) trees still stand. It was in this area where the old Hermann Hotel (also known as Koster's Hotel) stood. If you visit in early spring, you will find long-ago-planted daffodils and vinca still blooming around the old home site. To visit the glass factory ruin, leave the hotel site and walk through the woods in an easterly direction. You will pass the foundation ruins of a sizable structure that may be the remains of a building associated with either the hotel (which is known to have had several outbuildings) or the glass factory. After walking approximately 100 yards, you will see a number of large dirt mounds where the foundation of the sprawling old glass works once stood. Still visible, though largely covered by earth, are the underground draft tunnels that once superheated the fires of the glass factory. The Hermann glass factory, also known as the Wapler's Glass Works, was designed to burn coal, unlike other 19th-century glass houses.

To visit the ruins of a nearby house site, walk eastward another 100 yards until you reach a dirt road. Walking toward the river, you will soon come upon a stone foundation of a house site overlooking the Mullica. According to archeologist Budd Wilson, this house foundation was built illegally during the early Wharton years, probably from stone pilfered from the glass factory site. Wilson believes this house was never completed. Nevertheless you can appreciate the builder's vision, given the sensational view.

To visit the rest of what remains of Hermann, return to the hotel site and walk to the barely discernable road that runs directly down to the river landing. Follow this road away from the river and toward Route 542. When you reach the highway, you will see several very

Ruins of the Sooy/Koster Homestead/Hermann Hotel.
(*Photo courtesy of Budd Wilson*)

Sooy/Koster Homestead/Hermann Hotel, 1935.
(*Photo by Augusta Weeks, courtesy of Budd Wilson*)

large oak trees, probably planted when the hotel was first built prior to the American Revolution. Bulltown Road will be directly in front of you. Using the site map, you should be able to locate the cellar hole of the old Hermann store and the boardinghouse ruins across the highway. Although nothing other than a clearing and some non-indigenous plants remain, at least 17 homes once stood on both sides of Bulltown Road near the ruins of the old boardinghouse. These were the homes of the workers of the Hermann glass works, many of which were abandoned when the glass works shut down in March 1874, six months after it began operation.

To drive to Hermann from Batsto Village, travel three miles east on Route 542 to where Bulltown Road intersects Route 542. At that point, directly across from the left turn onto Bulltown Road, is a blocked-off dirt road that leads directly to the Hermann river landing.

Ruins of Hermann glass works, 1913.
(*Photo courtesy of New Jersey State Archives*)

Ruins of a house at Hermann, 2004.
(*Photo by Gordon Stull*)

These houses at the intersection of Bulltown Road and
Route 542 are no longer standing.
(*Photo courtesy of Budd Wilson*)

A DEEPER LOOK

Sweetwater, where the Batsto and Mullica Rivers meet, is the place often referred to as The Forks. Once a name that encompassed the entire area, to include the hamlets of Pleasant Mills and Batsto, The Forks has a history as rich and wild as the river on which it is situated.

Settled in the early 18th century by Scots fleeing religious perse-cution, The Forks quickly grew into an important and prosperous trading center. Situated on a navigable river, yet inland and remote, The Forks was the perfect port for merchant vessels seeking to avoid the heavy tariffs of the British.

Near the fork of the Batsto and Mullica Rivers stood the once thriving industrial village of Batsto. Founded in 1766, the Batsto Iron Furnace held the distinction during the Revolutionary War years of being one of the principal munitions suppliers for the Continental Army. At Batsto Landing (now called Stone Landing), located on the north side of the Mullica at the place where the two rivers merge, vessels filled with the finished cast iron products of the furnace left the docks regularly during those prosperous years.

At the last bend of the Mullica, just before it merges with the Batsto River, once stood the Van Sant Shipyard. Operating for over 30 years, from 1760 to 1791, the shipyard contributed greatly to the prosperity of the region. Even though ships built at The Forks rarely exceeded 100 feet, the shipyards built one vessel after another, and many other businesses that supported the shipbuilding industry also lined the banks of the river.

When ships laden with goods landed at The Forks, merchants from near and far would crowd the dock. Horse wagons lined the sides of the wharves, waiting to take smuggled merchandise to the marketplaces of Philadelphia.

After the costly French and Indian Wars, the British decided the American colonies should bear the brunt of replenishing King George III's coffers. Noting, too, that it was costing the Crown 8,000 pounds annually to collect 2,000 pounds in custom duties, they decided it was time to launch serious efforts to collect import tariffs. Citing the tyranny of "taxation without representation," the Americans found even more ways to resist paying the high tariffs now demanded by the British. From bribing officials to forging clearance papers to mislabeling cargoes, the Colonists were creative in their response to the crackdown.

With the enforcement of the Navigation Acts and statutes against smuggling, The Forks of the Little Egg Harbor (an earlier name for the Mullica River) began to play an even more pivotal role as a clandestine port of entry.

With the Americans clearly outwitting the Mother country in its effort to win control over the colonies, the cold war between the two adversaries began to heat up.

On March 23, 1776, the Continental Congress in Philadelphia authorized privateering. In simple terms, a privateer was defined as a privately owned, armed vessel authorized by the Congress or state government to take prizes instead of carrying cargo. Privateers operating under sanction of "Letters of Marque" (license) were authorized to harass and prey on British merchant ships. A captured vessel and its cargo could then be sold at public auction and its proceeds divided among the ship's owners, officers, and crew.

By June 1776 privateers began unloading captured booty at The Forks of the Little Egg Harbor. Just as The Forks had been a haven for smugglers, along with Chestnut Neck, it quickly became a headquarters of the privateers. Soon advertisements like the following began to blatantly appear in New York and Philadelphia newspapers:

> To be SOLD by PUBLIC VENUE
> On Monday the twenty-ninth of this instant
> At the House of Mr. Richard Wescott, at the Forks of
> Little Egg-Harbor River.
> The Prize BRIG BLACK SNAKE; and the Schooner
> MORNING STAR, with their tackle, and apparel, & c.
> Captured by Captain William Marriner.
> ZACHARIAH ROSSELL, Marshall.
> (*The Pennsylvania Journal, May 24, 1780*)

Richard Wescott, a prominent and wealthy tavern- and landowner living at The Forks, had an interest, as did many of his contemporaries, in several of the privateers that were capturing and looting the British merchant ships off the coast of Little Egg Harbor. Rather than being thought of as villains, the prominent men of the area who made a fortune with their privateer ventures were considered great patriots who were helping to win the war against the British. In actuality, privateers did make a huge contribution to the victory in the War for Independence, capturing almost as many prisoners during the war as did the Continental Army.

Cargoes looted from the British also helped to outfit the Continental Army. Large warehouses were erected at The Forks in order to store those goods reserved for Washington's troops. A military post was established on Rabbit Island in 1777 to provide protection for the captured goods allotted for the army.

During the summer of 1778, American privateers captured 22 vessels, two of which had prizes that have been estimated at $500,000. The British had run out of patience, and soon The Forks, along with Batsto and Chestnut Neck, became a prime target of the British Navy.

On September 30, 1778, a British expedition under the command of Lieutenant General Sir Henry Clinton and Captain Patrick Ferguson left New York. Their task was to find and "clean out the nest of rebel pirates" at Chestnut Neck and The Forks and to destroy the colonial ironworks at Batsto, where armaments, camp kettles, and other equipment were being manufactured for the Continental forces.

Local patriots, anticipating an attack on Chestnut Neck by the British, had erected Fort Fox Burrows, a military post, the previous year. Fort Fox Burrows was defended by a local militia but had neither a cannon nor any other heavy artillery.

The British expedition reached the area of the Little Egg Harbor on October 5, 1778. Having learned of the impending attack, New Jersey Governor William Livingston sent express riders through the Pines to alert coastal residents of the danger. The townsfolk of Chestnut Neck acted quickly and moved much of the seized stores and vessels up to The Forks for safekeeping. General George Washington, also learning of the impending attack, sent Count Kazimierz Pulaski and his legion of 333 men to the area to assist local militia in fending off the British. Colonel Thomas Proctor's regiment was sent to The Forks to fortify the small military post situated there.

On October 6, British troops attacked Chestnut Neck. The local militia—outmanned and out-armed—quickly retreated to the woods to await reinforcements. Count Pulaski, having left Trenton on October 5, had not yet arrived in the area.

The British raided and burned all remaining ships and dwellings in Chestnut Neck. They had planned next to travel upriver to Batsto and The Forks, but intelligence reports warned them of the imminent arrival of Pulaski and his forces, and they opted to retreat.

The privateers of the Little Egg Harbor, although experiencing a setback from the British attack, were soon back in business.

Unsanctioned pirates had been sailing the Mullica for decades by this time. In the early 1700s Edward Teach, known widely as Blackbeard, was said to have frequented the Jersey Coast. Known as the fiercest of all pirates, Blackbeard is reported to have had a hideout on an island in the Mullica River.

Another well-known 18th-century outlaw, Joseph Mulliner, was also said to have had a camp near The Forks. Mulliner, who was of English extraction, settled in the area with his brother Moses before the American Revolution. Although Moses chose to join the Continental forces and to fight for American independence, Joseph used the confusion of the war years to his own advantage. Claiming to be a Tory, Mulliner and his gang of 100 men—referred to as the Refugees by the local populace—robbed and pillaged patriots and British loyalists alike at every opportunity.

Mulliner, sometimes referred to as the Robin Hood of the Pines, was tall and good looking and had an appetite for pretty women and good times. Even though it is said that he did not take part in the worst of his gang's crimes, such as rape and murder, there is no question that he was a participant in many of their tavern and stage holdups.

One particular incident attributed to Mulliner's gang occurred on a Sunday just as the Widow Bates and her family were returning to their home from services at the Pleasant Mills church. When they arrived at their home, they found a number of the Refugees rampaging through their farmhouse. Not one to hold her tongue, the

Widow Bates ordered the men off her property. Irritated, the Refugees told her to watch her mouth or they would burn down her house. Refusing to back down, the widow called the men a bunch of cowards, insisting that as long as she had breath in her body, she would not be silenced. The men responded by torching her home and, after tying the family to a tree, riding off with their few prized possessions.

Hearing of this dreadful event, Mrs. Bates's neighbors quickly came to her aid and helped her rebuild her homestead. Several weeks after the incident, a bag of gold coins was left anonymously at the Bates farm. Many believed the gold was left by Joseph Mulliner, who was disturbed by his gang's actions and felt the need to make restitution to the family.

Mulliner's love of a good time ironically led to his capture and subsequent hanging. In the summer of 1781, Mulliner, while enjoying some dancing and drink at a local tavern, was captured by Captain Baylin and his rangers from the local militia. Mulliner was taken to Burlington City, where he was tried and convicted for the crimes of robbery and traffic with the enemy. In August 1781 he was hanged in the prison yard. His body was returned to his family in Pleasant Mills, where he was buried.

Although the Refugees disbanded after the capture of their leader, Mulliner is said to still be a presence at The Forks. It is reported that his ghost roams the banks of the Mullica River looking for gold he had buried long ago.

Built by a retired sea captain, Samuel Crowley III, in 1851, Crowleytown grew into a thriving village that by 1857 consisted of an eight-pot glass house, 17 dwellings, a store, a blacksmith shop, and a school. It was here that the first Mason jar, designed by John Mason as an experimental canning jar, was blown by the best glass blower in the house, Clayton Parker of Bridgeton. Although canning had been done for years in tin, home canners had no container to use because the tin canning process was too complicated and not familiar to the general populace. John Mason solved the home canning problem by inventing a glass jar with a threaded opening on which a metal cap could be easily screwed; a rubber gasket under the cap kept the sealed jar airtight.

In an interview printed in the *Bridgeton Evening News* on November 15, 1954, Meade Landis quoted Clayton Parker's brother, Jonathan, offering his version of the advent of the Mason jar. In the interview, Jonathan also provided the reader with a vivid picture of the life of a 19th-century glass worker.

> I started to work in a glass factory at the age of 10, in the Crowleytown plant, which then had eight glass pots. I was paid $10 per month for twelve hours work a day, six days a week. When I was old enough to cut wood for the furnace I was paid $1 per day; and during the six years I worked in Crowleytown, I never saw a dollar in cash because the factory store extended credit on book and by the time payday came around I had used up all my pay on book account.
>
> Glassblowing was very different from what anyone living today knows or remembers. I am 92 and there are few of that age in any line of work still surviving. When I started, the blower did all of the work. He had to open and close his own molds and finish the neck of the bottle also. He had no glory holes in which to heat the neck for finishing. And the lone blower was a shop in himself, instead of the three men who later worked together—two to blow and the third to finish.
>
> A piece of cord attached to the mold handle ran up to the blower's foot-bench, and he had to pull the string and close the mold himself. In time, this was improved by a foot-treadle. The Mason jar required a tight-fitting top and the rim had to be ground on a grindstone. This grindstone was kept in motion by a horse hitched to a long pole that went round and round to generate power. In that factory we also made bottles for mineral water and soft drinks, also glass inkstands and other novelties.

The property on which the Crowleytown glass house was eventually built had first belonged to Samuel Crowley III's father, Samuel Crowley Jr. Samuel Jr. also sold some of his land in 1836 to Abe

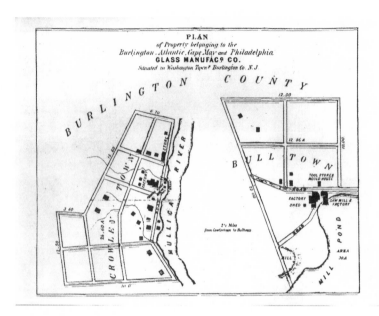

Crowleytown and Bulltown survey map.
(*Map courtesy of New Jersey State Archives*)

Nichols, who built a river landing there that still bears his name. Across from the landing, Nichols built a tavern where many town meetings were held until 1870. The tavern ceased operation sometime between 1870 and 1880, at which time census records list Nichols's occupation as farming.

By 1857 Samuel Crowley III found himself in some financial trouble. He agreed to lease his glass factory to Daniel Berlin of New York City for the term of one year. As part of the agreement, Crowley agreed to buy one-half of all the glass blown at the factory at specified prices, and Berlin agreed to erect a new glass factory. Documents located in the Wharton Land Records indicate that the property was leased to a variety of New York investors and eventually became known as the Atlantic Glass Works. In *Heart of the Pines*, John Pearce states that after several disastrous fires at the glass house, the New York investors abandoned the Crowleytown property in 1866.

When Samuel Crowley leased his glass factory in Crowleytown in 1857, he moved several miles away to Bulltown, where he had a local carpenter, Hazelton (Haze) Birdsall, build him a second glass factory. Around the five-pot glass house, Birdsall built a wheelwright-blacksmith shop, workers' homes, a gristmill, and a sawmill. He also built a large farmhouse nearby for Crowley and his family. Haze, who lived in town himself, ran the Bulltown wheelwright-blacksmith shop and was also the community undertaker, building coffins for many of the local populace. When the New York investors pulled out of Crowleytown, Samuel Crowley, with the support of other investors, formed the "Burlington, Atlantic, Cape May and Philadelphia Glass Company" and reopened the glass house. Although the grand name of the new company gives the impression that Samuel Crowley and his investors had plans to expand their enterprise, it appears to have included only the Bulltown and Crowleytown glassworks.

The Bulltown Glass Works, which made bottles and mason jars, closed down in 1870. The Crowleytown glass house is said to have blown down in 1874, although it appears to have been out of operation prior to that date. The Bulltown property was purchased in 1890 by Gustav Voss and converted into a cranberry farm. Even though the glass house was gone, Crowleytown remained a viable town until the Depression of the 1930s. Later the state acquired the property and created a picnic area and boat launch there.

Nearby was another beautifully situated riverfront property, which came to be known as Hermann. Hermann was first owned by the Sooy family. In 1771 John Sooy bought 151 acres of land there for $80 and erected the first section of a home that later was to be known as the Hermann Hotel. During their ownership, John and his wife, Abigail, added more sections to the house. Nicholas Sooy II—son of Nicholas Sooy, owner of the Washington Tavern and nephew of John—and his wife, Esther, acquired the property in early 1823. By the time Nicholas II acquired the old homestead, he owned thousands of acres of land in the area, a successful shipping business, several ships, and a glass factory. When Nicholas II died in 1851, he bequeathed the Sooy homestead to his son and namesake, Nicholas III. After living on the property for 18 years, Nicholas III sold his home and 240 acres of property to John H. Rapp and Luman B. Wing, two New York businessmen who had established a lucrative charcoal and lumber business in the vicinity of Green Bank. The products were manufactured along the banks of the Mullica River, then shipped to New York for sale and distribution.

In 1868 Rapp's daughter, Johanna Augusta, married an emigrant from Germany named Augustus Koster. In 1869 they moved into the old Sooy homestead, turning it into a hotel and installing themselves as host and hostess.

Rapp and Wing, who had purchased the Hermann land for $6,735, had decided to turn their property into a planned community that encompassed the existing towns of Bulltown and Crowleytown. A map of the planned community shows that it was to be laid out in a gridiron pattern with four large squares or parks and over 20 streets running from the river inland. In 1869 Rapp and Wing published a pamphlet titled the "Plan For Founding The Town Of Hermann On The Beautiful Riverbank Of The Little Egg Harbor River In The County Of Burlington State Of New Jersey."

The pamphlet, whose sole purpose was to draw in potential buyers, extolled the beautiful as well as utilitarian nature of the Mullica

Later view of Sooy/Koster Homestead/Hermann Hotel.
(*Photo courtesy of Budd Wilson*)

River tract. It indicated that its location on the Little Egg Harbor was easily navigable by large vessels and that two large wharves (with a third one planned) had been long established there. The pamphlet said that the steamer *Eureka* made regular trips from Hermann to New York, as did a number of coasting vessels. The pamphlet further described how four blocks had been laid out for public parks, with a number of acres laid aside for the building of a school, a church, and a cemetery, and 32 lots for the erection of public buildings and a marketplace.

Although the Hermann pamphlet describes the availability of single lots, the fifth paragraph of the document clearly shows its interest in attracting the corporate investor:

> For the establishment of factories, as it is certain that Hermann is better adapted than any other place on the whole river, two glass factories are already established here, together with two sawmills and one gristmill, the last mentioned are all run by water power, the water for which the two lakes furnish an abundance; there is also a church and a schoolhouse on the place. Great effort will be made to establish factories of all kinds, especially for the establishment of another glass factory for the manufacture of window glass. The expense for the transportation of raw material and manufactured articles cannot be compared with the enormous expenses incurred on manufacture in large cities. The climate is very healthy and the laborer who finds employment here must be happy especially if he builds his own home for his family, for which purpose he has a better chance here than in any other place.

The pamphlet went on to describe how a New Jersey and Philadelphia company had petitioned the state legislation for a charter to build a canal between the Little Egg Harbor River and Philadelphia, potentially shortening the shipping distance by a hundred miles. It discussed how a rail line was already being laid, with a depot within two miles of Hermann providing direct communication with both New York and Philadelphia.

The pamphlet also advertised individual riverfront lots, with 30-foot frontage and 130-feet depth, for $120. After a $5 registration fee and a first payment of $15, the balance could be paid off in monthly installments.

In order to encourage the sale of multiple lots, the sellers offered a discount of 10 percent off the published price for anyone buying five lots and a 15 percent discount for anyone buying ten lots.

John H. Rapp and Luman B. Wing & Co. were noted as proprietors at the bottom of the pamphlet, which was printed in both English and German.

Charles W. Wapler, a German emigrant who had arrived in New York in 1870 with a $50,000 inheritance from his father, formed a partnership with Frances Thill of the New York-based Empire State Glass Works. Together they purchased a large tract of land in Hermann for the purpose of building a glass house. Late in 1872 or early 1873, construction of the glass house was started, along with a company office and a company store. The store was to stand on the main road (now Route 542), and the office was to be located between the glass house and the store. Before the construction was completed, Thill pulled out of the deal, selling his half interest in the property to Wapler, who then owned the property outright.

Wapler's father-in-law, Charles Brome (also referred to as Bloomer or Brummer), apparently had considerable knowledge of glass production. He built the furnace and, after construction was completed, became the general manager of the factory. Wapler married Brome's daughter, Minna, in 1872.

Wapler not only invested his entire fortune into the Hermann venture but also took two large mortgages on his glass house, one for $25,000 and a second for $18,000.

The Wapler Glass Works opened in the latter part of 1873 and was said to be the second-largest factory of its kind in South Jersey. During its short time in operation, it made bottles, glass domes, smoke bells, lamp shades, lamp chimneys, vases, glass buttons, Christmas tree ornaments, and glass eyes. In spare time, ordinary offhand pieces were made, such as canes, rolling pins, pitchers, compartment bottles, and

HERMANN GLASS FACTORY

(Illustrated by Berminna Solem)

paperweights. The Wapler glass factory was primarily a clear glass house, though colors such as green, amber, cobalt, ruby, milk, and olive green were also used.

During the early 1870s, between 30 and 40 houses were started in the town of Hermann, though fewer than 20 were ever completed. A boarding house was constructed to accommodate the glass house workers, though many of the workmen lived in barrack-like structures.

In March 1874 the Wapler Glassworks failed and closed its doors for the final time. Charles Brome continued to live at Hermann, where he earned his living farming, serving as justice of the peace, and acting as a watchman over the abandoned glass house. When the glass house closed, most of the workers of the factory moved away. Those who stayed earned their living mainly by farming, fishing, or hunting.

Many reasons are given for the failure of Wapler's glass enterprise: the railroad's never being built as proposed, the depression of 1873, competition from other, better established glass factories, and even the freezing of the river, which prevented shipping wares and receiving necessary raw materials. The downfall of the business may have been best stated by Charles Wapler: "The reason for failure was simply because I could not sell my wares."

The old glass house stood for a number of years, abandoned and crumbling. The company office building was purchased and carted away to Nesco, and much of the wood of the large framed structure was pilfered. What was left of the building finally blew down during a storm in 1905. The tall brick chimney continued to stand until the early 1920s, when it was demolished by dynamite and its bricks used in the construction of a barn in Weekstown.

In the fall of 1884, Washington Township brought foreclosure proceedings against the nine-acre glass house property for $123.83 in unpaid taxes. On June 28, 1887, Joseph Wharton purchased the glass house tract from Washington Township for $500. Wapler and his wife still held the Hermann property deeds, which were surrendered to Wharton for $50. Wharton also purchased the first mortgage held on the property (which had been originally purchased at $25,000) for an additional $500. During the mid-1950s, the State of New Jersey purchased the Wharton share of the Hermann tract from the Wharton heirs.

The Hermann Hotel operated for a number of years after the closing of the glass factory. For a time steamboats continued to dock at the Hermann Wharf, bringing guests to the hotel. The Koster family stayed on through several generations until they, too, sold their property to the State of New Jersey in the late 1980s. In the summer of 1987 the old Hermann Hotel was burned to the ground by an arsonist, bringing a sad and final close to a long-ago dream of a metropolis on the banks of the Mullica River.

THE FORKS TO HERMANN SIDE TRIPS

THE SWEETWATER CASINO AND MARINA

While paddling or touring the area of the upper Mullica River, stop by the Sweetwater Casino and Marina, located several miles downriver from The Forks. The restaurant features several lovely dining rooms, all overlooking the historic Mullica River. In season and on weekends, there is an outside deck bar, where guests can enjoy a drink, a meal, or a snack while listening to live entertainment. There is a marina, a gift shop, and a pontoon boat in the marina that offers half-hour trips down the Mullica River (weather permitting). Although the restaurant uses the term casino as part of its name, it is not a gambling establishment. For information on hours of operation and directions, contact Sweetwater Casino at 609-965-3285 or www.sweetwatercasino.com.

BIKE RIDE TO BULLTOWN

To visit the site of the Bulltown Glass Works and village, drive or bike east from Hermann on Route 542 until you reach Belhaven Canoe Rental (three-tenths of a mile from Bulltown Road). Turn left onto Mill Road (the first road after Belhaven) and drive one mile to a fork, where you will bear to your left and travel an additional two-tenths of a mile. At the point where an old dam and cranberry bog are visible on your left, you have reached the site of the old glass works. The scarce remains of the glass works are located between two dirt roads, one of which parallels the cranberry bog. Scattered multi-colored glass and brick chips can be found on and around the dirt roads near the site.

Old Voss homestead, 2004.
(*Photo by Gordon Stull*)

A great bike road through the Pines runs from the T intersection of Bulltown Road and Route 542 through Bulltown and Tylertown to Batsto Village. On the Bulltown Road ride, you will pass the old, boarded-up Voss homestead, built in the late 1800s and now owned by the state. It is about a five-mile bike ride on Bulltown Road from Hermann to Batsto, an easy trip on a flat, relatively traffic-free road.

BELHAVEN CANOE RENTALS

To rent a canoe or kayak for a river trip on the Mullica (or another Pine Barrens river), contact Belhaven Canoe Rental at 800-445-0953 or visit its Web site at www.Belhavencanoe.com. Belhaven also offers a wide selection of new and used canoes and kayaks for sale.

REFERENCES

Beck, Henry Charlton. 1945. *Jersey Genesis: The Story of the Mullica River.* New Brunswick, NJ: Rutgers University Press.

Beck, Henry Charlton. 1937. *More Forgotten Towns of Southern New Jersey.* New Brunswick, NJ: Rutgers University Press.

Garuffi, Mildred. "Hermann: City of Many Names But Is Deserted Today." *Batsto Citizens Gazette*, Winter/Spring 1989.

Gaunt, David. "Privateers, Pirates and Chestnut Neck." *Batsto Citizens Gazette*, Spring/Summer 1990.

Green, C. F. n.d. *A Place of Olden Days, Nescochaque, Sweetwater, Pleasant Mills: A Historical Sketch.* Hammonton, NJ: Hammonton Printing Company.

Hermann Glass Works. n.d. (essay found in Edward Pfieffer Collection, Wharton Land Records, State of New Jersey Archives.)

Kemp, Franklin W. 1966, 1993. *A Nest of Rebel Pirates.* Egg Harbor City, NJ: The Batsto Citizens Committee, Laurette Press.

Landis, Meade. "1st Mason Jar Blown by Local Man; Invention Credited to Ex-resident of Vineland." (article found in Edward Pfieffer Collection, Wharton Land Records, State of New Jersey Archives) *Bridgeton Evening News*, November 15, 1954.

Pearce, John E. 2000. *Heart of the Pines: Ghostly Voices of the Pine Barrens.* Hammonton, NJ: Batsto Citizens Committee.

Pepper, Adeline. 1971. *The Glass Gaffers of New Jersey*. New York: Charles Scribner's Sons.

Peterson, Robert A. 1998. *Patriots, Pirates, and Pineys: Sixty Who Shaped New Jersey*. Medford, NJ: Plexus Publishing, Inc.

Pierce, Arthur D. 1960. *Smugglers' Woods*. New Brunswick, NJ: Rutgers University Press.

Plan For Founding The Town Of Hermann On The Beautiful River Bank Of The Little Egg Harbor River In The County Of Burlington, State Of New Jersey. 1869. (pamphlet found in Wharton Land Records, State of New Jersey Archives). New York: A. Marrer.

Solem-Stull, Barbara. 2002. *The Forks: A Brief History of the Area*. Medford, NJ: Plexus Publishing, Inc.

Wilson, Budd. "Hermann City Just Never Grew." *Batsto Citizens Gazette*, Winter/Spring 1981.

Brendan T. Byrne
State Forest
and Vicinity

Brendan T. Byrne State Forest and Vicinity

OVERVIEW AND DRIVING TOUR

By the mid-1800s new enterprises were needed to fill the economic gap created by the collapse of the bog iron industry. Developers were soon exploiting the other rich natural resources of the region and establishing glass houses and clay manufacturing companies throughout the land.

Within the boundaries of the Brendan T. Byrne State Forest and the adjacent Greenwood Forest Wildlife Management Area are the deteriorating remains of an industrial past. Although some of these former 19th-century sites have all but vanished, others have left behind evidence of a time when men relied almost totally on the natural resources of an area to carve out their livelihoods.

To begin the tour of Brendan T. Byrne State Forest and its vicinity, first drive to the park office, where you can obtain a free map of the forest. After picking up your map, leave the parking lot and drive in an easterly direction on Shinns Road for 2 miles. At the intersection turn left and drive 1.4 miles. Turn right at the next intersection and travel one-tenth of a mile. On the right side of the road is the site of the former Lebanon Glass Works. In 1851 Thomas Richards and his son Samuel erected a glass works here that supported 150 workers and their families. Today nothing remains of the glass works or village except a mound of dirt that covers the hearth of the factory and some scattered glass slag. Near the site of the glass works are the ruins of an old Civilian Conservation Corps camp that provided jobs for unemployed men in the 1930s.

During the years in which the Lebanon Glass Works was in operation, several large clay factories also operated nearby. The arrival of the railroad in 1861 had expanded the opportunities for new businesses interested in capitalizing on the rich clay deposits that existed in the area.

getting to brendan t. byrne state forest

From the East
Take Route 70 East to the Red Lion Circle (where Route 206 intersects Route 70) and continue on 70 East to the Four Mile Circle (approximately 8 miles). Take Route 72 East for 1 mile and turn left. Take the first right, and the Brendan T. Byrne Forest office will be on your left.

From the South via the Garden State Parkway
Take the Garden State Parkway to exit 63A. Take Route 72 West to mile marker 1 and turn right. Take the first right, and the Brendan T. Byrne Forest office will be on your left.

From the North via the Garden State Parkway
Take the Garden State Parkway to exit 63. Take Route 72 West to mile marker 1 and turn right. Take the first right, and the Brendan T. Byrne Forest office will be on your left.

From the North via the New Jersey Turnpike
Take the New Jersey Turnpike to exit 7 and follow Route 206 South to the Red Lion Circle (where Route 206 intersects Route 70). Take Route 70 East to the Four Mile Circle (approximately 8 miles). Take Route 72 East for 1 mile and turn left. Take the first right, and the Brendan T. Byrne Forest office will be on your left.

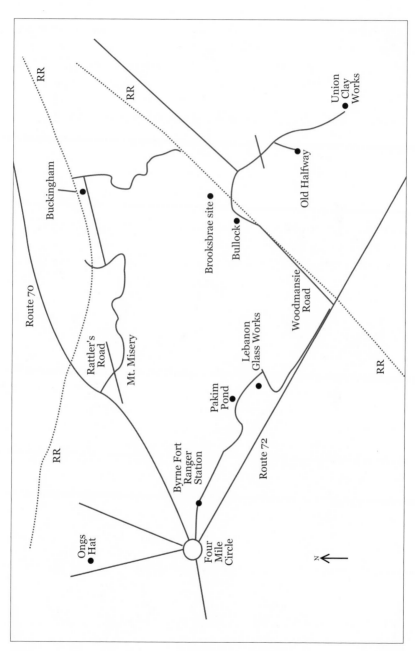

Brendan T. Byrne State Forest and vicinity tour map.

To visit the site of several clay manufacturing factories, leave the Lebanon Glass Works and drive in an easterly direction 0.7 mile to Route 72. Turn left onto Route 72, drive 2.6 miles, and make a left turn just before the railroad trestle. After driving approximately 1.8 miles (during which you will be driving parallel to the old Jersey Central railroad tracks), you will see a hunting cabin on your right. This cabin is all that remains of the old village of Woodmansie. In 1882 Woodmansie consisted of a hotel, post office, sawmill, school, and 12 dwellings. Like many other Pine Barrens ghost towns, Woodmansie was the site of a failed real estate venture.

After passing Woodmansie, drive another 1.5 miles to reach Bullock. At the dead end, turn right and cross the abandoned Jersey Central Railroad tracks.

At this point in the tour, you can choose to enter the Greenwood Forest to visit the sites of Old Halfway and the Union Clay Works or to turn left and head down to the Brooksbrae Brick Company (also known as the Pasadena Terra Cotta Company) ruins. If you choose to head into the Greenwood Forest, be aware that this is a wildlife management area where seasonal hunting is allowed. To avoid a hunting encounter and to learn about the rules of the wildlife management area, you can contact the Fish and Wildlife Land Management office at 609-259-2132. There is no hunting allowed in any New Jersey State Forest on Sunday.

When traveling to the Union Clay Works and Old Halfway sites, enter the Greenwood Forest on the dirt road farthest to the left, driving in an easterly direction. In four-tenths of a mile, you will reach a fork in the road. Take the road to the right and travel an additional 1.2 miles until you reach another fork. To travel to Old Halfway, park and take the right fork on foot (vehicles are prohibited beyond this point) four-tenths of a mile to the top of the hill. You will know you have reached Old Halfway when you come upon a large lake filled with aquamarine-colored water. The blue-green color of the water is due to the rich clay deposits found in the earth here. Two lakes are all that remain of the clay-mining enterprise that was located at Old Halfway in the second half of the 19th century. During the mid-1800s an inn was located at Old Halfway that provided rest and refreshment for weary stage road travelers journeying to and from the Tuckerton area.

To travel to the site of the Union Clay Works, return to the fork and head to the right. The Union Clay Works (the official name of which was Lewis Neill and Company) is 1.6 miles from the fork. The site of the factory is located in a clearing on the left side of the road. Several cellar holes, scattered bricks, and some broken pieces of terra-cotta pipe are all that remain at the site. Across a barely discernable dirt road near the factory site are the ruins of a house. During the 19th century, railroads were a crucial link to the major marketplaces of the big cities, and the Union Clay Works cessation of operations in 1877 was probably due to its considerable distance from the railroad.

To reach the ruins of the Brooksbrae Brick Company, leave Union Clay Works, backtracking in a westerly direction 3.3 miles to the Bullock intersection. At the Bullock intersection, turn right and travel seven-tenths of a mile. After parking, cross the old Jersey Central Railroad tracks and follow the path that leads to the ruins. This site is often used by paintball enthusiasts, so don't be surprised if you come across a group of individuals wearing military fatigues

Old Halfway clay pits, 2003.
(*Photo by Gordon Stull*)

Broken terra-cotta pipe found at the Union Clay Works site, 2004.
(*Photo by Gordon Stull*)

and carrying paintball guns. Paintball matches are forbidden in the state forest boundaries; however, it has been difficult for the rangers to enforce the prohibition.

The Brooksbrae Brick Company, built in 1905, is believed never to have operated because of its owner's untimely death. The ruins are a well-known local landmark, immortalized by Henry Charlton Beck as the Pasadena Terra Cotta Company in *Forgotten Towns of Southern New Jersey.* When visiting the area, Beck, who sought out information from locals wherever he went, was told a convoluted tale that was a mixture of fact and fiction. Recently, Scott Wieczorek, an archaeologist working in conjunction with Monmouth University, has unraveled much of the mystery of the Pasadena site.

When you explore the Brooksbrae ruins, it is helpful to be aware of some basic steps in the brickmaking process. In his work on the Brooksbrae Brick Company, Wieczorek cites Charles Thomas Davis, an authority on the brick and terra-cotta industries of the 19th century, who outlined the four steps of the brickmaking process: (1) preparation and tempering, (2) moulding, (3) drying, and (4) burning. Preparation and tempering involved mixing the clay and water to a workable consistency. Moulding was simply forcing the clay into

Brooksbrae Brick Company ruins, 2004.
(*Photo by Gordon Stull*)

Brooksbrae Brick Company ruins, 2004.
(*Photo by Gordon Stull*)

a wooden or frame mold. Drying took place in a variety of ways, but in the case of the Brooksbrae factory, an "artificial heat" drying system was used. Burning required baking the bricks in a kiln.

The brickmaking process at Brooksbrae was designed to begin at the pug mill, where the clay would be mixed with water to the

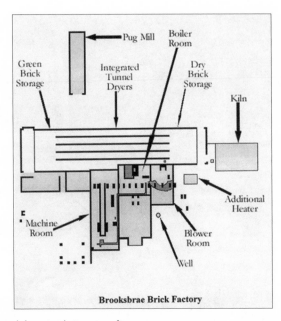

Map of the Brooksbrae Brick Company factory.
(*Drawn by Scott Wieczorek*)

Drying tunnels at Brooksbrae Brick Company ruins, 2004.
(*Photo by Gordon Stull*)

appropriate consistency. The raw clay would then move to the machine room, where the Chambers Brothers' brick machine was located. In the machine room, the clay would be extruded into a rectangular trench and cleaved into individual bricks by the brickmaking machine. The individual unbaked bricks could then be delivered to an interior rail system, which moved them through the integrated tunnel dryers. In the four drying tunnels, a current of hot air from a downdraft furnace would draw out any moisture within the bricks. The bricks would then be baked in a downdraft kiln. Using the Brooksbrae Brick Company site diagram, you should be able to easily identify and explore each area of the factory.

To continue on the tour after exploring the Brooksbrae site, drive in a northeasterly direction on Pasadena Road for seven-tenths of a mile. Make a left turn and cross the railroad tracks, where you will see a hunting cabin on your left side. Between the road and the cabin is a mound of earth that covers what remains of the Wheatland Manufacturing Company factory. The remains of the factory are on private property and should not be explored without permission. The Wheatland Manufacturing Company (first called the Townsend Clay Manufacturing Company) was established in 1866. The Wheatland Company made terra-cotta fence posts and sewer drain pipes, operating successfully for 13 years. Wheatland had a railroad station, established in 1866, and a post office, first operated in 1872. The Wheatland Railroad Station and Post Office were later called Pasadena Rail Station and Post Office, respectively, after a real estate venture in 1889 that renamed the town.

After passing the Wheatland site, continue on the dirt road approximately 1.5 miles to an intersection. At the crossroads make a right turn and travel another 1.5 miles. At the next crossroads make a left and drive a short distance to a clearing surrounded by some large Norway spruce trees. The clearing is the site of the ghost town of Buckingham, a former lumber camp established in 1880. Using the Buckingham site map, you will easily be able to explore what remains of the old town.

To reach Mt. Misery from Buckingham while experiencing an enjoyable ride through the heart of the Brendan T. Byrne State Forest, follow the dirt road that runs parallel to the abandoned

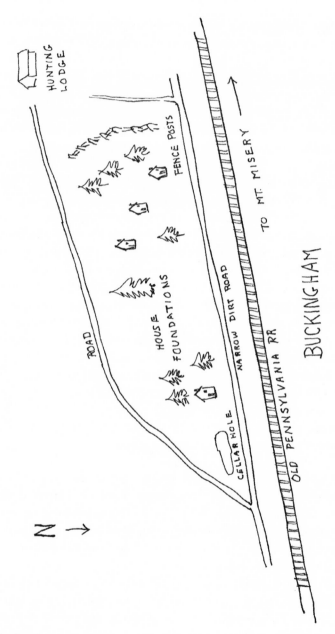

Buckingham site map.
(*Drawn by Berminna Solem*)

Pennsylvania Railroad tracks in a westerly direction. Travel 1.5 miles until you reach a crossroads. Make a left turn and follow this road for one-eighth of a mile. At the next crossroads, make a right, and follow this road approximately 2.7 miles to the center of Mt. Misery. Mt. Misery is now the site of the United Methodist Retreat Center and a few private residences. At one time a thriving lumber camp and village of 100 homes was situated here adjacent to Rattler's Road (right turn at the crossroads at the center of the settlement). Although Rattler's Road is a public thoroughfare, the property on both sides is private and should not be explored without permission. Rattler's Road heads down to a partially washed-out bridge and a barely discernable dam that once created the sawmill pond.

To finish the tour and enjoy some refreshment after your day in the Pines, head down to Cafe Apanay at Ongs Hat. To reach Ongs Hat, drive down the hill to Route 70 and turn left. Drive 3.8 miles to the Four Mile Circle and take the turnoff to Pemberton. Drive 1.5 miles until you reach the restaurant on your left, opposite the entrance to the Batona Trail on your right. Although there is nothing historical to explore at Ongs Hat, the settlement's name has been a curiosity for years and the cause of much local speculation. The folklore regarding the name of the town is fanciful and varied. The only certainty is that a stage tavern was located here at the turn of the 19th century.

A DEEPER LOOK

Today's Brendan T. Byrne State Forest, encompassing 34,725 acres of Pine Barrens forest, bears strong contrast to the barren, cleared land that existed here in the 1800s. During those years, the forest was cut down to provide fuel for the Lebanon Glass Works, an important local employer after the collapse of the bog iron industry and the closing of the nearby Hanover Furnace.

At one time, Atlantic white cedar covered vast areas of this forest, but this too was a valuable resource, and many lumber camps were established throughout the region by the early 1800s. In close proximity to the land that now comprises the Brendan T. Byrne State Forest was a clay stratum, 10 to 12 feet deep. The clay industry enjoyed a brief but successful period in the region beginning in the mid-1800s and lasting until the turn of the 20th century. The history of these long-ago industries and the towns that grew up around them is an important part of local legend, with stories passed down orally from generation to generation.

When the state of New Jersey purchased 2,437 acres of land in 1908 for the purpose of establishing a forest preserve, it was named Lebanon, after the glass works that operated here in the mid-1800s. The Lebanon Glass Works was the second glass factory erected by Thomas Richards and his son Samuel following the success of their glass works in Jackson, New Jersey. Thomas—the son of William Richards, the well-known ironmaster of Batsto, and the brother of Samuel Richards, who also owned a number of iron furnaces in the Pine Barrens—recognized that the iron days were over and smartly invested his family fortune in a more promising venture. The Lebanon Glass Works produced a high volume of glass that was said to have "enjoyed a reputation for clear crystal of superior quality." The glass works began by manufacturing bottles but eventually turned to producing window lights (window panes). At one point, 150 men were employed at the glass works, with a village of 60 houses, a store, a sawmill, and a blacksmith shop growing up around the factory. The town was considered so prosperous that a post office was established there in 1862. In 1860 Thomas Richards passed away, but the furnace continued to be operated by his heirs.

The Lebanon Glass Works prospered for 15 years but eventually exhausted the timber resources in the area. Faced with the loss of its fuel supply, the Richards family abandoned the town in 1866, closing up shop and moving away.

Many of the workers left Lebanon to seek new employment, but some stayed behind, and the town managed to cling to survival. By 1876 there were nine occupied homes in the town, housing 40 or 50 residents. The town at the time consisted of an icehouse, store, blacksmith shop, sawmill, and small cemetery, located a short distance from the town.

In 1881 the glass works property was leased to Samuel Lee, who operated a sawmill there until 1883. But by the turn of the century,

The Lebanon sawmill stood from 1872 to 1936.
(*Photo courtesy of Brendan T. Byrne State Forest office*)

with no employment opportunities in sight, most of the inhabitants of the town had moved away.

In May 1933 the Civilian Conservation Corps (CCC) erected a camp near the site of the old glass works. The CCC was created by President Franklin D. Roosevelt during the Great Depression to get unemployed American men back to work. The goals of the CCC program were twofold: to reduce unemployment and to preserve the nation's natural resources. Most of the men assigned to the area arrived at Lebanon on May 29, 1933, and Camp S-52 was completed during October 1933. Another CCC camp was erected at Mt. Misery in June 1935. One of the first jobs of the CCC at Lebanon was to salvage fire-killed oak, pine, and other woods. The wood was then sold to the public at $1 a load. Later the men planted trees and constructed buildings, roads, and bridges, as well as picnic tables, pavilions, cabins, and benches. The CCC work continued at Lebanon until July 1942, when the last camp ceased activity.

Today all that marks the site of the old town of Lebanon is a mound of earth that covers the hearth of the glass works, some scattered bricks

One of three cabins built by the CCC in the 1930s.
(*Photo by Gordon Stull*)

and glass slag, and a barely discernable cemetery hidden deep in the forest. Ruins of the CCC camp are also visible nearby. Standing behind the glass works site is a building used in a 1930s sawmill operation that today serves as a nature center for the Brendan T. Byrne Forest.

In the 1930s, when Henry Charlton Beck came searching for the old towns of the area, he was taken to picturesque ruins in the woods that locals referred to as the Pasadena Terra Cotta Company. Beck wrote about Pasadena in *Forgotten Towns of Southern New Jersey*, and from that time forward his work became the source for most of what has been written about this interesting site. Recently, Scott Wieczorek, an archaeologist working in cooperation with the Monmouth University Department of History and Anthropology, has unraveled the mystery and confusion surrounding the Pasadena Terra Cotta Company. Although Beck was right in regard to the existence of several mid-19th-century terra-cotta factories in the area, the name Pasadena actually referred to a failed real estate development rather than a company or a town, as described by Beck.

In reality, what has been known for years as the Pasadena Terra Cotta Company was actually the Brooksbrae Brick Company. Brooksbrae's story begins in 1890 with the mining of Owen's Hill by Alfred Adams. By 1901, Adams, with backing from investors, formed the Adams Clay Mining Company and soon obtained ownership of the mine. Adams Clay Mining was the main clay supplier for several large companies in Pennsylvania and New Jersey. The contract Adams had with one of these companies, the Eastern Hydraulic Press Brick Company, was about to expire and it was believed it would not be renewed. Attempting to capitalize on this situation, William Kelly, treasurer of Adams Clay Mining Company, decided to establish his own local brick company in the area.

In 1905 Kelly began construction of the new factory, which he named the Brooksbrae Brick Company. Kelly's brick factory was built using a design marketed by Chambers Brothers of Philadelphia, which specialized in the manufacture of brickmaking machines. Using the Chambers brickmaking machine, the factory would have the capacity to manufacture 50,000 bricks a day.

In 1908 Kelly died without ever operating his brick factory. After his death a clause in his will caused his estate (which included the Brooksbrae Brick Company) to be frozen. The clause stipulated that 20 years after his death, a school and residence for homeless Philadelphia youth between the ages of 16 and 20 was to be built in the area now known as Pasadena. The trustees of his estate were authorized to sell any part of the brick factory ten years after his passing to aid in the construction of this facility, which Kelly intended to be named the "Sarah Brooks Kelly Memorial Home for Boys and Girls," in honor of his mother. Kelly may have believed that his brick factory would have been a successful operation by the time of his death and therefore would have been able to fund the endowment of the proposed youth facility. Unfortunately, by the time of his death the Brooksbrae Brick Company was not a successful operation. The plant stood idle and abandoned for a number of years, and the Sarah Brooks Kelly Memorial Home was never realized.

One event that occurred in September 1915 probably sealed the fate of the proposed youth home. With a railroad strike looming in the area, caretakers for the Brooksbrae Brick Company were sent to the factory on September 13, 1915, to keep watch and prevent mayhem, which was often associated with angry strikers. That night, a fire burned down the quarters in which the caretakers were staying, killing them and destroying the brick factory. A police investigation following this tragedy determined that the fire was accidental, caused by a clogged chimney flue. Many locals, however, suspicious of the immigrant Italian railroad strikers, were not satisfied with this finding and were convinced the caretakers were murdered during a robbery.

In 1918, several years after the fire, the trustees of William Kelly's estate sold the Brooksbrae Brick Company property.

In *Forgotten Towns of Southern New Jersey*, Beck tells a story of two Pasadena residents who eventually became known in local folklore as the Pine Wizard and the Pine Witch. In the tale told by Beck, Bill Clevenger told his wife, Peggy, that when he died he would send her a sign telling her where he was spending his afterlife. Seems old Bill was a real hell-raiser—he liked to drink and brawl, and local preachers had been predicting for years that he would come to a bad end. On the night Bill died, the well behind his home began to bubble and boil, leaving no question as to where poor Bill was spending his afterlife.

Despite his carousing, Bill Clevenger left Peggy a wealthy widow. Unfortunately, Peggy couldn't resist showing everyone who stopped by her remote cabin the gold Bill had left behind. One night, as Beck reports the legend, someone broke into Peggy's home, stole her money, and burned down her house, killing her in the process. Soon afterward homesteads were burning all over the Pines, leaving locals to wonder if Bill had placed a curse on them. According to Beck's legend, the final fire that followed Peggy's untimely death burned down the Pasadena Terra Cotta Factory.

Although Beck's Pasadena story is considered folklore today, it does include many of the important elements of actual events and probably helped to keep the history of the local clay industry alive.

As Beck had written, two terra cotta factories were present in the area during the mid-1800s, though neither was named the Pasadena Terra Cotta Company.

In 1866 Daniel Townsend, a former sea captain, obtained title to 1,600 acres in the area known as Wheatland (now referred to as

Pasadena). In 1861 the Raritan and Delaware Bay Railroad (later called the Jersey Central) had laid rail through this tract of land, making it prime real estate for any company that wanted to have easy access to the major marketplaces of New York and Philadelphia. Townsend initially called his company the Townsend Clay Manufacturing Company, and there he made terra-cotta fence posts and sewer drain pipes. Townsend's company employed 11 men, and on his property he built several houses, a factory, and numerous terra-cotta muffle kilns. Daniel and his wife, Jemima, built a large home for themselves on the west side of their property.

In 1873 Townsend incorporated with the financial assistance of three local bankers. They named their new company Wheatland Manufacturing Company, and for six years the company was profitable. In 1879 Daniel Townsend, who was the principal stockholder, died, and without his leadership the company began to falter. In 1881 the county sheriff seized the Wheatland Manufacturing Company property for unpaid taxes. After bailing out the company, the stockholders held a meeting, at which they agreed to change the use of the property from clay manufacture to land development. By 1889 a map showing the property subdivided into 25 x 150 foot lots was filed at the county clerk's office. The new town's name was Pasadena, and by 1891 the Wheatland Railroad Station had also taken on this name. By 1906 the Pasadena real estate venture had failed without even one house being built. In 1915 a company calling itself Pasadena Farms purchased the land. The owners of Pasadena Farms hoped to develop the land agriculturally, but they, too, were unsuccessful. After several changes in ownership, the tract came into the possession of the American Smelting and Refining Company. Its principals hoped to mine the rich clay deposits of the area for a nontoxic chemical, titanium oxide, which was used as pigment in paint. Nothing seemed to come of this venture either, and the land was eventually sold to the Clayton Mining and Masonry companies, which still operate the mine today.

The Union Clay Works, also mentioned in Beck's work, was actually the first clay manufacturing enterprise to operate in the area. Located deep in what is today the Greenwood Forest Wildlife Management Area, the Union Clay Works first began operation in

1858. The factory was ideally located on the Old Egg Harbor Road—an important stage and trade route from Mt. Holly to Tuckerton. The clay used at the Union Clay Works came from a pit near Old Halfway. Although the operation was referred to colloquially as the Union Clay Works (due to its location within what was then Union Township), its trading name was Lewis Neill and Company. Owned by Lewis Neill, the company was a fire brick and terra-cotta operation whose principal product was sewer pipes.

Near the factory were the homes of Andrew McCall, who served as its manager, and Lewis Cassidy, a wealthy Philadelphia politician who owned interests in Neill's operation.

In 1865 the company was sold to Joseph Keaseby Brick, a New York-based firebrick manufacturer. Keaseby operated the company until his death in 1868, after which his widow, Julia, operated the company with Joseph's business partner, Edward White. The factory ceased operation sometime in 1877. Julia Keaseby maintained ownership of the tract for the next two decades and, upon her death in 1897, bequeathed it to the Brooklyn Memorial Hospital. The land was eventually acquired by the state of New Jersey's Division of Fish and Wildlife.

Old Halfway, the source of clay for the Union Clay Works, was the site of a rest stop used by stages and carters hauling goods to and from Tuckerton in the mid-1800s. During those years the settlement consisted of an inn or rest house, several service buildings (barns and sheds), and three or four other dwellings. The rest stop was located on a spur of the Egg Harbor Road that connected the Mt. Holly-Burlington-Trenton area with Barnegat and Tuckerton. The name of the settlement indicates that the rest stop was probably situated halfway between the two destinations.

Clay mining began in Old Halfway sometime between 1860 and 1870. Today the clay pits, long ago abandoned, have become lakes tinted an aquamarine color due to the clay deposits that can still be found in the surrounding sand.

Clay wasn't the only important 19th-century industry operating in the area. In 1880 John Buckingham and his wife came to the wilderness of southern New Jersey to start a lumber camp. Buckingham came to harvest the American white cedars from the Pine Barrens swamps. The cedar was considered the most valuable tree in the area because it was lightweight and resistant to weather and disease. Cedar was (and still is) prized for roofing, fence posts, and boat building, among other uses.

Buckingham, as the camp was known, was situated on the Pennsylvania Railroad line, and soon a siding was established that provided the company with access to the major marketplaces of the big cities.

A modern sawmill was erected at Buckingham, along with a number of homes for the mill workers, woodcutters, and teamsters who hauled the wood to the railroad siding. Barns and stables were constructed to provide shelter for the company's horses and oxen, needed to cart the cedar from the swamps. A school and a store were built in the town to provide all that was needed by the growing village. John Buckingham and his wife lived in the town and eventually had a daughter, who became John's pride and joy.

Buckingham prospered for 15 years until one day a terrible tragedy struck. Buckingham, who tried to provide his family with every comfort, bought a cow in order that his young daughter might have fresh milk every day. Unfortunately, the poor cow was driven mad by the mosquitoes that swarmed from the nearby swamps. One day Buckingham's little daughter, frolicking in the field, was spied by the cow. Suddenly old "Bessie" went berserk and started to chase the little girl across the field. Although the child ran as fast as she could, the cow quickly caught up and stomped her to death. From that time on, John Buckingham and his company began to fail. Within a month the Buckingham sawmill shut down, and John, grief-stricken, shortly passed away. His wife soon left the town, and all the workers departed to seek employment elsewhere. The village of Buckingham thus became another Pine Barrens ghost town.

All that remains of Buckingham today is a clearing in the forest. Surrounding the clearing are a number of huge Norway spruce trees, planted long ago when hope for the town's prosperity ran high. A number of cellar holes and foundations and a few old fence posts are all that are left to remind the infrequent visitor that a thriving village once existed in this remote and lonely place.

Buckingham as it looks today.
(*Photo by Gordon Stull*)

On the edge of Brendan T. Byrne Forest on a 100-foot rise is the site of the village of Mt. Misery, once a prosperous logging settlement. Called Mt. Misery to this day, the area is now home to the United Methodist Camp and several private residences. In his book *Sign Posts: Place Names in the History of Burlington County, New Jersey*, Henry Bisbee states that the name Mt. Misery was actually shortened from Misericorde—a name likely bestowed by the founder of the town, Peter Bard.

Bard, a French emigrant from Montpelier, France, who had come to America to escape religious persecution, was the first known settler at Mt. Misery. Bard had spent years as a merchant in Burlington and began to buy and sell land as a sideline around 1717–1721. Sometime during this period, he purchased a tract of land encompassing the area now known as Mt. Misery. Soon after purchasing the land, he settled there with his family and built a sawmill that became known as Peter Bard's Cedar Mill. Bard is said to have named his settlement after his birthplace, Montpelier Lands.

One hundred years later, in 1834, the mill was described in *Gordon's Gazette of New Jersey* as a hamlet with four or five houses, a tavern, and a sawmill.

George Upton of Boston later purchased the property and decided to enlarge the mill. With the assistance of Upton's foreman, Charles Pittman, the town soon grew to include over 100 homes, a store, a hotel, and a school that doubled as a place of worship on Sundays. Pittman and his wife, "Aunt Sallie," were owners of the Mt. Misery Hotel. By the time Henry Charlton Beck came to Mt. Misery in the 1930s, "Aunt Sallie" and her daughter Caroline (also known as Cad) were the only residents left in the town. Charlie and Sallie's son Asa (Rattlesnake Ace), who lived in the nearby town of Upton, served as a guide for hunters during deer season and, in off months, caught and sold pine and rattlesnakes, which were once common in the area.

The author is in possession of a hand-drawn map created by Howard P. Boyd noting the site of the old hotel, sawmill, pond, mill race, and house foundations. Today these sites are on private property and should not be explored without permission. Rattler's Road (the road running past the old village site and over the old mill stream) is still open to public access, although in sections it is overgrown and difficult to discern. At the top of Mt. Misery, the gravel road (which is not passable by car) intersects with Mt. Misery Road and eventually connects with Route 72.

On the edge of Brendan T. Byrne Forest, at the entrance to the Batona Trail, is the curiously named place known as Ongs Hat. First mentioned in county newspapers in 1818, the town's name has held a fascination for locals for years. Although nothing is left to mark the location of the old settlement, there are a number of differing stories that explain how the town received its name.

In one account, Ongs Hat is mentioned as the host site of a popular 1890s dance hall. It seems a dashing young man named Ong used to attend these dances on a regular basis. Ong, who was considered quite the lady's man, always came to the dances wearing a shiny tall silk hat. One night, a young lady who was desirous of Ong's undivided attention, ripped the hat off his head and stomped on it in the middle of the dance floor. Another version of this story has a drunken Ong tossing his hat high into the trees at the center of the village, where it hung for many months.

Another account relates the story of a Chinese cook named Ong, who lost his hat while passing through the area with his employer on the way to the seashore. As the story is told, when Ong's hat blew off his head, his employer shouted to the stage driver to stop. When Ong got off the stage to retrieve his hat, his employer, ever the man on the lookout for a new business venture, decided to get off himself and look around. Realizing that this was the halfway point between the Delaware River and the Atlantic Ocean, he decided it was an ideal spot for a stagecoach tavern. The tavern was built shortly afterwards and called Ongs Hat.

One story has Ong as an Indian. One day he disappeared, and evidence suggested he had been murdered. His bloody hat was found in the brush near a crossroads in an area that soon became known as Ongs Hat.

Yet another version states that Ong was actually a Dutchman who lived in Tuckerton. Once a year, Ong would travel with his family from Burlington to Tuckerton. As this was an arduous two-day stagecoach trip, Ong decided to build his family a shelter or "hoet" (which in English is "hut") at the halfway point, where they could rest before continuing their journey. Ong called his shelter Ong's "hoet," which was later corrupted to Ongs Hat.

With all these stories it is hard to determine the truth, but what we do know is that there really was a man named Jacob Ong, who owned about 100 acres in the vicinity of what is now referred to as Ongs Hat. We also know that this was the site of a tavern owned by Issac Haines in 1800.

Today Ongs Hat can still be found as a location on a map. Aside from a restaurant and the entrance to the Batona Trail, nothing exists there today but forest. The truth behind the name seems destined to remain a mystery.

Brendan T. Byrne State Forest and Vicinity Side Trips

Forest Office to Pakim Pond Hike

To gain appreciation for the diverse flora and fauna of the Brendan T. Byrne State Forest, take a hike on the Batona Trail from the park office to Pakim Pond. The terrain is easily hiked, and the round-trip distance, from the office to the pond and back, is approximately 6.5 miles. Pack a lunch to enjoy at Pakim Pond, where picnic tables, grills, and restrooms are available. After lunch take a walk around the pond and see if you can find the rare and elusive curly-grass fern that reportedly grows in this area. Near Pakim Pond are three rustic cabins that can be rented in season for a nominal fee. Inquire at the park office (609-726-1191) for information about renting the cabins or reserving a camping site.

PAKIM POND

(Illustrated by Berminna Solem)

VISIT THE PYGMY PINES

An unusual ecosystem of the New Jersey Pine Barrens is the area commonly referred to as the Plains. The stunted pine trees growing here, also known as the Pygmy Pines, are thought to have developed as the result of physiological adaptation to frequent fires, unfavorable soil conditions, or both. The Pygmy Pines are unique to the New Jersey Pine Barrens, with a few exceptions—small patches of similar trees can be found near Albany, New York; on Long Island; and in Mendocino County, California.

Pygmy Pines.
(*Photo by Gordon Stull*)

During the 1960s, the Plains area was proposed as the site of a supersonic jetport, designed to be four times as large as Newark Airport, LaGuardia, and Kennedy combined. If the jetport proposal (which was paid for by the federal government) had been realized, it would have certainly destroyed this amazing ecosystem we now call the Pygmy Pines.

To view the Pygmy Pines, drive east on Route 72 from the Four Mile Circle (where Route 70 and Route 72 intersect) to mile marker 10. As you approach this mile marker, you will begin to see the change in the forest.

"SACRIFICIAL BOG" AT WEBBS MILL

To enjoy a view of a typical Pine Barrens bog without getting your feet wet, travel over to Webbs Mill on Route 539. A boardwalk is built over the water so that visitors can walk out into the bog and view many of the plant species unique to the New Jersey Pine Barrens. Species such as the carnivorous pitcher plant and sundew can be found in the bog, as can bog asphodol and curly-grass fern.

Spring is a particularly spectacular time to go because many of the Pine Barrens wildflowers are in bloom. When visiting the bog, be sure to bring along Howard P. Boyd's *Wildflowers of New Jersey* to aid in identifying the various species (and please stay on the boardwalk so as not to disturb the flora and fauna). Locals call the Webbs Mill location Sacrificial Bog, believing that by making this site accessible to the public, other bogs will be spared. To reach Sacrificial Bog from the Four Mile Circle, travel approximately twelve miles on Route 72 to Route 539 and make a left. Go approximately 6.3 miles until you see a Greenwood Forest sign on your left side. Park and look for a narrow path (across the highway from the Greenwood Forest sign) leading into the woods to the boardwalk.

BIKE RIDE FROM BULLOCK TO MT. MISERY

To enjoy a bike ride on a paved road through the heart of Brendan T. Byrne Forest, start at Bullock. The ride to Mt. Misery from Bullock is approximately five miles on a virtually traffic-free road. The forest road from Bullock to Mt. Misery is found on Brendan T. Byrne Forest maps distributed at the park office.

REFERENCES

Baer, Christopher T., Coxey, William, and Schopp, Paul W. 1994. *The Trail of the Blue Comet: A History of the Jersey Central's New Jersey Southern Division.* Palmyra, NJ: The West Jersey Chapter, National Railway Historical Society.

Beck, Henry Charlton. 1936. *Forgotten Towns of Southern New Jersey.* New Brunswick, NJ: Rutgers University Press.

Beck, Henry Charlton. 1937. *More Forgotten Towns of Southern New Jersey.* New Brunswick, NJ: Rutgers University Press.

Berger, Jonathan, and Sinton, John W. 1985. *Water, Earth and Fire: Land Use and Environmental Planning in the New Jersey Pine Barrens.* Baltimore, MD: Johns Hopkins University Press.

Bethman, Christian M. 1989. *The History of the Lebanon State Forest.* New Lisbon, NJ.

Bisbee, Henry H. 1971. *Sign Posts: Place Names in the History of Burlington County, New Jersey.* Willingboro, NJ: Alexia Press Inc.

Comellas, Bob. 1979. "Industry: Clay Works." (hand-written notes probably from presentation). Toms River, NJ: Ocean County Historical Society, January 25, 1979.

McMahon, William. 1980. *Pine Barrens Legends and Lore.* Moorestown, NJ: Middle Atlantic Press.

Miller, Pauline S. 2000. *Ocean County: Four Centuries in the Making.* Toms River, NJ: Ocean County Cultural and Heritage Commission.

Pepper, Adeline. 1971. *The Glass Gaffers of New Jersey.* New York: Charles Scribner's Sons.

Pierce, Arthur D. 1964. *Family Empire in Jersey Iron: The Richards Enterprises in the Pine Barrens.* New Brunswick, NJ: Rutgers University Press.

Schoening, Gary. "Pasadena: Its Past Hidden in the Pines." *Asbury Park Press,* July 27, 1978.

Wieczorek, Scott. 2002. *Of Myth and Brick: Explaining the Legendary Pasadena Terra Cotta Company.* (Master's Thesis) Monmouth University.

Wieczorek, Scott. 2002. *The Ruins in the Woods: The History of the Legendary Pasadena Terra Cotta Company: Fact and Fiction.* (Master's Thesis) Monmouth University.

whitesbog village
and double trouble

on the cranberry trail

Whitesbog Village and Double Trouble

WHITESBOG VILLAGE

OVERVIEW AND WALKING TOUR

Although technically not a ghost town—the village currently contains eight private residences and is headquarters to three organizations—Whitesbog is clearly representative of the early industries of the Pinelands. When exploring interesting historic sites in the New Jersey Pine Barrens, Whitesbog is definitely a must-see. Once an agricultural plantation of the industrial period, the old company town of Whitesbog is now owned by the state of New Jersey and is part of the Brendan T. Byrne State Forest. Prior to being sold to the state in the 1960s, Whitesbog had been a family-owned cranberry farm for over five generations. In 1857 James Fenwick purchased 108 acres of Pinelands along Cranberry Run, a tract of land previously mined for bog ore by the nearby Hanover Furnace. After acquiring an additional 485 acres needed to assure adequate water supply, Fenwick fenced off his property and began to develop his land into a cranberry farm.

Approximately 10 years later, young Joseph Josiah (J. J.) White began to clear land given to him by his grandfather with plans of planting cranberries. In the process of clearing his land, J. J. met Mary Fenwick, daughter of James Fenwick, and they soon married. Thus began the Fenwick-White Pinelands cranberry dynasty that exists to this day.

The Fenwick-White cranberry bogs eventually became known as Whitesbog, trading under the company name of J. J. White, Inc. During its peak years of the early 1900s, Whitesbog was considered the largest and most innovative cranberry farm in the state. During those years it employed 40 year-round workers and 600 pickers during the six-week harvesting season. The villages of Florence and

getting to
whitesbog village

From the West
Take Route 70 East to Route 530. Take Route 530 one mile. Turn right into Whitesbog Village.

From the East via the Garden State Parkway
Take the Garden State Parkway to exit 88. Take Route 70 West to Route 530. Take Route 530 one mile. Turn right into Whitesbog Village.

From the South
Take Route 206 North to Red Lion Circle (where it intersects Route 70). Take Route 70 East to Route 530. Take Route 530 one mile. Turn right into Whitesbog Village.

From the North via the New Jersey Turnpike
Take the New Jersey Turnpike to exit 7. Take Route 206 South to the intersection of Routes 206, 38, and 530. Turn east onto Route 530 and follow to mile marker 13. Entrance to Whitesbog Village will be on your left.

Village of Florence.
(*Photo courtesy of Burlington County Library*)

Rome were erected to house the large influx of Italian migrant workers that came to work the fall cranberry harvest.

In 1916 Elizabeth White, J. J.'s oldest daughter, working with Dr.
Fredrick Coville of the U.S. Department of Agriculture, cultivated
the first blueberry, bringing national recognition to Whitesbog.

In 1982 the Whitesbog Preservation Trust, a nonprofit organization whose purpose is to preserve the village, began to restore many
of the buildings of the old company town. The village as it stands
today offers a good representation of a cranberry and blueberry farm
of the late 19th and early 20th centuries. To begin a tour of
Whitesbog Village, first walk to the kiosk located on the commons
(the open area to the east of the Whitesbog General Store). A map
of the village as well as information about events occurring at
Whitesbog can be picked up at the kiosk. Using the map, start your
tour at the Whitesbog General Store. The current building was
erected in 1924 to replace the original store, which was moved to
another location within the village. The Whitesbog General Store

also served as the village post office, and it was from here that Elizabeth White shipped her blueberry bushes to farms across the United States.

The original Whitesbog General Store and Whitesbog Pond.
(*Photo courtesy of Burlington County Library*)

Today the Whitesbog General Store serves as a gift shop selling Pine Barrens books and crafts. The upstairs of the General Store serves as offices for the Whitesbog Preservation Trust and the Pinelands Institute for Natural and Environmental Studies (P.I.N.E.S.). The P.I.N.E.S. program provides on-site historical and ecological Pine Barrens field experiences for school groups as well as in-school presentations. The P.I.N.E.S. program is administered by Burlington County College in cooperation with Brendan T. Byrne Forest and can be reached at 609-893-1765. The General Store is operated by the Whitesbog Preservation Trust as a fundraising enterprise and is staffed by volunteers.

Behind the general store is the town's 85-foot water tower, built in 1914 to provide fire suppression for the village. The water tower was

The Whitesbog General Store, 2003.
(*Photo by Gordon Stull*)

connected in the 1920s to a series of fire hydrants in key locations throughout the village. Holding 30,000 gallons of water, the water tower was also the lookout tower from which the farm's bogs could be easily observed.

Walking in a southwesterly direction, head toward the four workers' cottages. Originally each of these cottages was built to house four families. Each of the four units within the cottage had two 8 x 8 foot rooms (one upstairs and one down), with a separate entrance and stairway to the second floor. There was a shared privy behind the house for each quad, and all cooking was done outside. Eventually these houses, which were for the fulltime workers of the village, were made into duplexes, and by the 1950s they were turned into single-family homes.

Continuing in a southwesterly direction, walk to the berry processing section of the village. The largest and most important building in the village was the cranberry sorting and packing house. As it stood in 1910, this structure was 38 feet wide, two and a half stories high, and consisted of three sections. Each section was 196 feet long, with protective firewalls dividing each wing of the building. A gravity pushcart

Whitesbog worker's cottage, 2003.
(*Photo by Gordon Stull*)

track ran down the middle of the plant through each of the sections. The eastern section (which stood on what today is the parking lot) was built in 1890, and the middle and western sections were constructed in 1900. The eastern and western sections of the building were used for storage, and the middle section housed the sorting, packing, and shipping operations. The storage area of the building could hold 60,000 one-bushel crates (nearly the whole year's harvest). The eastern section of the cranberry sorting and packing house burned down in 1970, and the middle section burned down several years earlier. The Whitesbog Preservation Trust subsequently made efforts to obtain funds to refurbish the western section (which is now in ruins) but was unable to raise the $500,000 necessary for the restoration. Today, unfortunately, the building has so deteriorated that restoration is no longer feasible.

Across from the ruins of the cranberry sorting and packing house stand the barrel factory and the barrel storage building. Cranberries grown at Whitesbog were packed and shipped in barrels that held 100 pounds of berries. Twenty thousand barrels were made annually

Whitesbog cranberry sorting and packing house.
(*Photo courtesy of Burlington County Library*)

Sorting cranberries at the Whitesbog cranberry sorting and packing house.
(*Photo courtesy of Burlington County Library*)

in the off-season by itinerant coopers (specialty barrel makers) and by the fulltime workers of the village. After the barrels were made, they were stored in the barrel storage building to await the following year's harvest season. The barrel storage building was designed to accommodate additional cranberry harvest and, like the sorting and packing house, had a push cart track running through its center.

Barrel factory, 2003.
(*Photo by Gordon Stull*)

Leaving the berry processing section of the village, return to the commons. In the commons is a small structure referred to as the pay house. This building was J. J. White's office and is where the workers of the village came to pick up their pay. Behind the pay house is the boardinghouse, which is now used as a double residence. The boardinghouse was divided into two sections, with one side providing shelter to the unmarried male workers of the village and the other to the unmarried female workers.

Use the village map to walk to the site of the original general store. This building was built in 1899 and moved to its current location in 1924. After the building was moved, it was used primarily as a residence.

The two-story cottage next to the original store is believed to have been the residence where Dr. Coville stayed on his visits to Whitesbog Village. The next structure served as the Whitesbog School from 1908 to 1918. After 1918, the children of the village attended school in nearby Browns Mills, and the school building served as a residence. The white building across from the school was erected in the 1920s from a kit ordered through the Sears catalog. During the 1920s it served as the Cranberry Research Center. The two small cottages at the end of the road facing one another were workers' homes and may also have been purchased from the Sears catalog. The three larger homes on this road are now private residences.

Returning to the area of the commons, use the map to locate the house of the superintendent. This house, built in 1912, became the home of J. J. White's superintendent, Joseph Haines, and later the home of Haines's son Isaiah, who also served as a superintendent at Whitesbog. The superintendent's house is now a private residence.

The home across from the superintendent's house is known as the Darlington house or the entomologist house. This was the home of J. J. White's daughter Mary and her husband, Emlen Darlington. Emlen Darlington was a physician and an entomologist, and it was hoped that his expertise in insect control would serve an important function within the company. The alliance did not seem to have lasted long, however, as the Darlington family only briefly lived in this house. Later the house served as the residence of Harold Haines, Isaiah's brother, who managed the blueberry operation at Whitesbog during the later years. The Darlington home is a private residence today.

Walking in an easterly direction on the dirt road between the Darlington house and the superintendent's house you will shortly come to Suningive, the home of Elizabeth White. The name "Suningive" was reportedly the name of a European chalet that Elizabeth had become familiar with. In 1923 Elizabeth built Suningive, at a cost of $23,000, on the site of her first blueberry field and next to her grandfather's original cranberry bog. The first floor of Suningive was laid out to function as the company's office, and the second and third floors as Ms. White's living quarters. Special features of the house include an elevator and windows that, when open, recess into the walls.

Elizabeth cultivated a native Pine Barrens garden at Suningive, filled with acid-loving plant species. Elizabeth's garden, designed to be in harmony with its surroundings, was widely known and had many visitors. The Whitesbog Preservation Trust Garden Club is in the process of restoring the Suningive gardens to a state similar to when Elizabeth lived there. Today Suningive serves as an office of the local Nature Conservancy. The Nature Conservancy, which offers many special Pinelands programs, can be reached at 609-735-2200.

East of Suningive are some of the original bogs of Whitesbog. Many of these bogs, which are slowly returning to a natural state, abound with birds and wildlife native to the New Jersey Pine Barrens. To make the most of your experience exploring the bog areas, purchase a Whitesbog Driving Tour booklet at the General Store.

Guided tours of the village are offered by the Whitesbog Preservation Trust and the P.I.N.E.S. program. To find out about scheduling a tour, contact the Whitesbog Preservation Trust at 609-893-4646 or the P.I.N.E.S. program at 609-893-1765. Whitesbog also lists its special events and programs on the Web site at www.whitesbog.org.

A DEEPER LOOK

On land where the bogs were once mined for iron ore stands the old cranberry village of Whitesbog. Considered at one time the largest cranberry farm in the state, Whitesbog was also one of the most influential, due to the important botanical, agricultural, and technological advances that occurred there.

The Whitesbog story began in 1857 when Colonel James Fenwick decided to expand his farming operations to include the cultivated cranberry. Experiments in cranberry cultivation, occurring first in the 1820s on Cape Cod, Massachusetts, and later in New Jersey, had begun to show success by the 1850s. Hoping to capitalize on the newly developed cranberry market, Fenwick purchased 108 acres from his neighbor Samuel H. Jones, who was his cousin and the owner of Hanover Furnace. The tract he purchased was known as Cranberry Run, and locals for years had freely harvested the wild cranberries that grew there in profusion. Surveying his land, Fenwick soon realized he needed a better water supply if his cranberry venture was to be successful. With the purchase of an adjacent 490 acres, he had adequate irrigation to begin his new cranberry farm.

When the nearby Hanover Furnace closed its doors in 1865, the land and the local economy were prime for the cranberry business that followed. Fenwick filled the economic gap by hiring the remaining workers from the Hanover Furnace village to work at his cranberry farm. The former ore bogs of Hanover Furnace, once considered useless land, now had a new purpose. Under Fenwick's management a new and profitable cranberry business emerged.

In another part of Burlington County, Joseph Josiah (J. J.) White was growing up at Sharon, his father's Springfield Township farm. Sharon had previously belonged to Charles Read, the original founder of the Batsto and Atsion Iron Works as well as several other bog iron furnaces in the area now known as Medford Lakes.

In the 1850s Barclay White, Joseph's father, had begun to develop cranberry bogs at his farm and on land along the Wading River. Young J. J. was keenly interested in the cranberry venture and often accompanied his father when he visited his bogs. When J. J. was 14 his maternal grandfather gave him 100 acres of land. J. J. soon realized that some 30 acres of his new property was suitable for cranberry cultivation. About this time J. J. also received a monetary gift of $2,300. In 1866, when J. J. was 20 years old, he built a cabin on his land and began to develop the property for cranberry production. Seven years later, after acquiring an adjacent 100 acres of land that had been given to his brother, J. J. incorporated as the Rake Pond Cranberry Company with assets of $30,000.

While clearing his land, J. J. had become acquainted with Mary Fenwick, the daughter of James Fenwick. In 1869 J. J. and Mary married. During the first year of their married life, J. J. and Mary collaborated on a book they entitled *Cranberry Culture*. Mary created the illustrations for the book, and J. J. wrote the text. *Cranberry Culture* became the standard guide on cranberry cultivation, and J. J. soon became a frequent consultant to those interested in improving the production of their bogs.

In 1875 J. J. branched off into an entirely different line of work, apprenticing as a machinist for Hezekiah B. Smith. Smith was an inventor and manufacturer of woodworking machinery and the founder of Smithville, located in Burlington County. J. J. stayed at Smithville, living in one of the workers' cottages while he learned his new trade. J. J., whom Smith had taken under his wing, was also being groomed for a leadership role in Smith's company. J. J. had a knack for the work and had already received several patents of his own. In 1878 Smith incorporated, and J. J. became the company's general manager. In 1880 J. J. became manager of Smith's retail franchise in Philadelphia.

In 1882 James Fenwick died, leaving his cranberry farm to his wife and appointing J. J. as sole executor and manager of his bogs. J. J. moved back to the area and for the next 17 years commuted Monday through Friday by train and ferry to Philadelphia while working Saturdays at the cranberry farm.

Through the years J. J. continued to expand his cranberry farm by acquiring adjacent tracts of land. He was also able to improve the farm's efficiency by his mechanical inventions. In 1903 he invented the Cranberry Mill, a machine that separated the good berries from the bad by rolling them down an inclined plane with several plateaus built within the structure. The ripe, marketable berries rolled to the bottom while the damaged berries remained on the plateaus.

In 1912, when Mary inherited her father's cranberry bogs, J. J. joined both land tracts together and incorporated under the name of J. J. White, Inc. The Fenwick-White combined 3,000-acre tract (with 600 acres in bogs) was now referred to as Whitesbog. By now Whitesbog was considered the largest cranberry farm in the state as well as one of the most progressive.

During the week, a superintendent who lived in the village oversaw the daily activities of the farm. J. J. White and his family lived in the Fenwick homestead in New Lisbon, from where J. J. commuted by wagon to Whitesbog on weekends. Whitesbog Village had grown to include 28 households by the 1915 census. These 28 households included 41 workers and a total of 88 residents. The residents of Whitesbog Village were the fulltime workers of the farm and lived in houses provided by the company. In winter these workers were kept busy doing maintenance tasks such as sanding the bogs, pruning, weeding, repairing dams, and making barrels. Two other villages were constructed a short distance from the center of operation at Whitesbog to house the seasonal workers needed during the six-week harvesting period. These two villages came to be called Florence and Rome because of the many Italian immigrants (often entire families) who came to work and live at the cranberry farm in early September. Elizabeth White, J. J.'s oldest daughter, wrote that when she first came to work at the bogs in 1893, the farm workers were all from the Pines. After several years, when the local employees had all moved on to more lucrative work, Whitesbog began to employ Italian immigrants recruited from South Philadelphia. By the early 1900s, 90 percent of the 500–600 pickers employed by the farm were Italian.

Florence, which was located a quarter mile from Whitesbog Village, was the newer of the two villages and considered a model

Cranberry harvest, early 1900s.
(Photo courtesy of Burlington County Library)

workers' village of its day. There were seven multifamily houses, a foreman's house, a dance hall, separate toilet facilities for the men and women, and a covered cookhouse. The multifamily dwellings consisted of eight separate units, each consisting of two rooms (upstairs and down), each measuring approximately 10 x 10 feet. Each unit had a private entrance, stairway, and stove.

Rome, which was considered more Spartan, had five multifamily dwellings, a foreman's house, an assembly hall, and separate toilet facilities for men and women. Each multifamily house had 20 small rooms, measuring approximately 8 x 8 feet occupied by as many as five to six family members.

In the early years all members of a family, including young children, worked side by side harvesting the berries. Beginning in 1915, a nursery was established at Florence, and a social worker was hired to care for the young children of the seasonal workers while they were out in the fields.

WHITESBOG CRANBERRY PICKERS

(*Illustrated by Berminna Solem*)

Though the living conditions of Florence and Rome may seem cramped and unpleasant by today's standards, they were considered quite pleasant at the time when compared with other farms of the kind.

By the early 1930s, with growing opportunities for unskilled workers, it was becoming increasingly more difficult to hire the large seasonal work force needed for the harvesting season. Compensating for this loss of labor, cranberry farms developed and increasingly began to use the cranberry scoop for harvesting. With such a scoop, the crop could be harvested by 150 workers, compared with more than 500 picking the berries by hand.

By 1915 Franklin Chambers, the husband of J. J.'s youngest daughter, Ann, and a professor of mathematics at the University of Pennsylvania, had become vice president of J. J. White, Inc. Chambers's new position, in which he worked on a part-time basis, included mostly management responsibilities of the cranberry farm. Joseph Haines, the superintendent of J. J. White, Inc., since 1917, lived at Whitesbog and managed the farm on a daily basis. In 1924, J. J. White died, leaving his cranberry farm to his four daughters.

In 1948 Joseph Darlington, the son of J. J.'s third daughter, Beulah, became president of the company, with the management assistance of Joseph Haines's son, Isaiah. Unfortunately, shortly after taking over the helm of the company, Darlington was killed in a plane crash.

In 1950, Thomas Darlington, Joseph's younger brother, became president of the company. Thomas, a mechanical engineer and inventor like his grandfather, spent his time designing innovative machinery while Isaiah Haines and his brother Harold managed the farm. During his tenure at Whitesbog, Thomas invented the first successful dry-harvesting cranberry picker, decreasing the number of pickers needed from 150 workers with scoops to 15 men with machines.

In 1965, Bill Haines of Hog Wallow, owner of another nearby large cranberry operation, introduced the wet harvesting method to the state. This innovation, when introduced at Whitesbog, further reduced the number of workers needed to harvest the farm's 600 acres of cranberry bogs to five individuals.

The most well-known member of the family, Elizabeth White, J. J.'s oldest daughter, was to reach national prominence with her work in the cultivation of the first blueberry. Born in 1871, Elizabeth, as a young girl, would accompany her father on many of his trips to

Elizabeth White.
(*Photo courtesy of Burlington County Library*)

the cranberry bogs. Although she lived in an age when women of a certain means were not expected to have an occupation, she spent most of her life dedicated to the improvement of cranberry and blueberry culture of the Pines.

Elizabeth, who never married, first began working at her father's cranberry farm in 1893 at age 22. Her first job was handing out tickets that acknowledged the receipt of the boxes of berries picked by the workers. From 1900 to 1910 Elizabeth collaborated with Dr. John Smith, a government entomologist who studied ways to eliminate a type of katydid that was destroying the cranberry crop.

For years Elizabeth and her father had discussed the possibility of using their land to grow a companion crop to the cranberry, one that also would do well in the acidic soil of the farm. In 1910 Elizabeth came across a federal government bulletin entitled "Experiments in Blueberry Culture," written by Dr. Fredrick Coville, a botanist with the Department of Agriculture. Impressed by what they read, Elizabeth and her father decided to contact Dr. Coville and offer him their support in his work.

The wild blueberry grows profusely throughout the Pines in the same acidic soil as the wild cranberry. For years Elizabeth had been hearing from local farmers that the blueberry could not be cultivated, but here was an expert who thought it could be done. The blueberry would be the perfect companion crop to the cranberry as its berries ripen in July and it grows best on higher ground. With a blueberry companion crop, the work force could be occupied during the slack season, land not being utilized could be planted, and another harvest—during the middle of the year—would bring in additional income. Also when cranberries were having an off year, blueberries might have a successful one. Needless to say, the prospect of cultivating the blueberry was an exciting concept for J. J. and Elizabeth.

While Coville was responsible for the scientific work, Elizabeth and her father offered financial support and the Whitesbog infrastructure necessary to carry out the large-scale blueberry experiment.

Probably the most important contribution of Whitesbog to the cultivation of the blueberry involved Elizabeth's efforts to locate and transplant the choicest of wild blueberry shrubs. Although Coville had planted the first experimental blueberry fields at Whitesbog with seedlings from his summer home in New Hampshire, Elizabeth was sure the Pine Barrens had better specimens to offer. By 1914 she was advertising for and organizing locals to search for superior wild blueberry shrubs within a 20-mile radius of Whitesbog. Each searcher was supplied with labels, bottles filled with a preservative, and a gauge with a five-eighths-inch-diameter hole. Searchers were instructed to locate bushes with berries that were too big to fit through the five-eighths-inch gauge. Advertisements offered payment of $1–$3 per bush for bushes with such large berries. In addition to the money for the bush itself, Elizabeth offered to pay for any time the finder spent taking her to the bush and helping her dig it up. Elizabeth was interested in being involved in the whole process and would often accompany locals in a horse and buggy through the Pine Barrens swamps in search of a prime blueberry specimen.

As another way to award those who located the choicest blueberry shrubs, Elizabeth would name the bushes for the finder who brought them to her. During the research, approximately 100 blueberry bushes were found and named for their finders. One bush, discovered by Ruben Leek on March 15, 1913, was considered most outstanding of all. This wild blueberry bush, discovered near Chatsworth, was divided over and over and became known as the Rubel.

The first successful field plantings were made in 1912 on the site of what later became Elizabeth White's home, Suningive. In 1916 Dr. Coville and Elizabeth managed to cultivate and produce a blueberry crop for sale. The result of the collaboration was the production of a new crop for Whitesbog and the propagation and sale of blueberry bushes across the country. At its peak, Whitesbog had 90 acres of blueberries under cultivation.

Another of Elizabeth's contributions to the berry industry was her decision to use cellophane to cover the blueberry containers being shipped to stores. Having seen this covering on candy boxes she received from Europe, she realized it would protect the product while allowing the consumers to see what they were purchasing. Prior to the use of cellophane, brown paper was taped over the berry containers.

In addition to her blueberry work, Elizabeth started a nursery for cultivating the native holly tree and other plants. Plants not native to the area, such as the Franklinia, a rare type of Magnolia shrub named in honor of Benjamin Franklin, were also propagated and sold at the nursery. A Franklinia shrub can be located today on the right side of the front porch of the Whitesbog General Store.

In 1923 Elizabeth built a home at Whitesbog Village and called it Suningive. Here she planted a garden filled with a variety of native plants that was designed to be in harmony with its surroundings. Although much of the Suningive garden is overgrown today, many native plant species can still be found there. The Suningive garden is in the process of being restored by Whitesbog Preservation Trust volunteers.

Elizabeth never realized her lifelong ambition to be president of J. J. White, Inc., although she was involved in the company's functioning for nearly all of her adult life until her death in 1954.

In 1967 Whitesbog Village, encompassing 2,000 acres, was purchased by the state of New Jersey from the J. J. White company with Green Acres funds and incorporated into Lebanon State Forest (now Brendan T. Byrne Forest). The J. J. White company still exists and is

Cranberry harvest, 2003.
(Photos by Gordon Stull)

managed by J. J.'s great grandson, Joseph Darlington. The company owns and operates 150 acres of cranberry bogs at Buffin's Meadow, south of the village, and also leases (from the state) 150 acres of bogs within Whitesbog Village. Due to agricultural and technological developments, the company is now able to harvest 40,000 barrels of berries a year, twice as much (on half the property) as was produced during peak production in the early- to mid-19th century. Today J. J. White, Inc., employs 15 year-round workers, compared with the 40 full-time and 600 seasonal workers needed during the early years.

In 1982 the Whitesbog Preservation Trust was created as a non-profit organization dedicated to protecting and enhancing the village. The Trust also provides educational and interpretative programs and is currently renting eight of the houses on the property as a way to raise funds for further restoration within the village.

DOUBLE TROUBLE

OVERVIEW AND WALKING TOUR

To explore the site of another historic 19th-century cranberry village, explore Double Trouble State Park in nearby Lacey and Berkeley Townships, Ocean County. Double Trouble State Park encompasses over 8,000 acres of pristine Pine Barrens habitat including Cedar Creek, reportedly the cleanest river in the state.

The Double Trouble Historic District occupies over 200 acres and includes a complete company town, cranberry bogs, a cranberry sorting and packing house, and a working sawmill.

The park was the site of an extensive lumbering business that was started in 1767. Within the boundaries of the park is the site of a bog iron forge established in 1809 and operated until 1865. On swampland cleared of bog ore and Atlantic white cedar, cranberries were cultivated beginning in the late 1850s.

The Double Trouble village as it stands today is illustrative of a cranberry company town of the late 19th and early 20th centuries. Purchased in 1904 by the Crabbe family, the village housed a successful working cranberry farm until the 1960s.

The origin of the town's name is a matter of conjecture, though most historians credit Thomas Potter (owner of the tract in the late 1700s) as the first one to dub the tract the unusual epithet of Double Trouble. As the story goes, spring rain twice washed out the dam that controlled the flow of water to Potter's sawmill, causing him to lament "Here's double trouble." A second (and more colorful) story involves local muskrats that continually gnawed at the dam, resulting in frequent leakage. When these leaks were discovered, someone would yell, "Here's trouble" summoning someone to fix the dam. One fateful day, two breaks opened up in the dam, causing someone to shout, "Here's double trouble." This second story is the one most often told to explain the town's name.

After reaching Double Trouble State Park, walk a short distance from the parking area to a one-story white building that serves as the park's restrooms. A map of Double Trouble State Park Historic Village can be obtained on the porch of this building. Using the map, you should be able to locate each of the buildings within the village.

Getting to Double Trouble

From Whitesbog
Return to Route 70 and take Route 70 East for five miles, then turn right at the intersection of Routes 530 and 539. Shortly after the turn, the road will fork. At the fork, bear left onto Route 530 East. Follow Route 530 through Whiting for approximately 12.8 miles until you reach the intersection of Dover Road, at which point Route 530 East will veer off to the left. To continue on to Double Trouble State Park, go through the intersection (do not follow Route 530 East) and travel another 2.6 miles to the entrance of the park. You will pass the canoe access road about one mile before the park's main entrance.

Unfortunately, at the time of this writing, due to staff shortages, none of the park's historic buildings are open to the public, although the buildings can be viewed from the outside.

Begin your tour at the cranberry sorting and packing house, which was built in 1916. The hand-scooped berries were brought to the basement of the cranberry sorting and packing house. The house contained (as it does to this day) three Hayden cranberry separators, which largely eliminated the manual sorting of the berries. The separators, comprising a system of belts, bins, and rollers, brought the cranberries to the main floor of the plant. The berries would pass

Double Trouble cranberry sorting and packing house, 2003.
(*Photo by Gordon Stull*)

Cranberry sorting tables at Double Trouble, 2003.
(*Photo by Barbara Solem-Stull*)

through the Hayden separators, which removed undesirable berries and chaff. Then the berries were moved on a conveyor belt to tables on which women laborers hand sorted them for color and shape. Following the manual sorting, the berries were moved to the packing area for boxing and shipping.

When Edward Crabbe purchased the Double Trouble tract, he built a large new sawmill, run partly by steam and partly by water-power. When the sawmill burned to the ground in 1904, Crabbe replaced it, but a fire claimed the new mill in 1908. Another steam-powered sawmill (covered with corrugated sheet-metal siding as a fire precaution) was built in 1909 and is extant. By the 1920s Crabbe mechanized and began operating the sawmill with a single-cylinder, kerosene-powered, internal combustion engine. The sawmill built by Crabbe in 1909 has been converted to diesel power and is occasionally operated today.

The entrance to a 1.5-mile nature trail can be found next to the cranberry sorting and packing house. A guide booklet that provides interesting information on the flora and fauna found along the path can be picked up at a box at the trail's entrance.

To visit the site of Dover Forge, leave the park and turn left, returning to the Dover Road intersection. Turn left at the intersection and drive 1.3 miles, where a sign on the left side will indicate that you have reached the site where Dover Forge once stood.

A Deeper Look

Located in Berkeley Township, Ocean County, several miles upstream from Barnegat Bay, is Double Trouble State Park. At the center of the park is a historic village, once owned by the Double Trouble (cranberry) Company. The tract of land that became known as Double Trouble was the site of a sawmill owned by Joseph Sharp in 1767. Thomas Potter, a local sea captain, had acquired the land by 1777 and built another sawmill there. Potter is sometimes credited with giving the town its name when the water on Cedar Creek overran its banks and rushed against the gates of his dam, smashing it for the second time in a week. Viewing the damage caused by this recurring disaster, Potter is reported to have lamented "Here's double trouble."

Later William Giberson, another local sea captain, began to acquire the Double Trouble tracts. By 1850 he had acquired enough timberland to keep two sawmills running full time. Eventually Captain George Giberson inherited the land from his father. George ran a successful logging business on his land by turning out cedar siding and shingles for the local housing market as well as shipbuilding materials. His son-in-law, Thomas Cooper (who managed Giberson's sawmills), began to clear the swamp areas on the Double Trouble lands and to develop cranberry bogs. The swamp areas of the Double Trouble tract had previously been mined for bog ore by Dover Forge, located several miles upstream from the village site.

Dover Forge, erected in 1809 by William Smith, was in its time considered the largest forge in Ocean County (then a part of Monmouth County). Owned later by the Austin family, the forge was destroyed by fire sometime during the first quarter of the 19th century. After the fire, Joseph Austin Jr. moved to Burlington County, where he operated Hampton Forge until shortly before 1828. In *Early Forges and Furnaces in New Jersey*, Charles Boyer quotes from a letter he received from Joseph Austin's grandson Charles W. Austin:

I have learned that an old iron forge was in operation at a place called Old Hampton by my grandfather, Joseph Austin, and he demolished it and carried it to Dover with eight mule teams, rebuilt it, and put it in operation again. In what year this took place I do not know, but it was prior to 1830. I was born at the place called Dover in 1864 and my grandfather, Joseph Austin, was owner of the old forge at that time and was making iron there. The iron was manufactured into long bars called "pigs" and was shipped away and made up into wagon axles, cannon balls, shovels, picks, and other articles. There was a sawmill connected with the works, located on the south side of the forge in which many cedar shingles, siding frames, plaster laths, fence pickets, and posts were made. The iron ore in my day was gotten in different parts of New Jersey; some was dug along Atsion River between Batsto and Atsion, loaded on scows, and floated downstream to a landing on the Mullica River from whence it was hauled by mule teams to Dover Forge. After Joseph Austin died in 1868, the old forge was torn out, the inside floored over, and converted into a sawmill. Besides the forge there were four dwelling houses, one a log-house in which Joseph Austin lived and died, a large blacksmith shop, and three barns for the mules.

Boyer states that at the time of his investigation of the site (in the 1930s), only the remains of the old blacksmith shop were still visible. All other traces of the buildings mentioned in the letter from Charles Smith had apparently been destroyed in a forest fire in 1912.

The principal product of Dover Forge was bar iron, which was carted to Philadelphia over a dirt road through the woods known as the "Mule Road."

By the mid-1800s the timber industry was in decline, and George Giberson (owner of the Double Trouble tract) began to focus more on cranberry production. During the picking season, it took 50 people to harvest the cranberries at Double Trouble. In the early days, local families, women and children included, came to harvest the berries. Pickers averaged 2.4 bushels in 5–6 hours and received 40 cents a bushel. They received tickets rather than cash for the berries they picked. These tickets could be taken to the general store and exchanged for goods.

In the early 1900s, Italian immigrants living in Philadelphia were brought in to harvest the cranberries. These workers lived in the village during the harvesting season, sleeping in four-room lodges and cooking their food outside.

Although cranberry production became more of a focus, Giberson continued to operate his sawmill and to harvest the cedars growing on his land. He practiced sustainable forestry, cutting down only the mature trees and leaving the smaller ones to grow. Using this system, he was able to work the forest surrounding his sawmill throughout his lifetime.

After Giberson's death his heirs closed the mill, and the property was abandoned until Edward Crabbe purchased the Double Trouble tract in 1903. Crabbe rebuilt the sawmill and began to harvest the timber and cranberries growing on his land. A number of company houses had been built around the mill site by 1904. The Crabbe family did not live at Double Trouble but in Toms River; therefore no mansion was built in the little village. By this time there were five to ten children living in the village, and they were educated in a cedar-shingled one-room schoolhouse. School started late in the season at Double Trouble because the children of the village were expected to participate in the harvest season, which extended until mid-October.

In 1909 Crabbe formed the Double Trouble Company and expanded his cranberry operation by adding three more bogs. This expansion brought the Double Trouble land under cranberry cultivation to 260 acres.

The Double Trouble Company, one of the larger cranberry operations in the state during the early 1900s, continued to harvest the bogs into the 1960s. Although cranberry farming became the major industry at Double Trouble, mining of the Atlantic white cedar was still considered an integral part of the company's business until the 1930s.

One-room schoolhouse at Double Trouble, 2005.
(Photo by Gordon Stull)

Double Trouble remained in the Crabbe family for 60 years. In 1964 the family sold the company and 1,500 acres to the state through the Green Acres Program. After the state acquisition, the property became known as Double Trouble State Park.

WHITESBOG VILLAGE AND DOUBLE TROUBLE SIDE TRIPS AND EVENTS
FESTIVALS AND SPECIAL EVENTS AT WHITESBOG VILLAGE

On the last Saturday in June, the Whitesbog Preservation Trust holds its annual Blueberry Festival. The festival is a wonderful country fair featuring crafts, food stalls, musical performances, guided tours of the village, nature hikes, and everything blueberry.

On the first Sunday in October, Whitesbog hosts the opening celebration of Pinelands Month, the Pinelands Discovery Festival, sponsored by the Pinelands Preservation Alliance. If you want to learn about the New Jersey Pine Barrens, this is the festival for you. Over 40 exhibitors and vendors, guided walking and wagon tours, Pinelands presentations, musical performances, and children's activities focus on introducing the festival participant to different aspects of the Pinelands. The Pinelands Preservation Alliance can be reached at 609-859-8860 or at its Web site, www.pinelandsalliance.org.

Throughout the year the Whitesbog Preservation Trust sponsors events including moonlight hikes and cranberry harvest tours. To learn more about these events, visit the Whitesbog Preservation Trust at its Web site, www.whitesbog.org, or call 609-893-4646.

WHITESBOG DRIVING TOUR

A five-mile Whitesbog driving tour booklet featuring the village bogs, canals, reservoirs, and pine forests can be purchased at the Whitesbog General Store for a minimal fee. The booklet guides the visitor along winding dirt roads past old cranberry bogs and blueberry fields to different stations that interpret Whitesbog's natural environment while telling the story of its industrial and agricultural past. The driving tour (which can also be walked) is a wonderful way to explore the Whitesbog tract and to enjoy the flora and fauna of a land in the process of returning to its natural state. If you visit between the months of November and March, you may see hundreds of tundra swans that winter on Whitesbog's reservoirs and bogs. For information about purchasing the Whitesbog driving tour booklet, call 609-893-4646.

CROSSLEY PRESERVE

To visit the site of a late 19th- and early-20th-century clay mining operation, stop at Crossley, a 1,400-acre preserve managed by the New Jersey Natural Lands Trust. Located on Route 530 several miles east of Whiting, this lovely tract features a nature trail that winds through a Pinelands habitat dotted with ponds that were once clay pits. Interpretative signs describing the history and ecology of the area guide visitors along a 1.6-mile trail.

Clay pits at Crossley, 2003.
(*Photo by Barbara Solem-Stull*)

In the early years, the clay mines at Crossley were operated by the United Clay Mine Company, owned by George Crossley. At its peak, the company employed over 100 people, all of whom resided in Crossley in housing provided by the company. Initially the clay at Crossley was dug by hand and later by steam shovels and gas-powered machinery. After being dug, the clay was loaded onto small carts that ran on a narrow-gage railroad from the pits to loading areas. Remnants of the old "Donkey" (corrupted from Dinky) railroad tracks are still visible in the preserve today, as are the old clay pits that provide watering holes for the tract's many threatened and endangered species, such as the Pine Barrens tree frog and timber rattlesnake. To reach the Crossley Preserve, drive several miles past Whiting and turn left onto a dirt road just after passing the Getty Gas Station. After you travel a short distance through the woods, the road will dead-end at a small parking lot near the beginning of the nature trail. To learn more about the Crossley Preserve, contact the New Jersey Natural Lands Trust at 609-984-1339.

PADDLE CEDAR CREEK

To enjoy a paddle trip on Cedar Creek and through Double Trouble State Park, launch your canoe or kayak at the canoe access area located approximately one mile north of the park's headquarters. To shorten the paddle to three hours (if taking out at Dudley Park), launch from the village site at the beach area behind the sawmill. Dudley Park is located on Route 9 in Berkeley Township. Canoes and kayaks can be rented from Cedar Creek Camping and Kayak Rental, also located on Route 9 in Berkeley Township. To contact Cedar Creek Camping and Kayak Rental, call 732-269-1413.

REFERENCES

Adelizzi, Joe. "Preserving History (Berkeley trying to keep open tract in its natural state)." *Asbury Park Press*, March 30, 2000.

Bolger, William, Githens, Herbert, and Rutsch, Edward S. 1982. *Historical Architectural Survey and Preservation Planning Project for the Village of Whitesbog*. Morristown, NJ: The New Jersey Conservation Foundation.

Boyer, Charles S. 1931. *Early Forges and Furnaces in New Jersey*. Philadelphia: University of Pennsylvania Press.

Dash, Judi, and Schensul, Jill. 1994. *Country Roads of New Jersey: Drives, Day Trips and Weekend Excursions*. Lincolnwood, IL: Country Roads Press.

"Double Trouble State Park." *Asbury Park Press*, May 25, 2001.

Michalsky, Barbara. 1978. *Whitesbog: An Historical Sketch*. Browns Mills, NJ: Conservation and Environmental Studies Center Inc.

Miller, Pauline. 1994. *A Pine Barrens Preserve (An information booklet about one of the forgotten towns in New Jersey)*. Toms River, NJ: Ocean County Cultural and Heritage Commission.

Moore, Kirk. "Saving Pieces of the Past: Double Trouble State Park." *Asbury Park Press*, January 1, 1998.

Morgan, Elizabeth M. "Double Trouble Well Named." *Batsto Citizens Gazette*, Spring/Summer 1980.

Tice, Jill. "The Lost Village of Crossley." *Berkeley Times*, August 8, 1999.

Windisch, Martha. 1997. *Whitesbog Driving Tour*. Browns Mills, NJ: Whitesbog Preservation Trust.

weymouth, belcoville, and amatol

of iron, paper, and munitions

Weymouth, Belcoville, and Amatol

WEYMOUTH

OVERVIEW AND WALKING TOUR

On the banks of the Great Egg Harbor River, five miles above the head of navigation, stands the old iron and paper mill town of Weymouth. Unlike many other old company towns of the Pines, when the iron ran out, the Weymouth owners successfully switched to the manufacture of paper. With the creation of the local paper industry, the owners gave the village a new lease on life that lasted another 20 years. Today the ruins of the old mills are preserved as part of the Atlantic County Park system. The acreage encompassing the site of the owner's mansion has also been preserved and is now owned and managed by the New Jersey Natural Lands Trust.

The story of the town begins in 1801 with the purchase by five Philadelphia businessmen of 78,060 acres known as the Great Egg Harbor Tract. On this land the five partners built an iron furnace and forge, a gristmill, two sawmills, a company store, and dwellings for the workers and their families.

In 1808 Samuel Richards and Joseph Ball, cousins with years of experience in the iron industry, purchased a controlling interest in the Weymouth Furnace Company. Under their expert guidance, Weymouth flourished and the company grew, eventually employing 100 men and sustaining 600 to 700 residents.

In 1836, Samuel Richards's daughter Sarah married Stephen Colwell. Stephen, who was to play an important role in the company's fortunes, was soon involved in the management of the Weymouth operations. When Samuel Richards died in 1842, he left Weymouth to his two daughters by his first marriage, Sarah Colwell and Elizabeth Richards. Several years later Elizabeth married Walter Bell, and soon both he and Colwell were actively involved in the management of Weymouth.

249

getting to weymouth

From the West
Take Route 295 South to Route 42 South to the Atlantic
City Expressway. From the Atlantic City Expressway, take
exit 28 and turn right onto Route 54 South. Proceed
approximately 1.1 miles to the next light and turn left
onto Route 561 (also called Mays Landing Road). Take
Route 561 to Route 322 (Black Horse Pike) and turn left.
Proceed 4.7 miles to the Route 559 North jug handle.
Cross over the Black Horse Pike onto Route 559 and
drive two-tenths of a mile to the entrance of Weymouth
Furnace Park.

From the East
Take Route 30 West to Route 623 (Weymouth/Elwood
Road). Turn left and proceed approximately 5.2 miles to
the entrance of Weymouth Furnace Park, which will be
on your left.

From the South
Take Route 50 North to Route 322 (Black Horse Pike)
and turn left. Drive approximately 4.5 miles and turn
right onto Route 559 North. Proceed two-tenths of a mile
to the entrance of Weymouth Furnace Park.

From the North
Take Route 206 South to the intersection with Route 30
(just above Hammonton). Turn left and proceed approximately 2.3 miles to Weymouth Road. Turn right onto
Weymouth Road and drive 7.2 miles. (Weymouth Road
will change from Route 640 South to Route 559 South
after several miles.) After 7.2 miles the road will curve to
the right. Follow the curve and drive one-tenth of a mile
to the entrance of Weymouth Furnace Park, which will be
on your left.

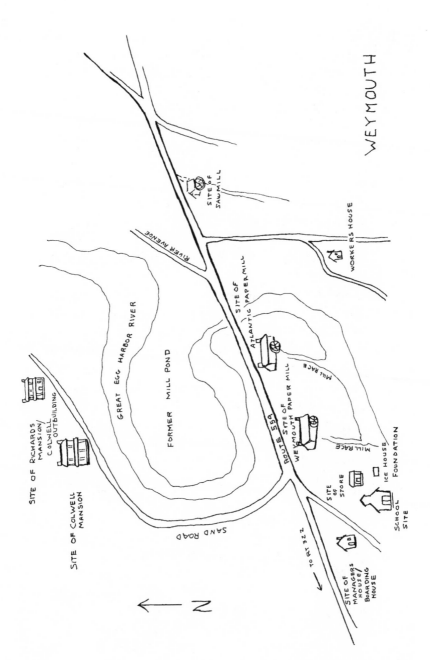

Weymouth site map. (*Drawn by Berminna Solem*)

Although Weymouth was in operation longer than most other iron-works in South Jersey, it too was forced to shut down in the early 1860s.

In 1864 Stephen Colwell built a paper mill on the site of the former furnace. The new mill was leased for a 10-year period to three businessmen with prior experience in the paper industry and was called the Atlantic Paper Mill. By 1865, after several deaths in the Bell family, the Weymouth properties came entirely into the possession of the Colwell family. In 1869 Colwell erected another paper mill on the site of the old forge. This mill was called the Weymouth Paper Mill and was managed by the Colwell family.

Both mills ran successfully until 1880, when the paper industry went into a decline. By the spring of 1887, the Weymouth Paper Mill went bankrupt, ending forever a 90-year manufacturing dynasty.

The village of Weymouth exists today as a small residential community. The busy manufacturing years, when the ironworks and paper mills controlled the destiny of the town, are only a memory. Today, the ruins of the old company town are located in the boundaries of the county park and can be easily located using the Weymouth site map. The site of the former Colwell mansion is situated on land owned and managed by the New Jersey Natural Lands Trust and may be freely accessed by those interested in exploring the remains of the old country estate. To start your tour, begin at the extensive ruins of the Atlantic Paper Mill.

Upon arriving at Weymouth, the visitor first notices the impressive 60-foot-high smokestack of the old Atlantic Paper Mill and its millrace, running through lovely brick archways. Although some archaeologists say this paper mill was built on the site of the old iron furnace, others say it was more likely built on the forge site. The Atlantic Paper Mill consisted of two sections, one of which was a stone building with walls 18 to 24 inches thick. This section contained four pulp engines and a paper machine. Behind the front section was a two-story frame building that included the boiler room on the first floor and the rope cutter and "devil" (the machine that tore the rope apart) on the second.

Approximately 50 feet to the south of the paper mill foundation is a capped-off wellspring encased in a concrete base. This well was drilled in 1886 to provide clear water for the manufacture of paper.

Nearby are the Weymouth Paper Mill ruins, which have been fenced in to prevent further deterioration of the stone walls. The former millrace (which at one point runs through a brick arch) is still clearly visible. The Weymouth Paper Mill (the second paper mill to be built on this site) was a T-shaped building divided into two sections. The front section of the T contained the turbines, pulp engines, rope cutter, and devil. The rear part of the T contained the paper machine and the calendar room (where the paper was smoothed and finished). Two boiler rooms (where the ropes were boiled) were

Atlantic Paper Mill smokestack.
(*Photo by Gordon Stull*)

Ruins of the Atlantic Paper Mill.
(*Photo by Gordon Stull*)

located in the southwest corner of the T-shaped building. In 1886 the Weymouth Paper Mill was altered to allow for the production of paper from wood pulp. Although it is not known what alterations were made, additional rooms to house a new boiler and wood processing machines were probably added.

An example of the housing provided for the workers of Weymouth can be seen two-tenths of a mile in on Gale Street. The abandoned former worker's home is in an advanced state of deterioration at the time of this writing and may completely collapse (or be torn down) in the near future. The foundations and debris of other workers' homes can be found in the wooded lot located on the north side of this structure.

An 1872 Beers map shows 25 residences located on three streets on the east bank of the Great Egg Harbor River. Of the 25 houses, 11 were two-family dwellings. After the paper mill closed, it appears that some families continued to occupy their homes. A 1900 census shows 11 families living in homes that they did not appear to own or rent. By the time the property came into the possession of the Mays

Abandoned worker's house at Weymouth, 2004.
(*Photo by Gordon Stull*)

Landing Water Power Company in 1921, the Weymouth residents had lived there for 25 years and had established squatters' rights.

To visit the site of the Colwell mansion, walk across the road (Route 559) from the paper mill ruins and locate a dirt road with a chain across the entrance. The site of the mansion ruins is located down this road about 1,200 feet northwest of the industrial complex. Shortly after entering the lane, you will pass the site of the gate-keeper's house on your left. The gatekeeper acted as the caretaker of the mansion and was also responsible for raising and lowering the floodgates of the dam. Nothing remains of this structure except a short segment of concrete footing located on the side of the road. A pump house (postdating the period of historical significance) is located nearby between the river and the road.

The Colwell house remains consist of foundation walls and some scattered building materials. Built by Stephen Colwell in the mid-1800s, the mansion was given this illustrious (though brief) description in a Hammonton newspaper in 1874:

The house and grounds of Mr. Colwell are probably the finest in South Jersey. The former is large and commodious, and located upon a ground a few rods from the pond, elevated some fifteen or twenty feet higher, with a lawn sloping toward the water, shaded by many old and beautiful ornamental trees, and adorned with numerous flower beds. The road to the house winds around the pond and is well graded.

In 1938 the *Atlantic City Press* offered the following more comprehensive description of the house:

This building has three stories with a two-story tower above. The first tower holds a water reservoir, the top tower being used as an observatory. The third story was used as a servants' quarters, and had many small rooms. One room contains an interesting wheel shaped round window with 12 spokes in it. All have separate bathrooms put in by the Rutherfords (ca. 1912). The Colwells and Richards had to use large tin bathtubs.

There were two story porches on three sides of the house, but when recently repaired the top balcony porch was done away with and a railing put around as the roof had rotted away.

On the second floor are two large and several smaller bedrooms, halls and bathrooms. Most of the rooms contain white painted fireplaces, made of wood so hard as to resemble iron. The first floor contains a large salon living room and two fireplaces. This room runs the entire width of the house and has long French windows. The lovely wide hall formerly contained a beautiful old fashioned staircase, but was removed by the former owner Mrs. Rutherford, who expected to install an elevator for the use of her invalid daughter, Elizabeth, but this was never done. The floors are of wide boards ten or twelve inches and kitchen with pantries, linen closets and patios galore.

The Colwell mansion, after standing vacant for a number of years, was destroyed by fire in 1956. The stone foundation located just north of the Colwell mansion is believed by some to have been the Samuel Richards mansion, erected in 1808. Others believe that the Samuel Richards mansion was actually what became known as the Manager's House or Boarding House. Robert Johnson, author of *Weymouth, New Jersey: A History of the Furnace, Forge and Paper Mills*, believes that the foundation found behind the Colwell house may have been a large dog kennel. The Colwells were actively involved in the breeding of American mastiff dogs.

After exploring the mansion site, head back across the highway and walk down the paved street behind the Weymouth Paper Mill ruins. On the westerly side of the road (which was formerly called Main Street) on the wooded lot near several large buttonwood (sycamore) trees is the site of what is known as the Manager's House or Boardinghouse. Some historians believe this was originally the site of the Samuel Richards mansion and only later was used as the manager's house and later still as a boardinghouse for the single workers

Colwell mansion after abandonment.
(*Photo courtesy of Burlington County Library*)

Ruins of Manager's House/Boardinghouse, 1930s.
(*Photo courtesy of Burlington County Library*)

of the village. If visiting in early spring, you will find vintage daffodils and vinca blooming around the house site.

Located behind the Weymouth Paper Mill are the stone foundations and stone-lined vault remains of the company store. Other stone foundations (probably including that of the icehouse) can be found behind the store, near the Weymouth Paper Mill tailrace (the lower millrace). The store, which also housed a post office, was a one-story frame structure with a full basement. The stone-lined vault located on the northern end of the building was used as the company safe. The modern-looking private residence located next to the store ruins was originally the Weymouth School, built in the mid-1800s. The second floor of the schoolhouse was also used for paper bag assembly from 1864 to 1876. A second school was built in 1877 near the Weymouth Church. Both schools were converted to private residences after the mills closed in 1897.

Prior to the 1930s, when the construction of the highway changed its configuration, Main Street extended across what is now Route 322 (Black Horse Pike) and connected with Deep Run Road where

Remains of the company store vault, 2004.
(*Photo by Gordon Stull*)

the Weymouth Church sits. Today, the way to reach the Weymouth Church is by driving south on Route 559 for seven-tenths of a mile to Deep Run Road. Turn left and drive a quarter of a mile to the church and cemetery on your right side.

The church, which was built either by George Ashbridge in 1806 or by Samuel Richards in 1808, is relatively unaltered and is still used to this day.

A DEEPER LOOK

In a remote Atlantic County park sits the picturesque ruins of one of South Jersey's busiest and most enduring 19th-century company towns. At one time an important stagecoach stop on the Long-A-Coming stage road (originally an Indian migration trail to the shore), the sleepy little village of Weymouth has a story as rich as the area's natural resources on which the town's fortunes rose and fell. It was here, in 1801, five miles above the head of navigation of the Great Egg Harbor River, that five partners (all related through blood or marriage) purchased 78,060 acres of prime Pine Barrens land. The

Weymouth Church, 2004.
(*Photo by Gordon Stull*)

property, known as the Great Egg Harbor Tract, had a ready supply of water, an abundance of bog ore, and vast stands of pine forest, all needed for the manufacture of bog iron. The tract stretched north as far as Elwood and extended south to include much of what is now Mays Landing. George Ashbridge, Charles Shoemaker, David Robeson, John Paul, and Joseph M. Paul purchased the vast tract from the West Jersey Society for the purpose of establishing an iron-works. By the spring of 1802, the furnace and forge were built, and Ashbridge (who managed the plant) began advertising for workers. The following ad appeared in the *Trenton Federalist* on June 8, 1802:

FORGE MEN WANTED: Wanted immediately, a full set of Forge-men to work new forge now erected and in complete order, with four fires and two hammers on the

Great Egg Harbor River. The Stream is powerful and can never want water in the driest season. Good encouragement will be given for workmen. Apply to Robeson and Paul's merchants, No. 43 North Water Street, Philadelphia, or to the subscriber at the works, Gloucester County New Jersey.

One of the new company's first contracts came from the Philadelphia Watering Committee for 56 tons of cast iron pipes to replace wooden mains on Water Street between Vine and Head House Square. Cast iron pipes would shortly become Weymouth's stock in trade, although other items, such as stoves, firebacks, pots, skillets, and other hollowware, were produced there during the early years.

In 1807, Ashbridge died, leaving his children a quarter interest in Weymouth. Samuel Richards, son of William Richards, ironmaster of Batsto, and Joseph Ball, Samuel's cousin and former manager of Batsto during the Revolutionary War years, were named executors of Ashbridge's estate.

Soon after Ashbridge's death, the Weymouth Furnace Company ceased operation, and the remaining partners decided it was a good time to sell the ironworks. After some investigation of the property on behalf of the Ashbridge heirs, Samuel Richards and Joseph Ball decided to buy out the four remaining partners. In 1808 Richards and Ball purchased a three-quarter interest in the Weymouth property for $34,500 while the Ashbridge heirs retained their one-quarter interest.

As recorded by the Weymouth time books (the ironworks' journal of daily events), Ball and Richards had the forge back in action ten days after their purchase and the furnace in blast a month later.

The following description of the property, written by Richards in 1811 (possibly during a financial crisis when he may have been considering selling the ironworks), provides an interesting view of the Weymouth tract:

> On the Great Egg Harbor River, thirty-five miles from Philadelphia: There are upwards of fifty thousand acres of

land. The works consist of a furnace now in blast, a Forge with four fires, a Grist Mill and a Saw Mill all on one dam for which there is plenty of water in the driest season, and a good boatable navigation to Mays Landing which is six miles, from which Vessels are constantly sailing to New York and Philadelphia.

There is at said works a good dwelling house and barn, a store and twenty tenements to accommodate workmen. There is also a Saw Mill four miles from the works called Penepot, at which there is a good dwelling house and barn, and three small tenements to accommodate workmen. There are also several other houses and improvements on said tract of land. There is a canal from the Furnace to the Ore beds so that ore is brought to the Furnace at small expense. The Iron made at said Works is of excellent quality. The Furnace went Eleven Months last year during which time she made eleven hundred and fifty tons of Iron.

The canal to the ore beds—still visible in some sections—was 1.3 miles long and ten feet wide. The ore, after being dug out of the swamps and bogs, was loaded onto scows and poled down the canal to the furnace. Bog ore, dug at Penny Pot (five miles northwest of the village), was boated down to the furnace on the Great Egg Harbor River.

In 1811, Ball and Richards, who were busy running their many other business affairs in Philadelphia, hired Lewis Walker, in his early 20s, to manage the furnace. Although Ball and Richards made frequent visits to Weymouth and in some cases stayed for extended periods of time, they chose to reside most of the year in Philadelphia. According to the Weymouth time books, Ball and his family spent several summers in the village, although it is unclear where they resided during their visits. (Historians and archaeologists who have investigated the site differ in their opinion of where the owner's mansion was located during the Ball-Richards years. Some believe it was located near the site of the later-built Colwell mansion, and others believe the house occupied by Richards and Ball during their visits was what became known as the Manager's House or Boardinghouse.)

By 1818 the ironworks had transitioned from making smaller-sized pipe, which it had made on a sporadic basis, to a more steady production of larger-sized pipes. By that time cast iron pipes had become the chief product of Weymouth, although iron plates, lamp posts, stoves, firebacks, and other essentials were also produced there. By 1809 (and continuing through the War of 1812) munitions were also being made at Weymouth.

Recognizing the importance of maintaining a happy and healthy workforce, Richards and Ball ceased all work at the ironworks on Sundays (an unusual practice for most foundries). Workers were free to attend religious services at the Weymouth Church or to spend the day relaxing with their friends and family. The ironworks also closed for Christmas. Weymouth had a school as early as 1818, 50 years before public schooling was being offered in most parts of the state.

In 1820 Lewis Walker left Weymouth and was replaced by Samuel's cousin, John Richards. John, who had previously managed the Atsion Ironworks, would eventually become a partner in the nearby Gloucester Furnace.

In 1821 Joseph Ball died, and his share of the property passed to his aunt, Sarah Hastings, and his uncle, William Richards (Samuel's father). By 1839 Samuel managed to purchase all shares of Weymouth not in his possession, thereby owning the property outright.

During the 1820s and 1830s, Weymouth prospered, but the supply of local bog ore was diminishing. As early as 1813, bog ore was being imported to the Weymouth ironworks from other parts of South Jersey and from out of state. During these years Weymouth employed 100 men and provided subsistence to between 600 and 700 people. Even though Batsto is generally considered the larger of the two furnaces, Weymouth, during the early 1800s, produced more castings and employed more workers.

The daily life of the workers of the village was chronicled in the Weymouth time books maintained by the company clerk. The time books, while keeping a general account of the operation of the ironworks, also noted the births, deaths, marriages, and other interesting life events of the villagers. On one day, Mrs. Woolfield beat Dan Beaty with a broomstick because he was drunk; on another day, the schoolmaster was taken away to jail but was back the next day conducting school; and on another, three Indians passed through town. Even a budding romance is noted: On November 10, 1820, the company clerk writes, "S. B. Finch in love with a young lady. He has a notion of making a grab. Nights rather cold to sleep alone." Seems the company clerk also had a sense of humor.

In 1836 Samuel Richards's daughter, Sarah Ball Richards, married Stephen Colwell, a widower with a law degree from the University of Pennsylvania. Soon after getting married, Colwell, who had spent his early career working in the field of merchandising, became involved in the management of Weymouth Furnace. Recognizing Colwell's competence, an aging Samuel Richards began to turn over more and more of his Weymouth business dealings to his son-in-law.

In 1842 Samuel Richards died, leaving his Weymouth property to his two daughters from his first marriage, Sarah Ball Richards Colwell and Elizabeth Ann Richards. In 1844 Elizabeth married, and her husband, Walter Dwight Bell, soon became involved in the business affairs of Weymouth.

Shortly after 1844 Stephen and Sarah Colwell began to build a manor house at Weymouth. The Victorian country house was built across the road from the ironworks, down a lane on a rise overlooking the millpond. The Colwells lived most of the year on 16th and Locust Street in Philadelphia but would reside in their Weymouth residence during the summer months.

In 1846 a six-mile mule-drawn tram railroad was built from the Weymouth Furnace to Mays Landing. Each of three tramcars was pulled by a mule team that carried goods daily to the docks in Mays Landing. In later years a one-horse passenger car was added to the tramway system. Prior to the installation of the tramway, goods from the furnace were transported to ships by scows down the Great Egg Harbor River to Mays Landing or by wagon over dirt roads.

In the late 1840s, Elizabeth Bell passed away, and in accordance with an agreement signed after her marriage, her one-half share of Weymouth passed directly into the hands of her daughter, Mary.

COLWELL MANSION

(Illustrated by Berminna Solem)

By 1850 the Weymouth Furnace (including the town's gristmill and sawmills) employed 80 men in addition to those who were loggers, carters of materials, and farmers. During that year the Weymouth enterprises made a profit of $48,625 while workmen earned from $25 to $30 a month. Although the ironworks prospered during the 1850s, the Weymouth ore deposits were depleted, and ore had to be brought in from other locations. During this period Weymouth was also using imported coal, as well as charcoal, as fuel during the smelting process.

With Weymouth doing so well, Colwell and Bell could turn their minds to other endeavors. In 1852 both invested heavily in the Camden and Atlantic Railroad that, when completed in 1854, ran through the Weymouth tract. The railroad provided a better transportation system for the industries on its route, and a station serving Weymouth was built five miles northeast of the ironworks. Colwell became the director of the Camden and Atlantic Railroad during the 1950s. During this period Colwell was also involved in many other endeavors. He was a prolific writer and produced over 27 pamphlets and books on economics and religion.

The year 1860 saw Weymouth having its most profitable year. By this time most other South Jersey ironworks had closed due to competition from Pennsylvania, where a richer ore and more efficient fuel in the form of coal had been discovered. But the waning days of the Weymouth Ironworks were just ahead, and in 1862, when the furnace burned down, Colwell decided not to rebuild. The forge continued on for two or three more years, but it too succumbed to fire in 1864 or 1865 and was not rebuilt.

In 1864 Stephen Colwell built a paper mill on the foundations of the old furnace (some historians believe it was built on the site of the old forge). The new mill, known as the Atlantic Paper Mill, was leased to John McNeil, Thomas Irving, and George Rich for ten years. McNeil and Irving had previously been partners in another paper mill at Pleasant Mills. The new mill produced manila paper manufactured from old bagging, rags, and ropes. The production of the paper involved cutting the raw materials into small pieces, boiling them by steam, washing them, then grinding them into pulp, the result from which the paper was then manufactured.

The manila paper manufacture process at Weymouth was described in the *South Jersey Republican* newspaper in 1874:

> Manila rope is the principle material from which paper is made. ... This is cut up into short pieces ... and is carried by an apron to what is termed the "devil," or picker, where it is torn into fine atoms and from thence to a steaming apparatus, into which lime is thrown and the stock is softened and prepared for pulping.
>
> When sufficiently boiled by the steam, it is put into an engine where it is washed until it is cleaned, and then ground and worked over until it becomes a pulp, when it is ready for use. From the tub where the engine works, it is drawn off into a large reservoir from whence it is pumped into a vat in which revolves a cylinder on which is a wire cloth.
>
> The water passes through this wire cloth while the pulp adheres to it, and is carried over and deposited upon a felt cloth, which is continually moved along this cylinder, and carries the paper between heavy iron cylinders to press the

water out, and this pressure is continued until the paper is sufficiently dried to bear its own weight. Then it leaves the cloth and is carried over some six or more hollow iron cylinders, which are heated by steam. This is the drying process. When it leaves these cylinders it is dry. It is then rolled up as it comes out and from this roll it is carried through the cutting machines and is cut into such sized sheets as is wanted and bound up, and is ready to ship. Most of the paper is used in the manufacture of paper bags. About a ton a day is finished.

In 1865 Mary Bell died, and her share of the Weymouth estate passed into the hands of her aunt, Sarah Colwell, and two cousins. In 1866 the cousins were paid $75,000 each to release their interest in the company. About this time Stephen Colwell began to turn over more and more of his management responsibilities at Weymouth to his son, Samuel Richards Colwell (whom his family referred to as Richards). In 1867 Richards married his cousin, Annie, the daughter of William Richards, his mother Sarah's half brother. That same year, Charles, Richards's younger brother, married Laura Williams Ritz.

In 1869 Stephen Colwell and his son erected a second paper mill on the site of the former forge (some historians believe it was built on the site of the old furnace). This mill was called the Weymouth Paper Mill and would be managed by the Colwell family. Richards, who managed the paper mill, lived in Weymouth in the family mansion while Charles and Laura resided in Philadelphia.

An 1870 industrial census record indicates both the Atlantic and Weymouth paper mills each produced one ton of paper daily, although the Atlantic Paper Mill was more profitable.

In 1871 Stephen Colwell died at the age of 71. After his death, Sarah deeded each of her sons a one-third interest in the Weymouth property, retaining a one-third share for herself.

In the spring of 1873 Richards began to suffer from Bright's Disease (a disease of the kidneys). Richards and Annie soon left for Europe and began "traveling for his health," as was the custom of the day. Several months later Richards died in Switzerland, leaving his wife his one-third share of the Weymouth properties. The management of the Weymouth mills and other operations now fell to Charles Colwell. At the time of Charles's ascension to a leadership role in the company, each of the Weymouth operations, including both paper mills, the sawmill, the gristmill, and the charcoal business, was turning a profit.

In 1876 the Weymouth Paper Mill burned down, and with it went the Colwell family annual income. Realizing he needed to reorganize if he wished to save the company, Colwell formed a partnership with Elisha Fulton, a family friend whose father had been a business associate of his father. With the advice of his new partner, Charles decided not to renew the contract with McNeil, Irving, and Rich, whose 10-year lease on the Atlantic mill had just expired. Colwell hoped that by managing the Atlantic mill himself, he could regain an income for his family and raise the capital needed to rebuild the Weymouth Paper Mill. At the time he also bought out his sister-in-law Annie's one-third share in the company.

The new paper mill, built entirely of stone as a fire precaution, opened on May 22, 1877. By 1879 the Weymouth Paper Mill was making two tons of manila and roofing paper daily, which was twice the previous output. By 1880, however, the paper industry went into a decline, and the Weymouth Paper Mill had to cut back its production to stay in business. By 1880, both mills were in full production only eight months of the year. The remaining four months, they operated at either three-quarters or half production. Profits dove from $42,700 (for both mills) in 1870 to $9,104 in 1880. Charles had begun to borrow heavily to keep the Weymouth mills solvent.

In the early 1880s, with prompting from Fulton, Charles decided to convert the Atlantic mill to a wood pulp paper manufacturing plant. This new method, still in the experimental stage, was designed for making wood pulp from Jersey pine using the sulfite process. In order to convert the mill, a large amount of capital was needed, and Charles borrowed $100,000 from his mother (and later $27,000 from Fulton) to begin the necessary conversion, which required enlarging the mill and purchasing special machinery. During the conversion of the Atlantic Paper Mill, the Weymouth Paper Mill continued to make manila paper.

By the time the new mill opened in 1886, Colwell had mortgages in excess of $200,000. Also that year the Weymouth mill suffered a minor fire, which put it out of operation for several months. The new pulp mill was unable alone to produce the income needed to pay the mounting interest due on Colwell's debts. By the spring of 1887, the Weymouth Paper Mill was bankrupt, with debts of $315,207.

Although some attempts were made to revive the company, by March 1891 Colwell had sold the bulk of the Weymouth estate—excluding the mansion, church, and 250 surrounding acres—to a land developer. But by 1897 the Industrial Land Development Company was bankrupt, never having paid the mortgage held by Colwell. At a court-ordered sale in 1898, 30,000 acres of the Weymouth tract sold under mortgage foreclosure. A $50,000 payment went to the estate of the former treasurer of the Industrial Land Development Company, who had earlier loaned the firm $200,000. At the time of the sale, the 30,000-acre tract contained two paper mills (both stripped of their workings by creditors), a store, and 25 dwellings. Although the dwellings were supposedly each rented for $1,200 a year, no rents had been collected since 1895. With the sale of the property, the doors of the Weymouth works closed for the last time, and after nearly a century of good fortune, a manufacturing dynasty reached its end.

Charles and Laura Colwell continued to live at the Weymouth mansion until Charles's death on March 10, 1901. Many of the villagers moved on when the mills shut down, but some stayed, finding work wherever they could. No one asked for rent, so the 11 families that continued to reside in the Weymouth workers' homes lived rent-free. By the time the Mays Landing Water Power Company came into possession of the property in 1921, the Weymouth residents had lived there for 25 years and acquired squatters' rights.

Weymouth residents like Andrew Stewart, who moved to Weymouth in 1869 to manage the company store, stayed on, waiting for the town to boom again. He and his son, Charles Colwell Stewart, operated a sawmill out of one of the mills in the early 1900s, but this too shut down by 1912. Fountain Gale, who arrived in Weymouth when the paper mills were still operating, stayed on and earned a living managing a sawmill for the Mays Landing Water Power Company, doing some commercial fishing, and scooping cranberries in season.

Laura Colwell continued to live at the Colwell mansion after her husband's death, but in 1909 she leased the family homestead to her cousin Harriet Colwell Rutherford. The lease with Rutherford allowed Laura to live in the gatehouse down the lane from the mansion. By 1910 Laura had built a small cottage near the old Weymouth church, where she continued to teach Sunday school each spring and summer. In 1916 she wrote a book called *Sketches of Old Weymouth* in which she told the history of the Richards and Colwell families and their industries at Weymouth. Laura died on August 20, 1920, in Philadelphia, shortly after moving there from her beloved Weymouth.

In 1921 the Mays Landing Water Power Company drained the old millpond to provide more waterpower for Mays Landing.

The Colwell mansion, the Weymouth Church, and the surrounding acres came into the possession of Dr. John Henry Trescher in 1937. Although some claimed Trescher had planned to renovate the mansion and turn it into a convalescent center, the house stood vacant for a number of years until it burned down in 1956. The Weymouth Church was maintained by Trescher until 1949 and was deeded by his wife to the congregation in 1960.

In 1993, the 202-acre property that housed the old Colwell mansion and gatehouse was donated to the New Jersey Natural Lands Trust by Dr. Trescher's daughter, Marian Waldhaussen. The Mays Landing Water Power Company sold the interests it held in Weymouth to the Lake Lenape Land Development Corporation in 1950. In 1962 the Lake Lenape Land Development Corporation deeded 4.4 acres of its holdings, identified in the deed as "the site of an ancient furnace and mill," to the Atlantic Historical Society. Lacking the financial means to maintain the property, the Atlantic Historical Society deeded the land to Atlantic County in 1966. The old Weymouth tract that houses the ruins of both paper mills is now a park owned and maintained by the Atlantic County government.

BELCOVILLE AND AMATOL
OVERVIEW AND WALKING TOUR

In 1917, with the entrance of the United States into World War I, the country's need for war materials suddenly increased. Particularly needed were facilities for the loading of high-explosive shells. The U.S. government decided that six of 14 shell-loading plants needed to augment the country's arsenal of weapons would be built in New Jersey. Two of these plants were to be built in the southern part of the state in heavily wooded and remote regions of the New Jersey Pine Barrens. In the final days of 1917, the U.S. government awarded contracts to Bethlehem Steel and the Atlantic Loading Company for the loading of high-explosive shells.

Bethlehem Steel chose as its plant site a parcel of land located 3.5 miles south of Mays Landing. The new plant, along with the town that would house the workers of the factory, was christened Belcoville. It was situated on a strip of land approximately one mile wide and six miles long. The Atlantic Loading Company chose a 6,000-acre tract in Mullica Township, approximately four miles east of

Belcoville plant, 1918.
(Photo courtesy of Hagley Museum and Atlantic County Park at Estell Manor)

getting to Belcoville

From Weymouth

Drive south on Route 559 until you reach the center of
Mays Landing (approximately 6 miles). The road will
wind through a residential section prior to reaching the
downtown area of Mays Landing. At the light in Mays
Landing turn right onto Route 50 and follow this road
until you reach the main entrance of Estell Manor Park
(approximately 4.2 miles). Please note that Route 50 will
make a sharp left a little less than a mile after leaving the
center of Mays Landing.

Hammonton. This shell-loading plant and town was named Amatol, after the explosive mixture that would be loaded into the shells.

Both companies began construction of their shell-loading plants and company towns in the spring of 1918. Crews worked around the clock to erect the plants and their companion towns, and after only four months, both Belcoville and Amatol were sufficiently complete to begin production. The first shell was loaded in Belcoville in July 1918, and Amatol followed with its first shell one month later.

A poem published in the *Belco News* on November 18, 1918, offers a glimpse of the pride the Belcoville workers felt in their accomplishment and the important task ahead of them:

Belcoville
> Down in the wilds of Jersey
> Where you sink in mud to your knees,
> There is a town called Belcoville,
> And Belcoville's just the cheese.
>
> They built this town in the Jersey Pines
> At such an awful pace,
> That Old Hog Island and Elwood, too,
> Were never in the race.
>
> The Sun did shine and the rain did rain,
> And morning followed night,
> But the buildings kept on going up,
> It was a busy sight.
>
> They would build a house in a single day,
> From sunrise till it died,
> And before the morning dawned again,
> The house was occupied.
>
> They built this town in the Jersey swamps,
> Beside the E.H. river,
> And the wind can blow, and the snow can come
> But Belcoville will not shiver.

They had a Loading Plant there too,
Run by the B.L.C.
It loads the shells that do the work,
With the boys across the sea.

There may be other sights, I know,
That make one sit up too,
But take a look at Belcoville,
When the construction gangs get through.

While the effort to build both Belcoville and Amatol in such a short period of time is a testament to what can be done in the face of great necessity, the accomplishment had no long-term value because the munitions production at both plants was destined to be short lived. With the signing of the armistice in November, the war came to an end, and the two Atlantic County shell-loading plants shut down shortly thereafter. The U.S. government eventually took possession of both plants, salvaging what they could and tearing down the rest.

In 1926 the Atlantic City Speedway, a "wooden bowl" raceway (a wooden oval track), was built on portions of the Amatol plant site. The grandstand was said to have been 75 to 80 feet high, with the capacity to seat 60,000 spectators. The speedway failed to draw the expected crowds and closed down in May 1928. The speedway oval is still discernible today and can be accessed from a trail off Moss Mill Road near its intersection with Burdick Avenue. Although most of the former track is on land owned by the state, some sections are privately held. Some of the remains of the Amatol plant are still visible at the easterly end of the oval, and the extensive remains of the town of Amatol are located in the woods behind the Mullica Township Athletic Field off Pleasant Mills-Elwood Road (approximately seven miles north of the Weymouth Furnace Park). Much of this land is private property, and permission should be obtained before exploring the ruins.

The Belcoville plant ruins are located in the Atlantic County Park in Estell Manor and are easily accessed. The many crisscross trails in the northern end of the park are the former railroad beds of

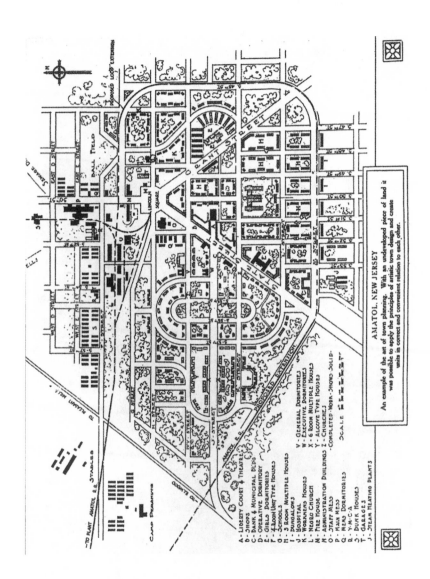

Town of Amatol. (*Map from* Construction and Operation of a Shell Loading Plant and the Town of Amatol, New Jersey)

Trail at Estell Manor Park (former railroad beds of
narrow gauge train that ran through Belcoville plant).
(*Photo by Gordon Stull*)

the narrow-gauge train that at one time connected all of the
Belcoville plant buildings.

On your way to Estell Manor Park, you will pass the former company town of Belcoville. Today, approximately 80 of the original homes of the old company town remain, though many have been greatly altered. The original Belcoville school (now the Marsh Center) and firehouse are located in the center of the village.

To explore the ruins of the Belcoville Shell Loading Plant, first pick up a trail map at the Estell Manor Park headquarters, located in the nature center near the main entrance. The southern section of the park can be accessed using the paved loop road that allows visitors to

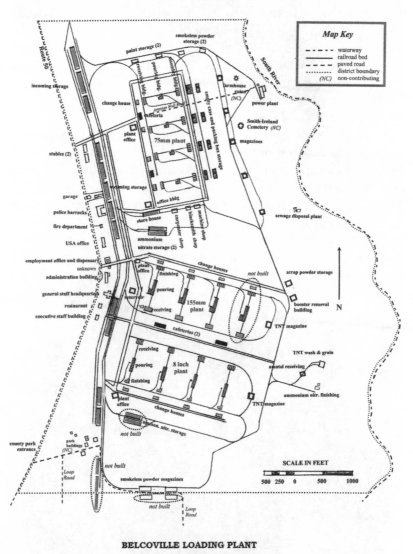

Map Key

- ─ ·· ─ waterway
- ─── railroad bed
- ── ── paved road
- ········ district boundary
- (NC) non-contributing

Route 50

incoming storage

paint storage (2)

smokeless powder storage (2)

change house

pouring bldg

South River

farmhouse ruins (NC)

power plant

cafeteria

Artesian Well Bldg

empty case and packing box storage

Smith-Ireland Cemetery (NC)

plant office

75mm plant

magazines

stables (2)

incoming storage

office bldg

garage

police barracks

fire department

store house

carpenter shop

machine shop

blacksmith shop

sewage disposal plant

USA office

ammonium nitrate storage (2)

employment office and dispensary

unknown

administration building

plant office

finishing

change houses

not built

scrap powder storage

general staff headquarters

reservoir

pouring

155mm plant

booster removal building

restaurant

receiving

executive staff building

cafeterias (2)

TNT magazine

N

receiving

TNT wash & grain

pouring

8 inch plant

finishing

amatol receiving

ammonium nitr. finishing

plant office

change houses

TNT magazine

ammon. nitr. storage

not built

county park entrance

park buildings (NC)

not built

Loop Road

smokeless powder magazines

SCALE IN FEET

500 250 0   500   1000

not built

Loop Road

BELCOVILLE LOADING PLANT

MAP DRAWN BY JOAN BERKEY

Belcoville plant.
(*Drawn by Joan Berkey*)

drive to the ruins of the Estellville Glass Works and other general points of interest within the grounds. Most of the Belcoville plant ruins can be found in the north end of the park, between the boundaries of Artesian Well Road and the main entrance and the South River and Route 50. A detailed schematic drawing of the layout of the three plants (most of which can be found in the boundaries just noted) is shown on page 277. Please note, however, that the dotted line shown cutting through the northern end of the 75 mm plant is today Artesian Well Road.

To begin your exploration of the Belcoville plant ruins, locate North End Road on your park trail map. North End Road runs parallel with Route 50 and is not automobile accessible. With the exception of the paved loop road in the southern end of the park and Artesian Well Road, roads and paths in the park are restricted to bike and foot traffic.

Walking (or biking) in a northerly direction on North End Road, you will see on the right blue signs marking the beginning of the 8-inch shell plant complex and after a short distance the 155 mm plant. The ruins of these two plants, with their numerous separate

Ruins at Belcoville of the 8-inch shell plant, 2003.
(*Photo by Gordon Stull*)

buildings, can be found east of the blue signs. The ruins extend deep into the park and can be partially viewed from the walking trails that crisscross the northern end. Other sections of the ruins require a walk off the established paths, sometimes into deep brush. Impressive ruins of the 8-inch shell plant can easily be seen from Shell Fill Road, whereas the equally extensive and interesting ruins of the 155 mm plant are hidden in the woods across from an open field on Crossover Road.

Walking in a northerly direction on North End Road, you will see on your left the foundations of 12 large buildings. These were the storehouses for the empty shells that had not yet been taken to the various plants to be filled with explosives. In front of the storehouse foundations fronting Route 50 are the ruins of a strip of nonindustrial buildings. Remains of the administration building, police barracks, general staff headquarters, employment office, and dispensary can be found in the mile-long strip between Artesian Well Road and the main entrance to the park.

To explore the extensive ruins of the power plant, go to the intersection of North End and Artesian Well roads and turn right, walking in an easterly direction. As you walk to the power plant, look for the remains of the 75 mm plant, which can be found on both sides of this road. After walking approximately seven-tenths of a mile, you will come to the South River boat ramp. The power plant ruins are located along the river to the south of the boat ramp.

Other historic and general points of interest within the park—such as the 18th-century Smith/Ireland cemetery—can be easily located by utilizing the park map.

A DEEPER LOOK

With the outbreak of World War I, the New Jersey Pine Barrens was once more set to play a pivotal role in the manufacture of munitions for the defense of the country. But, oh, what a difference a hundred years can make!

When America entered World War I in 1917, it was estimated to have less than a month's supply of field artillery ammunition on hand. With this realization, the Ordnance Department of the U.S.

Flag raising at Belcoville administration building, 1918.
(*Photo courtesy of Hagley Museum and Atlantic County Park at Estell Manor*)

Remains of Belcoville administration building vault, 2003.
(*Photo by Gordon Stull*)

Ruins at Belcoville of the 75 mm plant, 2003.
(*Photo by Gordon Stull*)

Belcoville power plant, 1918.
(*Photo courtesy of Hagley Museum and Atlantic County Park at Estell Manor*)

Army (whose responsibility it was to provide explosive shells, guns, tanks, and other weaponery) deemed it necessary to build 14 shell-loading plants in order to meet the munitions needs of the U.S. military. Two of these plants—Amatol and Belcoville—were destined to be built in Atlantic County within the wilds of the New Jersey Pine Barrens.

Near the end of 1917, the Bethlehem Steel Company was given a U.S. government contract to build and operate an ordnance plant for loading shells with high explosives. In February 1918 plans were drawn up to erect a new shell-loading facility on land previously purchased by Bethlehem Steel for an ordnance proving range. The site, located approximately 3.5 miles south of Mays Landing, would be situated on 12,947 acres—11,995 dedicated to the shell loading plant and 952 to the town that would house the 3,000-plus workers needed to operate the plant. A subsidiary company (with the same executive officers and departments as the parent company) called Bethlehem Loading Company was formed to operate the new shell-loading plant. The town that housed the workers was named Belcoville, a derivative of the new company's name.

The first order of business for the newly formed company was to build a railroad at the Mays Landing site. The railroad was essential for bringing in workers as well as the building materials needed to begin the construction of the plant and town. Eventually the railroad, which connected to an existing line in Mays Landing, would be used to transport the munitions produced at the plant to an army distribution center. The rail line serving the plant and village was over 30 miles long and included both broad- and narrow-gauge rail.

Concurrent with the building of the rail line was the building of the temporary camps and mess halls needed to house the 2,000 workers (both military and civilian) who were constructing Belcoville.

The first building materials arrived at the Mays Landing site on May 15, 1918, and construction began April 1, 1918. Construction occurred at a breakneck pace, with work continuing seven days a week, 24 hours a day. By mid-August the town of Belcoville was sufficiently complete to house 400 families and 3,000 single people. The homes and dormitories built for the workers came with the most modern conveniences of the time, including running water, indoor bathrooms, and heating—amenities not enjoyed by most local families. Belcoville, which was designed to be a totally self-contained community, had a grocery store, butcher shop, bakery, restaurants, laundry, tailor shop, department store, bowling alley, motion picture theater, pool room, YMCA, YWCA, school, bank, 100-bed hospital, post office, firehouse, and town hall. The amenities provided to the workers of Belcoville far surpassed anything offered by any Pine Barrens company town of the past. The company was so concerned with keeping its workforce happy that it sponsored numerous recreational activities, including dances and sporting events, on a weekly basis.

Not far behind the building of the town was the construction of the shell-loading plant. The shell-loading plant actually consisted of three plants, each with its own complex of buildings constituting assembly lines containing a receiving house, a filling-pouring house, and a finishing house. The three plants, which were arranged in a row running from north to south, were linked by conveyor belts, and a narrow-gauge railroad ran through the entire complex. The northernmost

Finished shells in storage at Belcoville, 1918.
(Photo courtesy of Hagley Museum and Atlantic County Park at Estell Manor)

shell-loading plant in the complex was the 75 mm plant. The 155 mm plant was in the middle and the 8-inch shell plant was located the farthest to the south. Nonindustrial buildings, including the administration building and police barracks, were located along Route 50, and behind these buildings, 12 huge storehouses were built to hold incoming shells prior to their being filled with explosives.

In 1921 William Bradford Williams offered the following description of the Belcoville plant and its extensive safety features:

> In explosives plants where the hazard is great and danger from fire and explosion is ever present, great care must be given to safe-guarding the lives of the employees. For this reason the village and magazines were placed considerable distances from the plant. The 75mm, 155mm and eight-inch plants were each divided into four units, with intervening spaces of about 500 feet. These units were again sub-divided into three units with a receiving building at one end in which were stored one day's supply of shell, and in which the shells were cleaned, painted, stenciled and prepared for loading. Exhaust systems for carrying off the paint fumes were installed. The shells were then carried by gravity conveyors to a central building. To this building was sent by continuous delivery in small quantities the T.N.T. and ammonium nitrate. The ammonium nitrate was crushed to a fine powder, thoroughly dried and delivered to the kettle rooms where it was mixed with melted T.N.T. These kettle rooms were separated from the other portions of the building by heavy fire-walls of brick. The mixed amatol was delivered to the extruding machines, each of which were separated from the others by heavy concrete walls so that any explosion would be confined to one compartment. Swinging doors, opening outward, were placed directly opposite the workmen's stations and from high floors sufficient slides were placed to permit the workman to get clear in the shortest space of time. In all cases explosives and loaded shells were handled in the smallest quantities that would permit

of rapid production. Ventilating systems were placed through out, keeping the air free from fumes and gases. Care was used that there was no ground obstruction so that workmen could get away from buildings without danger. There was a well-equipped dispensary with X-ray operating equipment and beds to take care of all accident cases, and ample ambulance service. This was in charge of a qualified surgeon and assistants.

Workmen were not permitted to wear their street clothing in the plant but were required to change to working clothes and also to bathe before leaving the plant. This was to prevent T.N.T. poisoning which is one of the results of careless handling of this material. Workmen also had to undergo an examination by competent physicians before being employed. So rigid were these precautions that not a single case of poisoning developed.

In July 1918 the first 155 mm shell was loaded at the Belcoville plant. The daily shell-loading capacity for the three plants was 25,000 from the 75 mm plant, 12,000 from the 155 mm plant, and 4,000 from the 8-inch plant. Production continued without interruption until November 1918, when the armistice was signed, bringing the war to a close. By the time the war ended, 70 percent of the buildings in the munitions plant had been built and 50 percent of the loading machinery had been installed. At a cost of over $14 million, the construction of the plant and town (which included 434 buildings) was accomplished in less than six months, a testimony to what can be done in the face of necessity.

Belcoville continued operation until February 15, 1919, when an order was issued that closed all loading operations at the plant. At that time, the U.S. government took control of the plant and changed the name to the Mays Landing General Ordnance Depot. Belcoville was destined to become an ordnance storage area for a short period. Eventually all the buildings were torn down or sold, and all metal, including the rail lines, was salvaged.

After the war, all of the houses of Belcoville were auctioned off, with most selling for $300–$500. Although 80 of the original houses of Belcoville remain on their original sites, many were dismantled and carted away to nearby towns. In 1921 the U.S. government divided and sold the Belcoville tract. As time went on, the land was further divided and changed hands many times. Today the largest section of the property, including the site of the shell-loading plant, is in the hands of the Atlantic County Park system. The old building foundations of the plant are still visible, scattered throughout the park.

About the same time that Belcoville was being constructed at the Mays Landing site, the Atlantic Loading Company was establishing the Amatol Shell Loading Plant and town four miles east of Hammonton. Amatol, which was constructed beginning on March 5, 1918, was named for the explosives to be used at the plant: ammonium nitrate and trinitrotoluene (T.N.T.). During the construction of the town and plant, 3,000–5,500 people, including 1,800 enlisted men, were employed at Amatol. As at Belcoville, the first efforts of the workers included establishing 50 miles of track, temporary living quarters for the construction workers, and heating, water, electric, and sewage systems for both the town and the plant.

The Amatol industrial complex, which would include a 75mm plant, 155 mm plant, 8-inch plant, 4.7-inch plant, booster plant, hand grenade plant, and rifle grenade plant, was destined to be the largest shell-loading plant of its day in the country. The plant complex would cover an area of 2,550 acres and include 642 buildings, while the town covered 350 acres and included 465 structures.

By July 31, 1918, enough factory buildings, residences, and utilities had been completed to start production, and on August 3, the first shell was loaded at Amatol. As at Belcoville the functions of the Amatol plant consisted of loading, assembling, and packing fixed ammunition. The Amatol plant had a daily capacity to load 60,000 shells of all sizes, plus 50,000 boosters, 50,000 hand grenades, and 20,000 rifle grenades.

The town, which was located two miles east of the plant, was designed to hold a potential population of 25,000, though it never included more than 5,500 and was only one-third complete by the time the war ended. Many of the Amatol workers were recruited from the local community, as noted by the *South Jersey Republican* in its publication of March 9, 1918: "The wages offered for ordinary help is 35 cents per hour, and up to something over a hundred dollars per month, are attracting help from (Hammonton) farms and those employed in clerical positions."

Although the town of Amatol was built in a matter of months, it was designed to be attractive and stimulating to its residents. The center of the town was Liberty Court, a shopping mall that lit up at night and included 21 commercial shops, several restaurants, grocery store, post office, and a 950-seat theater. The residential section of the town included single- and multiple-family dwellings, dormitories, cafeterias, bunkhouses, a school, and a church. There were four YMCAs, seven hospitals, a swimming pool, tennis courts, and a bowling alley. A description of a women's dormitory provided in Victor Hammel's *Construction and Operation of a Shell Loading Plant and the Town of Amatol, New Jersey* offers an indication of the care taken by the company to create an environment pleasing to its workers:

> Dignified, yet simple in its exterior, it is arranged throughout for comfortable living. A big living room 60 feet in length, has a fire place at each end and simple but attractive furnishings. The room includes a piano, long tables, lounges and easy chairs and leading from it are numerous little alcove rooms for entertaining. The building is "H" shaped, its center being given to the living room, a sun parlor and general rooms, while its two side wings contain the dormitory rooms, each for one occupant only; and its furnishings includes bed, bureau, table and chair.

Hammel goes on to explain that each dormitory included a laundry, kitchen, infirmary, telephones, and shower and toilet facilities—certainly a greater range of conveniences than were available to most local citizens at the time.

As the company recognized that Amatol would have to be dismantled sooner or later, all construction was of a temporary nature. The general method of construction of the buildings in the residential area was cement stucco applied on a composite metal lath. The lath was a mesh of steel wire over which clay had been pressed and baked. The material was flexible and came rolled in strips 40 inches

LIBERTY COURT

(Illustrated by Berminna Solem)

wide and 16 feet in length. In the wall construction of the buildings, the stucco/metal lath was nailed to studding and the lath then covered with stucco.

Like Belcoville, Amatol was to have a short though productive life. By the time the armistice had been signed in November 1918, the Amatol plant had loaded 9 million rounds of ammunition. In March 1919, the U.S. government took title to Amatol and began to dismantle the town and plant, salvaging what it could. Some of the houses were moved to Hammonton and Elwood, but most were simply torn down. Only the administration building survived, later becoming a barracks for the New Jersey State Police. Today the town site, where the foundations of many of the old structures are still visible, includes a large sandpit used for recreational purposes by ATV and dirt bike riders.

In 1926 Charles Schwab, president of the Bethlehem Steel Company, purchased a portion of the land on which the Amatol plant had been situated. He built a "wooden bowl" speedway—an oval 1.5 miles long and 50 feet wide—to handle speeds of 60 miles per hour. The track, called the Atlantic City Speedway, was billed as "the fastest board track in the country" and was considered the largest one on the East Coast. The speedway, which opened on May

1, 1926, boasted automobile, stock car, and motorcycle races. The grandstand was reportedly 75 to 80 feet high and capable of seating 60,000 fans, with standing room for 250,000 spectators. Great names of the racing world drove at the Atlantic City Speedway, and a number of world records were established there. In spite of the promise it seemed to hold, the track never drew the crowds expected and was forced to close down on May 30, 1928.

After the speedway closed, the track was used as a testing ground for automobile manufacturers. In 1933 the oval track was torn down and the lumber sold. Later, the Hammonton Fire Company burned down what remained of the speedway.

Today the oval track of the speedway can still be seen in aerial photos of the Hammonton area. Some of the remains of the Amatol plant are still visible within the oval of the old speedway. Although portions of the track are owned publicly by the Division of Fish and Wildlife, other sections, including the Amatol plant ruins, are in private hands.

WEYMOUTH, BELCOVILLE, AND AMATOL SIDE TRIPS

VISIT THE HISTORIC RENAULT WINERY

To enjoy a wonderful meal and learn about winemaking, stop off at the historic Renault Winery in Egg Harbor Township. Established in 1864, it is the oldest continuously operating winery in the United States. The Renault Winery complex now includes two restaurants, a gift shop, a wine store, a four-star hotel, and an 18-hole golf course. Tours of the winery, which run daily, take you through the winemaking process and culminate in a wine tasting. To get to Renault Winery from Weymouth Furnace Park, travel north on Route 559 a short distance until the road forks. At the fork, stay to the right and take Route 623 (Weymouth/Elwood Road) for approximately 5.7 miles (passing over the White Horse Pike) until you reach Route 561 (Moss Mill Road). Turn right on Moss Mill Road and drive six miles until you see a large wine barrel and sign for the Renault Winery on your left. Turn left on Bremen Avenue and drive approximately half a mile to the entrance of the Renault Winery on your right. The

Tuscany House Hotel and Joseph's Restaurant (both part of the Renault complex) are located across the road from the winery. To contact Renault Winery, visit its Web site at www. renaultwinery.com or call 609-965-2111.

PADDLE THE GREAT EGG HARBOR RIVER

There is no better way to arrive at Weymouth than by canoe or kayak. To enjoy a relaxing and scenic paddle down the Great Egg Harbor River, launch your boat at Penny Pot, located approximately 4.5 miles west of Weymouth. The trip will take approximately three to four hours if you take out at Weymouth Furnace Park. To reach Penny Pot from Weymouth, drive west on the Black Horse Pike (Route 322) 4.5 miles to the Route 561 spur. Bear right on Route 561 and drive a short distance to the light. Turn right onto Eighth Street, and the boat launch area (Atlantic County Park at Penny Pot) will be a short distance on the right. Canoes and kayaks can be rented from Winding River Campgrounds, located two miles south of Weymouth on Route 559. To contact Winding River Campgrounds, call 609-625-3191.

LAKE LENAPE

If you're looking for a great place for some bird-watching, hiking, or camping or to just enjoy a scenic picnic lunch, visit Lake Lenape, located 5.4 miles south of Weymouth. Swimming is not permitted at this Atlantic County park, but boats may be launched from the park's boathouse dock. Any boat with a motor, however, must apply for a yearly permit. To reach Lake Lenape from Weymouth, drive south on Route 559 for approximately 5.4 miles. The park entrance will be on your left side. For information about the park, call 609-625-8219.

ESTELLVILLE GLASS WORKS RUINS

Located within the boundaries of the Atlantic County Park at Estell Manor are the interpretive ruins of the Estellville Glass Works. In 1825, John H. Scott built the glass works on land owned by the Estell family. In 1834, Daniel Estell bought the glass works from Scott, operating it successfully for the next two decades. Glass was shipped (in sailing vessels owned by the Estell family) to New York and Philadelphia via Stephen's Creek. The glass works was made up of about 15 buildings, which included 10 to 12 houses lived in by the workers of the village. The glass works ruins that remain today include those of the pot house, the melting house, and the flattening house. Signage that interprets the making of glass at Estellville is displayed in front of the remains of each of these buildings. The owner's mansion and company store still stand today on Route 50, in the nearby village of Estell Manor, just south of the park entrance.

The Estell family sold the glass works in 1860. After passing through many hands, the glass works closed its doors in 1887. The Estellville Glass Works ruins can be easily accessed on the paved loop road that circles through the southern end of the park. For more information about the Atlantic County Park at Estell Manor, call 609-645-5960.

Ruins of Estellville Glass Works, 2003.
(*Photo by Gordon Stull*)

REFERENCES

Beck, Henry Charlton. 1937. *More Forgotten Towns of Southern New Jersey*. New Brunswick, NJ: Rutgers University Press.

Berkey, Joan. 2003. "Nomination to the National Register of Historic Places, Bethlehem Loading Company Historic District (draft)."

Berkey, Joan. 2003. "Nomination to the National Register of Historic Places, Weymouth Archaeological District (draft)."

Bernstein, Herbert, and Wilson, Joseph. "Amatol: Last of the Pine Barren Ghost Towns." *Batsto Citizens Gazette*, Spring/Summer 1981.

Boucher, Jack. 1963. *Absegami Yesteryear*. Egg Harbor, NJ: The Atlantic County Historical Society.

Connolly, Charlie. *Amatol, Hammonton, NJ*. apnostalgia.crosswinds.net/amatol.html

Csere, Stephen. 1995. *The History of Weymouth Township*. Somers Point, NJ: Atlantic City Historical Society.

Dash, Judi, and Schensul, Jill. 1994. *Country Roads of New Jersey: Drives, Day Trips and Weekend Excursions*. Lincolnwood, IL: Country Roads Press.

Gise, Wayne. "The Town That Came from Nowhere." *Atlantic City Press*, November 18, 1979.

Hammel, Victor F. 1918. *Construction and Operation of a Shell Loading Plant and the Town of Amatol, New Jersey*. New York: Atlantic Loading Company.

Johnson, Robert F. 2001. *Weymouth, New Jersey: A History of the Furnace, Forge and Paper Mills*. Kearney, NE: Morris Publishing.

Pepper, Adeline. 1971. *The Glass Gaffers of New Jersey*. New York: Charles Scribner's Sons.

Pierce, Arthur D. 1964. *Family Empire in Jersey Iron: The Richards Enterprises in the Pine Barrens*. New Brunswick, NJ: Rutgers University Press.

Rigby, Paul, and Benner, Robert. *Amatol History Site Home Page*. July 24, 2003. William J. Spangler Library at Atlantic Cape Community College, Mays Landing, NJ, December 19, 2003. venus.atlantic.edu/amatol

U.S. Army Corps of Engineers. "Finding for the Former Bethlehem Loading Company." Mays Landing, NJ, January 1997 (Project No. CO2NJ097301).

Williams, Bradford. 1921. *Munitions Manufacture in the Philadelphia Ordnance District*. Philadelphia: A. Pomerantz & Company.

Wilson, Michael. *Belcoville Loading Plant*. Stockton State College, 1979.

Winslow, Carl. "Amatol—World War I Marvel." *Batsto Citizens Gazette*, Summer/Fall 1990.

Batsto, Allaire, and wheaton villages

Living History in the Pines

Batsto, Allaire, and Wheaton Villages

When visiting the old ghost towns of the Pines, it is often difficult to envision the glory years when these self-sufficient villages were brimming with life. Where once a towering furnace and a grand mansion stood, today little more exists than a few cellar holes, a barely visible sluiceway, and some scattered brick and iron slag. Although little has been done to safeguard what's left of most of these rapidly vanishing remains, the state of New Jersey has managed to preserve at least two of the old iron towns of the Pines. Complete with a restored sawmill, gristmill, company stores, workers' homes, mansions, blacksmith shops, a blast furnace, and other structures, the villages of Allaire and Batsto provide living history museums for anyone interested in learning more about the history of the Pine Barrens.

Along with visits to Batsto and Allaire, those interested in the old industries of the Pine Barrens should plan an excursion to the replicated Victorian village of Wheaton, located in Millville, New Jersey. Here visitors can watch as artisans demonstrate and discuss traditional glassmaking techniques.

At each of the villages, free maps are available that will guide the visitor and provide interesting information about each of the buildings on the grounds. Demonstrations by individuals proficient in 19th-century carpentry, blacksmithing, glassblowing, pottery making, and lumber milling are scheduled regularly. Tours of both mansions (at Batsto and Allaire) are also regularly scheduled. Both Batsto and Allaire have small museums offering exhibits and information about the two villages. The recently renovated visitors center at Batsto also houses a theater, which features a 10-minute film on the history of the village. A museum housing 6,500 American glass objects, including many historical pieces, is located at Wheaton Village.

Generally, tours of the three villages are self-guided. In addition, tours for groups can be arranged by contacting the visitor center at each location.

BATSTO VILLAGE

OVERVIEW AND WALKING TOUR

On land used by Native Americans as early as 5,000 years ago, the industrial village of Batsto grew during the 18th and 19th centuries. Destined to have a crucial role in the Revolutionary War as a principal munitions maker for the Continental Army, Batsto was the site of one of the earliest bog iron furnaces to be built in southern New Jersey.

In 1766 Charles Read, recognizing the bounty of resources located on the site, built an ironworks on the banks of the Batsto River. Four years later John Cox, a Philadelphia businessman, acquired the ironworks. During the war years, Cox, who was involved in the patriot cause, made munitions for the Continental Army. William Richards acquired the ironworks around 1784, thus beginning a family dynasty at Batsto that would last 92 years.

Under William Richards's leadership, Batsto enjoyed its most prosperous years. During the peace years, the Batsto Furnace made pig iron, stoves, and a variety of hollowware. In 1809 William Richards retired, turning over the management of the ironworks to his son, Jesse.

In 1846, anticipating the end of the iron years, Jesse Richards built a glass works at Batsto. The glass works, which produced window glass, was so successful that Jesse built a second glass works there in 1848. That same year the iron furnace went out of blast for the last time, but the glass works continued to function successfully until Jesse's death in 1854. The Batsto Glass Works, under the management of Jesse's son, Thomas, continued to operate until 1867. During its later years of operation, the company encountered a series of calamities that brought it into receivership by 1868. In 1874 Batsto experienced a disastrous fire that ended all hopes for the revival the village as an industrial center.

In 1876 a Philadelphia industrialist, Joseph Wharton, purchased Batsto. Wharton had plans to dam the rivers and streams of the Pine

getting to Batsto village

From the West
Take Route 73 to Route 30 (White Horse Pike) East. After passing the intersection of Routes 206 and 54 near Hammonton, continue on Route 30 approximately 1.2 more miles to Route 542. Make a left turn and drive 6.9 miles to Batsto Village.

From the South via the Garden State Parkway
Take the Garden State Parkway North to exit 50 (New Gretna). Take Route 9 North and proceed for approximately 1.1 miles. Turn left onto Route 542 and continue for approximately 11.7 miles. Batsto Village will be on your right.

From the North via the Garden State Parkway
Take the Garden State Parkway South to exit 52 (New Gretna). Turn right at the stop sign onto East Greenbush Road (CR 654). Make a left at the next stop sign onto Stage Road. After two small wooden bridges, Pilgrim Lake Campground will be on your right. Bear left onto Leektown Road (CR 653). Take Leektown Road to Route 542. Turn right onto Route 542 West. Stay on Route 542 for approximately nine miles. Batsto Village will be on your right.

From the North
Take Route 206 South to mile marker 3 and make a left onto CR 613. Proceed 2.4 miles to the first intersection (a brown Batsto sign is at the intersection). Turn left and drive two-tenths of a mile to the "T." Turn left onto Route 693. Continue on Route 693 until the deadend (approximately 2.7 miles). Turn left onto Route 542 and travel 4.4 miles to Batsto Village.

Barrens and pipe the water to Philadelphia. Thwarted in this attempt by
the New Jersey legislature, Wharton instead farmed the land. Wharton
also remodeled the mansion, which he used as a weekend and summer
residence. After Wharton's death in 1909, the Girard Trust Company
(acting on behalf of the Wharton heirs) managed the property. The state
of New Jersey purchased the Batsto tract from the Wharton heirs in the
mid-1950s for the purpose of developing it into a historic site.

After arriving at Batsto, obtain a village map at the visitors center. Batsto guidebooks are also available for sale in the visitors center
if you are interested in a more in-depth description of the village and
its existing buildings.

A good place to start your tour of Batsto (after spending some time
in the small museum in the visitors center) is at the mansion, or "Big
House." When it is open, the Batsto historians or volunteers offer
regular guided tours of the mansion throughout the day. The guided
mansion tours include interesting information about the village as
well as the house.

The Batsto mansion was the home of the Richards family for 92
years. The present structure, believed to have been built by the
Richards family in sections, may also include a portion constructed

Batsto mansion, 2004.
(*Photo by Gordon Stull*)

prior to their ownership. When Wharton purchased the property, he extensively remodeled and enlarged the dwelling to include the front and side porch that exists today. Wharton also divided the dwelling into two sections, the main house to the west and the caretaker's quarters on the east. The mansion, which is today furnished as it would have looked during the Wharton era, has 36 rooms, including a secret room that, legend has it, who was once used to house runaway slaves. This seems unlikely as both William and Jesse Richards owned slaves who worked in the mansion.

Down the hill from the mansion is the Batsto general store/post office. The store was built in two sections, the eastern end predating the Revolutionary War and the western end added in 1846–1847. Originally the company store was on the second level, where the post office is located today, and the first floor was used for storage and the sale of flour and meal milled at the Batsto gristmill. The store sold groceries, clothing and fabric, crockery and glass, toys, medicine, soap, boots and shoes, hardware, stationery, candy, animal feed, tobacco, and garden seeds. During the prosperous years, four or more ships docked at Batsto Landing (located one mile below the town)

Batsto general store, 2004.
(*Photo by Gordon Stull*)

every week, laden with goods for the village store. Most of the wages paid at Batsto were paid in store credits, by which the workers and their families could make purchases at the company store. A post office located in the store was established at Batsto in 1852 and operated until 1911.

Across from the store is the gristmill—an important structure in all Pine Barrens villages of the 18th and 19th centuries. This Batsto gristmill was built in 1828. It was originally operated by a water wheel and later (sometime after 1832) driven by a turbine (a horizontal,

Batsto gristmill, 2003.
(*Photo by Gordon Stull*)

metal waterwheel). The Batsto gristmill is still in working condition, able to grind corn into meal and wheat into flour.

The blacksmith and wheelwright shops—also integral parts of every self-sufficient community of the 18th and 19th centuries— were built at Batsto around 1850. The two separate structures were combined and moved to their present location during the Wharton years. The blacksmith shod horses, fashioned iron rims for wagon wheels, made iron rings for barrels, and forged hand-wrought nails. He also made special bolts and parts for machinery and wagons, window grating, and scale weights. The wheelwright made wooden wagon wheels from the lumber milled at the sawmill.

Joseph Wharton erected the present Batsto sawmill in 1882. The village sawmill produced the lumber to build many of the structures and other wooden items needed by the plantation. Lumber products such as planking and shingling, as well as cordwood and charcoal, were produced at Batsto and shipped to the major cities for sale. The equipment within the present Batsto sawmill can still be operated to produce cedar shingles, siding, and other wood products. During the warmer seasons, demonstrations are offered on weekends several times daily.

The 1846–1871 Batsto rent rolls indicate there were 77 workers' houses located on six different streets. Today only 17 houses on two streets remain. The most common worker's house in Batsto was a two-story single frame dwelling with two rooms on the first floor, one that served as a common room (or kitchen in the early years) and one that was used as either a parlor or an extra bedroom. In the mid to late 19th century, an addition was built onto the back of the houses and used as a separate kitchen. There were two bedrooms and a hall on the second floor, and a privy was located behind the house. Each tenant had a good-sized garden plot, and everyone kept a few chickens or had a pigpen in the backyard.

On the average each household consisted of a married couple, four children, grandparents, and possibly a single male boarder. Today several of the cottages have been furnished as typical Batsto workers' homes of the mid-1800s and are open to the public. Several of the other worker cottages—open to the public on occasion—have been set up to house craftsmen such as weavers and potters.

Batsto sawmill, 2003.
(*Photo by Gordon Stull*)

Batsto workers' homes, 2003.
(*Photo by Gordon Stull*)

A DEEPER LOOK

The name Batsto, derived from the Swedish word "Badstu," meaning "bathing place," is believed to have been used by the Lenni-Lenape, who first inhabited the area, to describe the land that would eventually become an industrial center of the 18th and 19th centuries. Some historians believe that the Lenape adopted the word after coming into contact with early Swedish settlers. Others, however, believe it was the Native Americans who first used the word, pronouncing it "Baastoo" or "Baatsoo," and that it was the Europeans who borrowed the expression after hearing it from the Lenape. Regardless of the name's origin, Batsto was a place rich in natural resources, as was quickly discovered by early European settlers in the area.

Charles Read, South Jersey merchant, legislator, and land speculator, knew he had found the perfect place for an iron furnace when he became acquainted with the Batsto tract. The land boasted miles of forest, an abundant water supply, and numerous swamps and streams filled with bog ore just waiting to be mined. The land was also close to tidewater, offering an ocean transport system for the goods that Charles Read planned to produce at the ironworks. The tract had previously been the site of several sawmills, one built as early as 1739.

Soon after receiving permission from the legislature to dam the Batsto River in 1766, Charles Read built his furnace. Although the fledgling ironworks prospered, within two years Read had sold his share in the Batsto enterprise to his four business partners. Read (having invested heavily in three other ironworks) was soon to leave the area after declaring bankruptcy.

In 1770 John Cox, in partnership with Charles Thompson, purchased the Batsto Ironworks. By 1773 Cox had hired William Richards, a foundry worker from Eastern Pennsylvania, to manage his furnace. Richards, who had spent a year working at Batsto five years earlier, now came to stay and moved his family to the area. Richards also brought with him his young nephew, Joseph Ball, who would soon play an important role in the management of the ironworks.

By 1775 Richards, who was committed to the patriot cause, had moved back to Pennsylvania to be closer to the conflict that was quickly heating up between the American colonists and the British.

After Richards's departure, Ball succeeded his uncle as manager of the Batsto Ironworks.

During the prewar years, Batsto made pig iron, stoves, hollowware (such as skillets and kettles), and other household necessities such as pestles, mortars, and sash weights. Soon, however, Cox, who was also involved in the patriot cause, began making products for the Continental Army. Turning away from peacetime products, the furnace began to produce cannons, cannon balls, iron fastenings and fittings for wagons and ships, large shallow pans (for evaporating ocean water to obtain salt for use by the troops to preserve food), and numerous other products needed by the military. Batsto soon became so important to the war effort that the workers of the village were given exemption from military obligation. Cox was authorized to establish a company of 50 men and two lieutenants, with himself as captain, to be activated only in the case of invasion.

By 1778 Batsto, along with The Forks, became the object of a military invasion planned by the British. Even though the British were on their way upriver, they turned back before reaching the area. (See Chapter 6, "The Forks to Hermann," for more about this episode.)

Around 1779 Joseph Ball, who was only 32 at the time, and two partners—both high-level officers in the Continental Army—acquired the Batsto Ironworks. Today the involvement of two military officers in the ownership of an ironworks that was producing large quantities of munitions for the army would be considered a serious conflict of interest; in 1779 it apparently did not even raise an eyebrow.

In 1781 Joseph Ball dammed the Nescochaque Creek (on the site of a sawmill built there in 1739) and built a forge. The iron produced at Batsto could now be shaped into useful wrought iron products.

By 1781 the Americans had won their struggle for independence from the British. John Cox had become a person of great importance during the conflict with the British, having been elected lieutenant colonel of the 2nd battalion and later being appointed assistant quartermaster general. It is also believed that William Richards spent the winter of 1778–1779 with George Washington at Valley Forge.

In 1781 William Richards returned to Batsto, first as manager and later, in 1784, as owner of the ironworks. Richards rebuilt the furnace and erected a mansion on the hill for himself and his family. The mansion soon became known as the Big House to the workers of the iron village.

Under William Richards's leadership, Batsto prospered and, at its peak, had a population of over 500 people. It is reported that although Batsto was run like a feudal village, a citizen of the town had only to put in a request at the Big House if medical or legal assistance was needed. It is noted in the Batsto account books that a schoolmaster was hired to provide education to the children of the village as early as 1782. The nearby church in Pleasant Mills provided the villagers with spiritual comfort, and the company store provided the necessary staples of life, including food and clothing.

By 1784 Batsto returned to making peacetime products, such as stoves and hollowware.

William Richards continued to operate the ironworks until 1809, when he turned over management to his son Jesse. William, who was by then 71, retired to Mt. Holly with his second wife, Margaretta, and several of their children. He continued to lead a full and busy life in retirement, and not the least of his later accomplishments was the fathering of two more children.

When William retired and moved to Mt. Holly, Jesse, with his family, moved into the Big House. With the advent of the War of 1812, Batsto once more turned to the task of supplying the American military with munitions.

In 1823 William Richards died at the age of 84. By the time of his death, he had been married twice and sired 19 children. After his death, Batsto was sold at auction to one of his grandsons, Jesse Richards's nephew, Thomas S. Richards. Thomas promptly hired his uncle Jesse to manage the ironworks. Jesse continued to live in the Big House with his family and within six years was able to purchase a one-half share of the ironworks.

Recognizing that the South Jersey bog iron industry was in decline, Jesse built a glass works at Batsto in 1846 and a second one in 1848. In 1848 the iron furnace went out of blast for the last time due to depletion of raw materials, obsolescence of methods and equipment, and transportation problems. During the 1840s Batsto had its own brickworks and even engaged in some shipbuilding, launching its own schooner, the *Frelinghusen*, in 1844.

In 1852, during the heyday of the Batsto Glass Works, the town had a population of 376 people, who lived in 75 houses scattered over six village streets. Both glass works continued to operate successfully until 1854, the year of Jesse's death.

After Jesse's death, his son, Thomas H. Richards, continued to operate the Batsto Glass Works, although his main interests lay in politics and public life rather than in industry. Soon the Batsto Glass Works began to decline, and the workers of the village began to demand cash instead of store credit. Transportation problems also developed as an anticipated rail line failed to materialize. Thomas tried to prevent bankruptcy by selling off tracts of land to pay creditors, but his efforts were too little, too late. Soon, workers whose income had been cut or was nonexistent began to leave, and the buildings of the village began to fall apart. By 1868 Batsto, with its enterprises at a standstill, was in receivership, and the Richardses' 92-year dynasty had come to an end. In 1874 a fire burned down what was left of the glass works and iron furnace as well as 17 workers' homes.

Two years later the village was sold to Joseph Wharton, a Philadelphia industrialist, for $14,000. Wharton had begun buying up properties in the New Jersey Pine Barrens, hoping to dam its rivers and streams, thereby creating vast reservoirs of water, which he planned to export to Philadelphia. When the New Jersey legislature got wind of Wharton's intentions, it quickly passed legislation to prohibit water from leaving the state. With his waterworks plan thwarted, Wharton began to focus on agriculture, raising sugar beets and cranberries and taking up livestock breeding on his New Jersey properties.

Wharton transformed the Batsto ironmaster's mansion (at a cost of $40,000) into an elegant Victorian country house. The Batsto country residence was used by Wharton and his family on weekends and during summer vacations. During the Wharton years, the workers' houses were rented for $2 a month.

By the time of Wharton's death in 1909, he had accumulated 112,000 acres of land within the New Jersey Pine Barrens. Some 6,000 acres of the Wharton tract, located near Elwood, were eventually sold

Batsto mansion during the Wharton years.
(*Photo courtesy of the Burlington County Library*)

to the Atlantic Loading Company for the erection of the Amatol munitions plant.

In 1912 the Wharton heirs attempted to sell 112,000 acres of their New Jersey land holdings to the state for $1 million. This deal was defeated in a referendum in 1915. In the early 1950s the United States Air Force attempted to establish a giant jetport supply depot on 17,000 acres of land immediately surrounding Batsto. Recognizing the treasure of the Wharton tract, the New Jersey government quickly dismissed this plan and once more began making efforts to purchase the Wharton tract. By 1956, in two separate land acquisition deals, the state of New Jersey had purchased the 96,000-acre Wharton tract at a cost of $3 million. Within the year the state launched an ambitious restoration project for the historic village of Batsto.

ALLAIRE VILLAGE

OVERVIEW AND WALKING TOUR

On land once inhabited by the Lenni-Lenape sits the historic village of Allaire. Recognizing the area as rich in natural resources, the early European settlers established a sawmill on the site that became known as Allaire by 1750. By 1800 the ironmongers came to take advantage of the rich beds of bog ore that could be found along the rivers and streams of the area. The Williamsburg Forge was erected on the property in 1803, and in 1812 the Monmouth Furnace was established there. In 1822, James Allaire, a New York City businessman, bought the Monmouth Furnace and its surrounding 5,000 acres.

During the period of his ownership, Allaire made many improvements to the ironworks, which he renamed the Howell Works. By the 1830s, the Howell Works and the self-sufficient village that Allaire created there provided a living for as many as 400 people. The ironworks and village prospered until 1836, when a series of calamities, including the death of Allaire's first wife, Frances, and the financial panic of 1837, caused him to suffer both personal and financial setbacks. Shortly thereafter the discovery of anthracite coal near the magnetite rock ore deposits of Pennsylvania and Northern New Jersey caused the New Jersey bog iron industry to go into decline. By 1846 the Howell Works ceased operation, and by 1850, Allaire had lost financial control of his company in New York City.

In 1846 Allaire remarried and, after being ousted from his New York firm, he and his wife Calicia and young son Hal retired permanently to his country home at the Howell Works. After Allaire's death in 1858, his wife and son continued to live at the Howell Works among the crumbling buildings of the former industrial center. By the time of Hal's death in 1901, only 16 of the original 25 buildings of the old village were still standing.

In 1907, Arthur Brisbane, a well-known journalist of the Hearst newspaper chain, purchased Allaire Village. Brisbane revitalized the village by building a large country estate on its grounds and refurbishing many of the old buildings as housing for his large staff. After Arthur's death, his wife, Phoebe, deeded 1,200 acres to the state to be used as a forest preserve and historic center.

getting to Allaire village

From the West
Take I-95 East to exit 31-B (Farmingdale/Allaire State Park). After you exit, turn right at the first traffic light onto Atlantic Avenue (Route 524). Continue on Atlantic Avenue for approximately one mile. The entrance to Allaire Village is on the right.

From the South via the Garden State Parkway
Take the Garden State Parkway North to exit 98. Follow the signs for I-95 West/Trenton. Take I-95 west to exit 31-B (Farmingdale/Allaire State Park). After you exit, turn right at the first traffic light onto Atlantic Avenue (Route 524). Continue on Atlantic Avenue for approximately one mile. The entrance to Allaire Village is on the right.

From the North via the Garden State Parkway
Take the Garden State Parkway South to exit 98 and turn onto Route 34 South. Turn right at the first traffic light onto Allenwood Road. Follow Allenwood Road to a "T" intersection. Turn right onto Atlantic Avenue (Route 524). Continue on Atlantic Avenue, crossing over the Parkway, for about one mile. The entrance to Allaire Village is on the left.

Today 13 buildings within the historic Village of Allaire have been restored, providing visitors with a good view of a 19th-century ironworks village. Allaire Village is a living history museum where, in season, volunteers in period dress provide tours of buildings and offer narrated demonstrations within the old carpentry and blacksmith shops.

The Allaire visitors center and museum is located in a restored row of 11 workers' homes. The interior of the first house in the row has been set up to resemble what a worker's home would have looked like in the 1830s. This row of houses, which includes the largest of the homes established for the workers of the village, was inhabited by the most skilled or privileged employees. These privileged few enjoyed the luxury of private kitchens. There were four blocks of row houses at Allaire, including two units of eight homes, one unit of 11, and one unit of five. The workers of the village did not own their homes but paid rent for them, about $1 to $2 a month.

The museum features information on the life of James Allaire, the ironmaking process at the Howell Works, and the development of the village. An interesting highlight within the museum is a diorama that

Allaire visitors center and row of workers' homes, 2004.
(*Photo by Gordon Stull*)

depicts workers inside the casting shed (the building that housed the blast furnace).

Obtain a map of the village and walk to the church, which served as a schoolhouse during the week. The church-schoolhouse was built in two parts, the southern half in 1832 and the northern half in 1836. The minister of the church also served as the schoolmaster and in 1835 was paid $500 a year for his dual responsibilities. At times there were more than 100 children attending the school, with all grades being taught in the same room. The school used the Lancasterian method, in which the older children taught the younger children, with the teacher acting as overseer. Today the Allaire chapel, which is open regularly to visitors, may be rented for functions such as weddings, christenings, and memorial services.

Some other highlights of the village include the general store, blast furnace, and the Big House, where James Allaire and his family lived after his retirement. The general store, standing four stories high, was built in 1835 at a cost of $7,000. At the time it was built, the Howell Works was said to have had the biggest store in New Jersey, rivaled only by the largest stores in New York and

Allaire church, 2004.
(*Photo by Gordon Stull*)

Philadelphia. During the iron years, general merchandise, such as dry goods, hardware, tools, shot, and medicine, was sold from the main floor of the store. The basement (which maintained a temperature of approximately 50 degrees Fahrenheit year round) contained a butcher shop and also served as cold storage for dairy products and the fruits and vegetables grown on the Allaire farm. The second floor was for larger items, such as furniture, and the third floor contained unpacked merchandise and huge bins of grain. Today the general store serves as a gift shop and bakery.

The blast furnace standing today at Allaire Village was built in 1831 and is the most complete remaining example of the early iron industry in New Jersey. At one time the blast furnace was enclosed in the casting shed, nicely depicted in the diorama located in the museum. Other buildings within the ironworks included a wheel-house, which housed large air chambers powered by a waterwheel, and a bridge house, where the raw materials were measured and stored prior to being wheeled across a trestle bridge to the furnace stack. About once every 12 hours, the furnace was tapped at the base, allowing liquid molten iron to flow out into a series of trenches or to

Allaire general store, 2004.
(*Photo by Gordon Stull*)

Allaire blast furnace, 2003.
(*Photo by Gordon Stull*)

be ladled into molds for casting purposes. The furnace operated 24 hours a day, seven days a week, for approximately nine months out of the year.

The Big House, restored in 1997, is one of the oldest buildings in the village, dating from the Monmouth Furnace era. In the 1830s it was the home of the superintendent of the Howell Works and his family. A brick dormitory was constructed in 1835 and attached to the house to provide rooms for the single workers of the Works. The

Big House at Allaire, 2004.
(*Photo by Gordon Stull*)

Big House was the residence used by James Allaire when he visited the village in the early years and also the home he resided in after his retirement. During Brisbane's tenancy, the Big House served as a caretaker's residence.

A DEEPER LOOK

Located on the banks of the Manasquan River in Monmouth County, the historic village of Allaire is situated on land once inhabited by the Lenni-Lenape Indians. By 1750 a sawmill was located there, and by 1800 European settlers, interested in the rich iron deposits to be found in the riverbanks and swamps of the area, had arrived. The Williamsburg Forge was established in 1803, and by 1812 the Monmouth Furnace had gone into its first blast. In 1820 William Newbold acquired Monmouth Furnace, and in 1822 he leased the ironworks to Benjamin Howell.

James Allaire, who was a business acquaintance of Benjamin Howell, had been having trouble acquiring the iron stock he needed for his manufacturing operations located in New York City. Allaire, who owned a brass foundry and a machine engine building shop, wanted to control his business from the raw materials to the finished product. When he learned of the rich resources that were to be found on the land surrounding the Monmouth Furnace, he believed he had found the solution to his problem. In 1822 Allaire purchased the Monmouth ironworks and 5,000 acres of surrounding woodland and ore beds for $19,000. The ironworks was not far from New York City and included close proximity to shipping, an important consideration with regard to getting goods to market and for importing all the necessities of life to the isolated iron village.

At the time of Allaire's purchase, the ironworks consisted of a furnace, sawmill, and 14 or 15 wooden buildings. These buildings included crude housing for the workers of the village. A larger frame house, which would later be known as the Big House, was also included and would later serve as housing for the management of the ironworks and eventually for the Allaire family.

Shortly after the purchase of the ironworks, Allaire changed the name of his new property to the Howell Works. After his purchase, Allaire began to make improvements to the little village surrounding the ironworks. Under his stewardship the village would eventually grow to include a carpenter shop, blacksmith, bakery, gristmill, additional and larger housing for the workers, a general store, a school that served as a church on Sundays, and a boarding house for single workers. By 1827 the first brick dwellings were built, including a foreman's cottage and eight small row houses. A factory for making screws and nails was added in 1831, providing employment for the women and children of the village. Children as young as eight or nine worked at the screw factory and later in the grinding and polishing mill where they could earn up to $6 a week cleaning iron wares from the furnace before they were sent to market.

The Howell Works produced the raw materials for Allaire's steam engine works in New York City and also made hollowware products, architectural castings, and water pipe. The Howell Works farm produced fresh produce for the village; excess produce was shipped to New York for Allaire's personal use and for sale. Initially, sailing ships were used to transport the Howell Works products to market; steam ships were later used, including several owned by Allaire.

Nearly 400 people were living and working at the Howell Works by the mid-1830s. Of these, 40 to 50 were fulltime workers who also lived at the ironworks. The remaining inhabitants were the family of the workers and the supplemental help who were employed seasonally. As did many other company towns, the Howell Works began issuing scrip notes as payment for wages and redeemable only in the company store.

Initially the Allaire family continued to live in New York City while James visited the village when necessary. A superintendent and foreman managed the ironworks on a daily basis. By 1834 the Allaire family had moved to the Howell Works in hopes that country living would improve Mrs. Allaire's health and to escape the cholera outbreak that was occurring in New York City and Philadelphia. James worked in New York during the week and would join his family at the Howell Works on weekends or when the ironworks required his presence. In order to provide his wife with assistance in managing the household and taking care of their children, Calicia Allaire Tompkins (a cousin of James's), joined the Allaire household.

In 1836 the Howell Works was in maximum production, but trouble lay ahead. In March 1836, Frances Allaire, James's wife of 32 years, passed away. Within two years of Frances's death, several of Allaire's steamships would run aground, causing them to be damaged beyond repair and, in one case, resulting in the loss of 90 lives.

The Panic of 1837 (which threw the nation into its first depression) created further financial problems for Allaire. Demand for his machine engine products began to dry up, and severe damage to the furnace at the Howell Works caused it to be out of blast for one and a half years. By the time the Howell furnace was back in blast, the discovery of large iron and coal deposits in Pennsylvania was having a catastrophic effect on the New Jersey bog iron industry. By 1846 the Howell furnace went out of blast for the last time. That same year Allaire remarried, choosing Calicia Tompkins—who had remained at the Howell Works after Frances's death—as his bride. At the time, Allaire was 61 and Calicia was 35. The marriage caused a great deal of upset to the Allaire children as well as to John Haggerty, Allaire's brother-in-law and main source of financial backing. Whether it was the concern over Allaire's choice of a bride or concern about the state of affairs of his businesses, Haggerty refused any further financial assistance. Apparently by 1849, through Haggerty's manipulation, Allaire had lost all financial interest in the Allaire Works, his New York City business. By 1850 the Howell Works had declared bankruptcy.

Throughout Allaire's business struggles, Calicia and their son, Hal, born October 5, 1847, lived at the Howell Works while James commuted between the Howell Works and his New York City brownstone. By 1851 Allaire was forced to give up his New York company-owned home and retired permanently to the Big House at the Howell Works. Although the company was bankrupt, Allaire had managed to buy back the property.

In 1858, at the age of 78, James Allaire died, leaving the bulk of his estate to his second wife, Calicia, and his 11-year-old son Hal. After Allaire's death all but one of his children from his first marriage contested his will. The family would be in and out of court for the next 16 years, with the court eventually deciding in favor of Calicia and Hal. By this time there was little left, as the estate was burdened with mounting debts and unpaid taxes. In 1879 Calicia died, and Hal, who had graduated from Columbia University in 1869 with a master's degree in architecture, continued to live at his family's homestead. Hal, who had never married or had children, had returned to live with his mother at the nearly deserted village of the Howell Works after finishing his education. Hal was a talented architect but spent most of his life focused on the Howell Works village and trying to pay off the estate's debts. As a way to generate income, Hal rented out houses in the dilapidated and nearly deserted village. In 1890 he allowed the former carpenter shop to be turned into a country inn, and in 1895 he created the Allaire Water Supply and Land Company. These endeavors, however, did not become the major source of income Hal had hoped for.

Prior to his death in 1901 at the age of 51, Hal sold the Allaire property to his friend William Harrison. After paying off the taxes that had long encumbered the estate, in 1907 Harrison sold the property to Arthur Brisbane, a newspaper editor at the *New York Evening Journal*, a publication of William Randolph Hearst.

Brisbane and his wife, Phoebe, built a large, contemporary home at Allaire and created a luxurious country estate that at one time included 10,000 acres. During his tenancy Brisbane renovated many of the village dwellings as homes for his large in-residence staff. Throughout the 1920s and 1930s, Arthur and Phoebe Brisbane and their five children made Allaire Village their permanent home.

In the 1940s, after Arthur Brisbane's death, 1,200 acres of the Brisbane estate were deeded by Phoebe to the state of New Jersey "to be used as an Historical Center and Forest Park reservation ... and for no other purpose." In 1944 Phoebe deeded the family home to the state to be used as a child treatment center, as it remains to this day. For nearly 14 years, the village remained deserted, decaying, and overrun with dense vegetation. It was not until 1957 that New Jersey had the necessary funds to begin restoration efforts at the historic village. The original 1,200 acres deeded to the state for use as a state park has now grown to include over 3,000 acres, thanks to New Jersey Green Acres funding.

WHEATON VILLAGE

OVERVIEW AND WALKING TOUR

Wheaton Village, located in the old glass and textile town of Millville, was originally built in honor of Theodore Corson Wheaton, pharmacist, physician, and local founder of the Wheaton Glass Company. Although not a Pine Barrens ghost town, it is included in this work for anyone who may be interested in the traditional art of glassmaking, an important early industry of the Pinelands. The highlight of Wheaton Village is a replica of the original glass works established in 1888 by Theodore Wheaton in Millville, a major area for glass production in the 19th and 20th centuries.

A visit to Wheaton Village is a pleasant day outing and learning experience for the entire family. After picking up a map at the entrance gate, head over to the T. C. Wheaton & Co. Glass Works to see narrated demonstrations of traditional glassmaking techniques by skilled artisans. The glass factory is a fully functioning studio modeled

getting to wheaton village

From the South via the Garden State Parkway

Take the Garden State Parkway North to exit 20. Take Route 50 North to Tuckahoe, turn left on Route 49, and drive for approximately 15 miles to the second traffic light in Millville. Turn right onto Wade Boulevard and follow the brown village signs to the main entrance.

From the North via the Garden State Parkway

Take the Garden State Parkway South to exit 38A. Go west on the Atlantic City Expressway toward Philadelphia to exit 12. Take Route 40 West to the intersection of Route 40 and Route 552 West. Turn left onto Route 552 and stay on this road for approximately 15 miles until reaching Millville. At the first traffic light in Millville, turn right onto Wade Boulevard and follow the brown village signs to the main entrance.

From the North

Take Route 206 South to Route 30. After crossing Route 30, Route 206 will become Route 54. Follow Route 54 to Buena, crossing Route 40. After the Route 54 and Route 40 intersection, go around a curve and bear to the left onto Route 655 (Lincoln Avenue). Stay on Route 655 until it intersects with Route 555 (Main Street). Follow the brown village signs from this point to the main entrance.

From the New Jersey Turnpike

Take the New Jersey Turnpike to exit 4. Take Route 73 North to I-295 South. Stay on I-295 until it intersects with Route 42 South. Take Route 42 to Route 55 South to exit 26. Follow the brown village signs from the exit to the main entrance.

T. C. Wheaton & Co. Glass Works, 2004.
(*Photo by Gordon Stull*)

after Wheaton's original 1888 factory. Watch glassblowers create pitchers, bottles, bowls, vases, and paperweights, all of which are available for purchase at the village.

Next to the glass factory is the Crafts Studio, where you can learn about crafts long associated with South Jersey. The Woodcarving Studio is located nearby, in front of the railroad depot. Craft workers, including potters, woodcarvers, and flameworkers, demonstrate their unique skills throughout the day as they create original works of art.

Another must-see of the village is the Museum of American Glass, home to the world's largest bottle (seven feet eight inches high, with capacity to hold 188 gallons). The Museum of American Glass is reported to house the most comprehensive collection of American glass in the country. The collection, which includes 6,500 objects on exhibit at any given time, includes examples of early American flasks and bottles as well as Tiffany masterpieces. Two Mason jars created at Crowleytown and several gothic pickle jars attributed to the Bulltown Glass Works are on display in the museum.

Within the village are the restored Palermo Railroad Station (built in 1897) and a half-scale 1863 C. P. Huntington Train, which

Glassblower at Wheaton Village, 2003.
(*Photo by Gordon Stull*)

C. P. Huntington Train at Wheaton Village, 2003.
(*Photo by Gordon Stull*)

Centre Grove Schoolhouse in Wheaton Village, 2004.
(*Photo by Gordon Stull*)

offers visitors rides through the grounds. Wheaton also features the restored 1876 Centre Grove Schoolhouse.

The Down Jersey Folklife Center, located across from the Museum of American Glass, offers exhibits and displays focused on South Jersey traditions and folk art.

The five museum stores in the village offer the visitor beautiful art objects such as one-of-a-kind crafts created by the village artists. The PaperWaiter Restaurant, located right next to the village, is a pleasant place to enjoy a meal. If the weather is good, bring a picnic lunch and eat at the tables in the picnic grove.

A DEEPER LOOK

Wheaton Village, first conceived by Frank Hayes Wheaton Jr. as a tribute to his grandfather, Theodore Corson Wheaton, was originally planned as a replicated Victorian village. A highlight of the village, which has now evolved into a center for glassmaking and other local crafts, is a replica of the glass works established by Theodore Wheaton in 1888. In comparison with other glass factories of its time, T. C.

Wheaton & Co. Glass Works initially was a small operation that stayed with the traditional method of making glass by hand until 1938, long after most glass factories had automated.

Before Theodore Wheaton entered the business of glassmaking, he explored several other career paths. As a young boy growing up in South Seaville in Cape May County, he often helped his father deliver bagged flour to the docks and wharves. Dreaming of sea adventures, Theodore left home in 1871, when he was just 19, to crew on a sailing schooner. By the third day of the voyage, terribly ill with seasickness and tired of the hazing by his crewmates who jibed him about his inexperience, he vowed that this would be his last journey. Theodore returned home and took work first as a farm laborer and then as a railroad worker before he apprenticed himself to Dr. Way, a local pharmacist and physician. By 1872 Theodore had saved $1,000—a remarkable feat considering his employment and the times—and he enrolled at the Philadelphia College of Pharmacy and Science. After completing his pharmaceutical studies, Wheaton enrolled in the University of Pennsylvania Medical School and earned his MD in 1879. Soon after finishing his education, he married and returned to South Seaville, settling into the life of a country doctor. Several years later his first son, Frank Hayes Wheaton, was born.

In 1882 Wheaton moved his family to Millville, then a thriving industrial city with a population of 9,000, where he opened a pharmacy and general store while continuing to practice medicine. While Theodore operated the pharmacy and practiced medicine, Mrs. Wheaton managed the general store and took care of the family. At the time Wheaton first opened his Millville store, glass and textile workers from local industries largely populated the town.

Managing his own pharmacy and medical practice and living in a glass town, Dr. Wheaton understandably became interested in the manufacture of pharmacists' and physicians' glassware. Five years after moving to Millville, he became involved in the financing of a Millville glass factory. In 1888 this six-pot glass furnace, so small that it covered barely an acre and a half, employed 50 men and boys. Before child labor laws came into effect, boys as young as eight worked in glass factories doing odd jobs. They were paid 46 cents a day and worked six days a week from 7:00 A.M. to 4:30 P.M. In 1890 some meager child labor laws were enacted that required any boy under 14 who worked to attend 60 nights of school in conjunction with holding down a fulltime job. Once boys reached 18, they could become apprentices to learn glassmaking skills. In payment the apprenticed workers were obligated to remain with the company for an additional four to five years after they had completed their training.

When the owners of the new glass plant that Wheaton had helped finance ran into financial difficulties, he was obliged to take over to save his investment, and by 1890 Wheaton had become the sole owner of the glass works. Calling his business T. C. Wheaton and Company, he specialized in making pharmaceutical bottles and glass tubing. Wheaton soon divested himself of his other professional and business interests to devote himself entirely to the operation of the glass works.

Under Wheaton's supervision the glass works prospered, and in 1892 he purchased a large tract of land that surrounded the factory. Part of this land, which when laid out included 25 city blocks, was set aside as a residential sector for employees interested in purchasing their own lots. A Wheaton employee could select a building lot and pay for it at a rate of $5 per week. If the purchasers changed their minds, they could receive a cash refund or transfer the amount they had paid to be used as credit at the company store. In 1894 and 1896, additional furnaces were erected, and by 1898 the company was operating three 12-pot furnaces.

In 1899 Wheaton's oldest son, Frank Hayes, entered the family business. At the time items produced by the factory included bottles, tubing, and a general line of druggists' supplies. In 1901 Theodore and his son started a window glass factory, but it soon failed due to the competition from other glass factories that had recently automated. Making window glass by automation had just begun, and this new technology put many of the hand factories out of business.

The Wheaton glass plant continued to grow, and by 1915 it occupied 20 acres. By 1916, 164 men and 21 women worked at the plant and by 1918 there were 450 employees. As the years passed, T. C. Wheaton and Company (incorporated in 1901) prospered, so much so that it was able to buy out one of its competitors, the Millville Bottle Works, in 1926.

During the first quarter of the century, Frank Hayes Wheaton traveled widely, visiting customers and other affiliated glass works. He traveled so much during those early years that his son Frank Jr. would later lament, "I can remember as a boy growing up hardly ever seeing my father during the week. He would take the Sunday afternoon train out of Millville and arrive back home either Friday night or Saturday morning. He would spend a good part of Saturday conferring with Mr. Krause, his factory manager and Saturday night and Sunday morning with us at home. This went on continuously through my younger years."

Theodore Corson Wheaton remained at the helm of his company until his death in 1931. After Theodore's death, Frank Hayes Wheaton was elected president of the company and chairman of the board of directors. In 1932 his oldest son, Frank Jr., entered the family business.

For many years the company continued to make glass using traditional glassmaking techniques. Frank Sr. and his father had remained

WHEATON GLASSBLOWER

(Illustrated by Berminna Solem)

steadfast in refusing to supplant the skilled handworkers of the company with automatic glassmaking equipment. In spite of having maintained these standards for so long, the company managed to stay profitable in the face of the competition that had already automated. Automatic glassmaking equipment was added, however, in 1938.

During World War II, Wheaton Glass produced the first blood plasma bottles. After the war, Frank Jr. established a subsidiary called the Wheaton Glass Company that specialized in the production of perfume and cosmetic containers, glass tubing, and ampoules. In 1950 the firm began experimenting with and producing plastic products. In 1958 Wheaton acquired a large old cotton mill in Mays Landing that had recently closed due to labor problems. After refurbishing the old mill, Wheaton Plastics Company began production. This division of the Wheaton enterprises grew to be so large that at one time it had three satellite plants and over 1,000 employees. At its height the factory was said to have manufactured 35 percent of all the plastic bottles used by American pharmaceutical firms.

Through four generations of Wheaton family management, the company became one of the largest privately held glass businesses in the United States. The T. C. Wheaton Glass Company was sold by the family in 1996 and today is controlled by foreign ownership.

BATSTO, ALLAIRE, AND WHEATON VILLAGES EVENTS

Batsto, Allaire, and Wheaton Villages each host a number of special events and programs throughout the year. In the following section are some of the events that occur annually at each village. For a complete list of events and programs at each of the villages, visit their Web site or call their visitor center.

BATSTO VILLAGE

One of the largest events held at Batsto Village is the Country Living Fair, held annually on the third Sunday in October. The event features crafts, exhibits, music, old time engines and cars, food, antiques, pony rides, and farm equipment. If you are interested in country art, music, and crafts, this is the festival for you.

The Antique Glass and Bottle Show is held at Batsto Village every September. The event is sponsored by the South Jersey Antique Bottle and Glass Club, Inc.

"Haunting the Pines" is a Halloween event for children 12 years old and younger. The event, featuring pumpkin carving and painting, hayrides, and apple dunking, is held annually on the Sunday before Halloween.

For more information about special events at Batsto Village, visit their Web site at www.batstovillage.org or call 609-561-0024.

ALLAIRE VILLAGE

Allaire Village annually reenacts several events that occurred at Allaire in 1836, including the marriage of Maria Allaire, the daughter of founder James Allaire. The wedding reenactment, which occurs in June, takes place in the Allaire chapel. A reception following the nuptials is held in the Big House, the former Allaire residence. A reenactment of the funeral of Frances Allaire (James Allaire's first wife) is held every March.

An annual Fall Harvest Festival is held at Allaire Village in early September. The event features cider pressing, wagon rides, apple bobbing and tossing, music, storytelling, puppet shows, and hearth cooking demonstrations.

Allaire Village hosts a Spring Crafters Market every May and an annual Fall Crafters Market every October.

For more information about special events at Allaire Village, visit its Web site at www.allairevillage.org or call 732-919-3500.

WHEATON VILLAGE

An Antiques and Collectibles Show is held every February and July at Wheaton Village. Many dealers from the mid-Atlantic states come to display and sell quality merchandise.

The Antique Fire Apparatus Show and Muster is held every August and includes a barrel slide, bucket brigade, and swap-and-sell flea market. The Antique Fire Apparatus Show and Muster is one of the largest such events on the East Coast.

The Festival of Fine Crafts is held every October at Wheaton Village. The festival is a juried show of fine traditional and contemporary crafts, with over 150 participating artists. The show runs for two days and offers craft demonstrations, children's activities, and great food.

To learn more about Wheaton Village's special events and programs, visit its Web site at www.wheatonvillage.org or call 856-825-6800.

REFERENCES

Boucher, Jack E. 1964. *Of Batsto and Bog Iron*. Batsto NJ: Batsto Citizens Committee.

Ewing, Sarah W. R. 1986. *An Introduction to Batsto*. Batsto NJ: Batsto Citizens Committee.

Historic Allaire Village: A Short History of the Life and Times of the Howell Works Co. 1999. Allaire, NJ: The Board of Trustees of Allaire Village, Inc.

McMahon, William. 1973. *South Jersey Towns*. New Brunswick, NJ: Rutgers University Press.

Pearce, John. 2000. *Heart of the Pines: Ghostly Voices of the Pine Barrens*. Hammonton, NJ: Batsto Citizens Committee, Inc.

Pepper, Adeline. 1971. *The Glass Gaffers of New Jersey*. New York: Charles Scribner's Sons.

Pierce, Arthur D. 1957. *Iron in the Pines: The Story of New Jersey's Ghost Towns and Bog Iron*. New Brunswick, NJ: Rutgers University Press.

Pierce, Arthur D. 1964. *Family Empire in Jersey Iron: The Richards Enterprises in the Pine Barrens*. New Brunswick, NJ: Rutgers University Press.

Rossi, John A. 1998. *Brief History of Glass Making and Its Impact on Southern New Jersey*. Vineland, NJ: Precision Electronic Glass Inc.

Sitkus, Hance Morton. 2002. *Images of America–Allaire*. Charleston, SC: Arcadia Publishing.

Weber, Martin C. n. d. Untitled document on history of Wheaton family found in archives of Museum of American Glass of Wheaton.

Wilson, Budd. "The Batsto Window Light Factory Excavation." *Archeological Society of New Jersey*, December 1971: 11–18.

Afterword

Researching the old towns of the New Jersey Pine Barrens has been an exciting and worthwhile journey that I would not have missed for the world. I hope in telling the stories of these old towns, I have motivated others to begin their own research because, heaven knows, I have just scratched the surface. *Ghost Towns and Other Quirky Places in the New Jersey Pine Barrens* can in no way be considered a complete inventory of the old towns of the Pinelands but, I hope, will serve as a representative sampling of the various industries that formed its culture. If I have accomplished that, then I have met my goal of introducing others to the rich history of this unique and remarkable place. I have heard it said that there are more ghost towns in the New Jersey Pine Barrens than there are in the American West. If that is the case, then we, the ghost town hunters of the New Jersey Pinelands, have some work to do! Places like Gloucester Furnace, Clark's Landing, Stafford Forge, Maryanne, Forked River, Hanover Furnace, and many other lost towns stand silent, slowly succumbing to the elements, waiting for their story to be told. But there is no time to waste! My friend, Budd Wilson, who has been researching the forgotten towns of the Pine Barrens for more than 50 years, tells me that more than half of what was there when he began studying these sites is now gone and lost forever. Much has been lost to vandals and those interested in taking home a souvenir or two. It is important to remember that these are historic sites, and no object, no matter how small, should ever be removed.

When searching for the old towns and places, always keep in mind that the Pine Barrens constitutes a unique and fragile ecosystem. The Pinelands are home to a wide array of plants and animals, and in this diverse community are more than 150 species of threatened and endangered plants and animals. We are all trustees of this valuable resource, and it is our collective responsibility to minimize our impact as we enjoy its natural and cultural wonders. Enjoy the experience, but be mindful not to disturb plants, animals, or habitat, and never remove a plant or animal from its home. Never take vehicles off-road, and don't trespass on private property.

I hope my book offers you another way to enjoy the New Jersey Pine Barrens. Though I have always loved the beauty of the Pinelands and have often hiked its many trails and kayaked its tea-stained rivers, I have found that learning about the people and searching out the old towns has further connected me to this special place.

So perhaps someday we will meet on one of the seemingly endless sandy roads of the Pinelands or at a site of some long-gone but not forgotten settlement. Or maybe you will drop me a line sharing a special story about one of the ghost towns in the book or about a town I failed to mention. Perhaps we will meet on a ghost town tour sponsored by the Woodford Cedar Run Wildlife Refuge, the South Jersey Outdoor Club, or the Pinelands Preservation Alliance—three wonderful organizations devoted to the preservation of the ecology, culture, and history of the New Jersey Pine Barrens. It is always good to make new friends, but more than anything, I hope by writing this book, I have made new friends for the New Jersey Pine Barrens, a treasure with a history well worth preserving.

About the Author

Barbara Solem-Stull has an undergraduate degree in psychology from The College of New Jersey (formerly known as Trenton State College). She has completed graduate work in education administration and has been a special education teacher, a trainer, a principal, and an administrator. Barbara retired from the State of New Jersey Department of Human Services, Office of Education, in 2002, having worked as an education administrator for 15 years.

Her love of the New Jersey Pine Barrens has grown over the last 20 years as she has hiked its trails, kayaked its little rivers, and explored its forgotten towns and places. She lives with her husband, Gordon, and two cats on the edge of the Pine Barrens in Shamong, New Jersey.

Please feel free to share comments or stories with the author at Barbara@njghosttowns.org.

Index

More Great Books
from Plexus Publishing

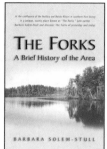

THE FORKS: A BRIEF HISTORY OF THE AREA
By Barbara Solem-Stull

Located on a navigable waterway, yet inland and remote, "The Forks" in South Jersey was a haven for smugglers at the dawn of the Revolutionary War. This short history describes the contribution of The Forks and its inhabitants to America's fight for independence and introduces a variety of colorful characters: early settler Eric Mullica, the treacherous Benedict Arnold, visionary citizens Elijah Clark and Richard Wescoat, ship builder Captain John Van Sant, highwayman Joe Mulliner, and the fictional Kate Aylesford—immortalized as "The Heiress of Sweetwater" in a popular novel first published in 1855.

48 pp/softbound/ISBN 0-937548-51-0/$9.95

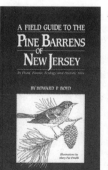

BROTHERTON: NEW JERSEY'S FIRST AND ONLY INDIAN RESERVATION AND THE COMMUNITIES OF SHAMONG AND TABERNACLE THAT FOLLOWED
By George D. Flemming; Foreword by Budd Wilson

In *Brotherton*, author George D. Flemming presents the history of the Brotherton Indian reservation (1758–1802)—the only Indian reservation ever established in the state of New Jersey—and the communities that followed. Following the exodus of the Brotherton Lenapes from the reservation, white settlements and industries began to dominate the area; Flemming chronicles the early churches and schools, hotels and taverns, forges, furnaces, mills, and notable citizens of "Old Shamong."

296 pp/hardbound/ISBN 0-937548-61-8/$34.95
296 pp/softbound/ISBN 0-937548-57-X/$24.95

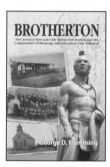

A FIELD GUIDE TO THE PINE BARRENS OF NEW JERSEY
By Howard P. Boyd

With his 420-page volume, author Howard P. Boyd presents readers with the ultimate handbook to the New Jersey Pine Barrens. Boyd begins his book by explaining and defining what makes this sandy-soiled, wooded habitat so diverse and unusual.

Each entry gives a detailed, nontechnical description of a Pine Barrens plant or animal (for over 700 species), indicating when and where it is most likely to appear. Complementing most listings is an original ink drawing that will greatly aid the reader in the field as they search for and try to identify specific flora and fauna.

423 pp/hardbound/ISBN 0-937548-18-9/$32.95
423 pp/softbound/ISBN 0-937548-19-7/$22.95

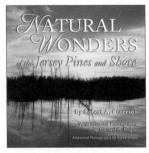

Natural Wonders of the Jersey Pines and Shore

By Robert A. Peterson with selected photographs by Michael A. Hogan and Steve Greer

In this exquisite book, fifty-seven short yet informative chapters by the late Robert Peterson celebrate a range of "natural wonders" associated with the Pine Barrens and coastal ecosystems of southern New Jersey. The diverse topics covered include flora, fauna, forces of nature, and geological formations—from birds, mammals, and mollusks, to bays, tides, trees, wildflowers, and much more. More than 200 stunning full-color photos by award-winning photographers Michael Hogan and Steve Greer bring Peterson's delightful vignettes to life.

312 pp/hardbound/ISBN 0-937548-48-0/$49.95

Down Barnegat Bay: A Nor'easter Midnight Reader

By Robert Jahn

"Down Barnegat Bay evokes the area's romance and mystery."
—New York Times

Down Barnegat Bay is an illustrated maritime history of the Jersey shore's Age of Sail. Originally published in 1980, this fully revised Ocean County Sesquicentennial Edition features more than 177 sepia illustrations, including 75 new images and nine maps. Jahn's engaging tribute to the region brims with first-person accounts of the people, events, and places that have come together to shape Barnegat Bay's unique place in American history.

248 pp/hardbound/ISBN 0-937548-42-1/$39.95

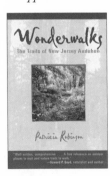

Wonderwalks: The Trails of New Jersey Audubon

By Patricia Robinson

Wonderwalks is the first book to present all of the accessible trails, sanctuaries, and nature centers owned by the New Jersey Audubon society. This delightful guide explores the 34 New Jersey Audubon nature preserves and sanctuaries throughout the state, with dozens of photographs, seasonal lists of birds and butterflies, trail descriptions, driving directions, and much more.

200 pp/softbound/ISBN 0-937548-53-7/$19.95

To order or for a catalog: 609-654-6500, Fax Order Service: 609-654-4309

Plexus Publishing, Inc.

143 Old Marlton Pike • Medford • NJ 08055
E-mail: info@plexuspublishing.com
www.plexuspublishing.com